GUIDE FOR PARTICIPANTS

IN PEACE, STABILITY,

AND RELIEF OPERATIONS

GUIDE FOR PARTICIPANTS

IN PEACE, STABILITY,

AND RELIEF OPERATIONS

Edited by
ROBERT M. PERITO
United States Institute of Peace

Steering Committee:

COLONEL JOHN F. AGOGLIA
U.S. Army Peacekeeping and
Stability Operations Institute

CHRISTOPHER J. HOH
U.S. Department of State

DAWN CALABIA
UN Information Center

ROY WILLIAMS
The Center for Humanitarian Cooperation

KAREN GUTTIERI
U.S. Naval Postgraduate School

UNITED STATES INSTITUTE OF PEACE PRESS
Washington, D.C.

The views expressed in this book are those of the authors alone. They do not necessarily reflect views of the United States Institute of Peace.

UNITED STATES INSTITUTE OF PEACE
1200 17th Street NW, Suite 200
Washington, DC 20036-3011

First published 2007

Printed in the United States of America

The paper used in this publication meets the minimum requirements of American National Standards for Information Sciences—Permanence of Paper for Printed Library Materials, ANSI Z39.48-1984.

Library of Congress Cataloging-in-Publication Data

Guide for participants in peace, stability, and relief operations / edited by Robert M. Perito.
    p. cm.
Includes bibliographical references and index.
ISBN-13: 978-1-60127-000-9 (pbk. : alk. paper)
ISBN-10: 1-60127-000-3 (pbk. : alk. paper)
ISBN-13: 978-1-60127-001-6 (hard cover : alk. paper)
ISBN 10: 1-60127-001-1 (hard cover : alk. paper)
1. Peacekeeping forces. 2. Disaster relief—International cooperation. 3. International cooperation. I. Perito, Robert, 1942-
JZ6374.G85 2007
341.5'84—dc22   2006017695

Contents

List of Illustrations and Maps

List of Graphs and Tables

Foreword

BRINGING LASTING PEACE and stability to regions devastated by violent conflict is a daunting and urgent task. Equally important is facilitating cooperation among the diverse institutions involved in peace, stability, and relief operations.

In discussing international interventions, terms go in and out of fashion, but, as I write these words (April 2007), what are referred to as "stability operations" are under way in Iraq and Afghanistan, societies still embroiled in violent conflict. Elsewhere, peace operations are carried out in situations where, for the most part, the violent phase of conflict is over. In these cases—as well as in instances of natural devastation, such as the Asian tsunami—the common challenge is to help people whose lives and societies have been devastated to build a firm foundation for stable peace. To accomplish this goal, international organizations must work together in ways that maximize their respective strengths, allowing each to retain individuality and initiative, while finding a unity of purpose based on mutual respect and understanding. Thus, as a basis for these efforts, I am proud to introduce a new Institute volume titled *The Guide for Participants in Peace, Stability, and Relief Operations.*

The guide introduces the Institute's *Framework for Success for Societies Emerging from Conflict.* The framework lays out five related objectives, or "end-states," that are mutually reinforcing and essential for success. The framework describes critical leadership responsibilities that are important to achieving these goals. The utility of the framework is its multiparty approach. It is designed to be used by interna-

tional military officers and civilian officials, as well as local
leaders involved in peace, stability, and relief operations.

This volume is a major revision, update, and expansion
of the Institute's *Guide to IGOs, NGOs, and the Military in
Peace and Relief Operations,* published in 2000. That volume
was the first handbook of its kind, and its many readers have
told us how valuable it was in helping members of the international community understand each other better—their
missions, their outlooks, and their styles of operations—
and thereby facilitating more effective working relationships. To produce the current text, the Institute established
a broad-based steering committee that has overseen the
process of making the guide as focused, accurate, objective,
timely, and user-friendly as possible and widening the scope
to include the civilian side of the United States government.

Producing the new guide reflected the same kind of
well-coordinated effort that is needed for success in field
operations. Robert M. Perito, senior program officer in the
Center for Post-Conflict Peace and Stability Operations at
the Institute, formed a steering committee of experts representing the U.S. State Department, the U.S. military, the
U.S. Naval Postgraduate School, the United Nations, and
non-governmental organizations, which worked diligently
to ensure that every aspect of the guide accurately reflects
the hard-won experience of those serving in Iraq and
Afghanistan. It was written by practitioners who had first-
hand knowledge of not only how things should work, but
how they do work, and how to make them work better.

New Departures in International Operations

In 2005, the U.S. government revamped the organizational structure that handles conflict interventions when

President George W. Bush signed National Security Presidential Directive 44, which ordered the State Department to coordinate the activities of other civilian agencies involved in conflict interventions. This responsibility was assigned by the State Department to a new Office for the Coordinator for Reconstruction and Stabilization. This office and its mission are thoroughly discussed in the guide's new section titled "Civilian Agencies of the U.S. Government," which highlights the expanded role that civilian agencies of the U.S. government play in peace and stability operations.

The military section describes the strengths of the U.S. military and provides a clear, sophisticated explanation of basic characteristics of the military and then explains how these characteristics relate to stability operations. The section on non-governmental organizations highlights the proliferation of these entities and the expanded role they play in providing all types of assistance to people in need.

Also new in this text is recognition of the grim threat of armed attacks and other types of violence directed at all actors in this field. The rise in the number of UN peace keeper deaths during the past seven years is an example of the increasing danger under which all participants in stability operations are working. In 2002, 52 UN peacekeepers lost their lives on duty. By 2005, the number of deaths more than doubled, as 121 peacekeepers died on mission. All participants in these operations have felt the impact of this increased insecurity on their respective roles and responsibilities—from personnel in NGOs and international organizations to those in military and civilian government agencies. In fact, the mounting danger and complexity of these operations has led to the increasing use of private security firms to protect NGOs and newly formed governmental offices.

Perito and the steering committee carefully describe the UN, the U.S. military, civilian U.S. government agencies, and non-governmental organizations and the roles they play. They did their utmost to keep pace with the developments in this ever-changing field, but this is a race with no finish line. We will be looking into the potential of Web-based updates as a way of addressing the challenge of timely information. But even in this electronic age, there is no substitute for a book—especially a book like this, which can be readily carried and used, whether in the field or the classroom.

It is clear that NGO, IO, military, and civilian government personnel will need to work together ever more closely as the challenges increase in future operations. The successful interaction of not only the key institutions, but more especially the individuals on the ground, can make the difference between the success and failure of an operation. In light of the new dangers and obstacles faced by NGOs, IOs, the military, and government personnel, it is critical that the guide be made available as widely as possible—to those in the field, at the headquarters level, and in the classrooms where new generations of peacebuilders are in training—to ensure that these disparate, yet equally vital, participants in peace, stability, and relief operations know each other and are able to communicate clearly, and operate together effectively.

RICHARD H. SOLOMON, PRESIDENT
UNITED STATES INSTITUTE OF PEACE

UNITED STATES INSTITUTE OF PEACE

1200 17th Street NW, Suite 200
Washington, DC 20036-3011

Phone: 202-457-1700
Fax: 202-429-6063
E-mail: usiprequests@usip.org
Internet: www.usip.org

Peacemaking: A Global Imperative

It is essential that the United States, working with the international community, play an active part in preventing, managing, and resolving threats to international peace. Interstate wars, internal armed conflicts, ethnic and religious strife, religious extremism, terrorism, and the proliferation of weapons of mass destruction all pose significant challenges to security and development throughout the world. The resulting human suffering, destabilization of societies, and threats to security make effective forms of managing conflict imperative. The United States Institute of Peace is dedicated to meeting this imperative in new and innovative ways.

United States Institute of Peace Mission and Goals

The United States Institute of Peace is an independent, non-partisan, national institution established and funded by Congress. Its goals are to help accomplish the following:

- Prevent and resolve violent conflicts
- Promote post-conflict stability and development
- Increase conflict management capacity, tools, and intellectual capital worldwide

The Institute does this by empowering others with knowledge, skills, and resources, as well as by directly engaging in peacebuilding efforts around the globe.

United States Institute of Peace
Programs and Activities

In order to achieve the above goals, the Institute "thinks, acts, teaches, and trains," providing a unique combination of non-partisan research, innovative programs, and hands-on support:

- *Providing on-the-ground support in zones of conflict,* most recently in Afghanistan, the Balkans, Colombia, Indonesia, Iraq, the Palestinian Territories, Liberia, Nigeria, Philippines, Rwanda, and Sudan. Specific work performed by Institute staff and grantees includes the following:
  - Mediating among parties in conflict
  - Facilitating interethnic, intersectarian and inter-religious dialogue
  - Promoting the rule of law
  - Helping build civil society
  - Reforming education systems
  - Building conflict management skills through training and workshops
- *Sponsoring a wide range of country-oriented working groups for policymakers in Washington,* including groups on Afghanistan, Haiti, Iran, Iraq, Korea, Somalia, Sudan.
- *Performing cutting-edge research* on the dynamics of conflict and on subjects relevant to policymakers and practitioners.
- *Identifying best practices and developing innovative resources* in support of conflict prevention, conflict resolution, and post-conflict stabilization.
- *Providing practitioner training* on conflict management, including mediation and negotiation skills, to government and military personnel, civil-society leaders, and the staff of non-governmental and international organizations.

- *Strengthening secondary school, college, and university curricula* and increasing the capacity of future generations to manage conflict.
- *Supporting policymakers* in the administration and Congress, as well as in the international community, by providing analyses, policy options, and advice.
- *Educating the public about peacebuilding* through events, publications, documentary films, radio programs, and an array of other outreach activities.

Expertise

The United States Institute of Peace draws on a variety of resources in fulfilling its mandate, including Institute staff, grantees, Jennings Randolph Fellows, and a broad set of governmental and non-governmental partners:

- *Institute Specialists.* The Institute employs more than seventy specialists with both geographic and subject matter expertise. These experts are leaders in their fields. They come from the government, military, non-governmental organizations, academia, and the private sector.
- *Grants.* The Institute invests more than 25 percent of its annual budget in grants to nonprofit, educational, and research organizations worldwide. Its grantmaking process is extremely competitive—only about 10 percent of proposals receive funding.
- *Jennings Randolph Fellows.* The Jennings Randolph Program awards Senior Fellowships (in residence) to outstanding scholars, policymakers, practitioners, journalists, and other professionals to conduct research on important issues related to conflict. Since the program's inception, senior fellows have produced more than 125 books and special reports. The Jennings Randolph Program also awards non-resident Peace Scholar Dissertation Fellowships to

students at U.S. universities researching and writing doctoral dissertations related to the Institute's work.

For further information on the United States Institute of Peace, please contact the Office of Public Affairs and Communications by e-mail at info@usip.org, by phone at 202-429-3832, or by visiting the Institute's Web site at www.usip.org.

Introduction

The Setting

In the wake of the attacks on New York and Washington, D.C., on September 11, 2001, the United States and the international community face an unprecedented security dilemma. The primary threat to international peace and security arises from virulent nonstate actors that have proven they can attack major world capitals with devastating effects. This new enemy is a global network based on ideology and a willingness to inflict massive civilian casualties to advance its cause. This enemy thrives in conflict zones where governments have failed to exercise effective control or where foreign intervention has failed to establish effective governance.

Today the United States is engaged globally against extremists. This conflict has involved U.S.-led military interventions in Afghanistan, where terrorists established a base of operations, and in Iraq, where a rogue regime appeared to threaten U.S. interests. In postcombat "stability operations," the United States has been both a combatant in an ongoing struggle against insurgents and a source of assistance to two emerging democracies. This dual role has required greater involvement of civilian government agencies and resulted in the creation of new government institutions. It also has impacted civil-military relationships to the point where traditional guidelines for interaction between the military and humanitarian relief organizations have been called into question.

Coincident with the war on terrorism, there has been a sharp increase in the number of UN peace operations. This has resulted from a consensus that sovereignty cannot shield rogue regimes from international intervention to end crimes against humanity. At the UN 2005 World Summit, world leaders formally endorsed the international community's responsibility to protect people from massive violations of international humanitarian law. This increased concern is reflected in the United Nations' involvement in nineteen peace operations with a total of 70,000 military and police personnel and the fact that new missions are based on the peace enforcement provisions of the UN charter. Today UN military and police forces are more likely to take action against spoilers than simply observe and report on the performance of indigenous personnel.

At the same time, the great Indian Ocean tsunami has demonstrated the massive challenges for humanitarian relief organizations that can result from natural disasters. On December 26, 2004, an undersea earthquake generated a towering tidal wave that devastated coastal regions in Indonesia, Sri Lanka, Thailand, India, the Maldives, and Somalia. Some 273,000 people died or disappeared. Millions more were injured or left homeless. Entire towns and villages were destroyed. Greater loss of life was averted, however, by the heartwarming and effective response to the call for international assistance. Fears that outbreaks of disease and collapse of social order would follow the initial destruction proved unfounded. Led by the United Nations, donor nations joined with non-governmental organizations (NGOs) to provide immediate relief. Contributions totaled billions of dollars and material assistance exceeded the assessed need. Remarkably, many agencies soon announced that they had received sufficient contributions. Effective action by international relief, humanitarian, and development organizations restored stability and launched the region on the road to recovery.

The Publication

This publication updates the Institute's highly successful *Guide to IGOs, NGOs, and the Military in Peace and Relief Operations,* which was based on peace operations in the Balkans following the Cold War. This edition reflects the operations that have occurred since 2000, particularly those in Iraq and Afghanistan and the response to the 2004 Asian tsunami. Its purpose is to help military and civilian personnel understand peace, stability, and relief operations so they can work more effectively. It seeks to introduce participants in these operations in a manner that promotes effective cooperation. Organizations that engage in peace, stability, and relief operations come from varied organizational cultures with different values, codes of conduct, and methods of operation. They speak different bureaucratic languages that use acronyms, terms, and jargon that are not mutually intelligible. Participants also have distinct mandates from different authorities and unique mission objectives. Cooperation among participating organizations is likely to be more dependent on personal relationships and circumstances than on formal arrangements. This book aims to dispel misconceptions and prejudices that can exist on all sides and to promote mutual respect and understanding. Our goal is to make cooperation more likely among the institutions that determine the success or failure of an operation.

The guide provides an introduction to the organizations that will be present when the international community responds to a crisis. It offers a series of short but informative scenarios of typical international involvement in peace missions, natural disasters, and stability operations. The guide offers descriptions of the United Nations, other international institutions, and NGOs that highlight the new challenge from international terrorism. It introduces civilian

U.S. government agencies in keeping with their increased role. It also describes the U.S. military and its role in stability operations.

The guide provides information that will be particularly relevant for those serving in the field. It is designed to fit easily into a pocket or backpack and has a durable cover. This book will also be helpful for headquarters personnel. It offers a general introduction to international organizations (IOs), NGOs, the U.S. government (USG), and the U.S. military—covering organization, mission, culture, operating procedures, and other characteristics—and a brief description of dozens of agencies and institutions. The guide also contains references to publications, databases, and Web sites that provide additional information. There is no need to read it sequentially. Users are encouraged to consult the table of contents and the index to locate specific topics. A unique educational resource, the guide may also be helpful to military and agency trainees and university students.

The Authors

The guide was produced by a steering committee that included Col. John Agoglia, director of the U.S. Army Peacekeeping and Stability Operations Institute; Christopher J. Hoh, deputy coordinator of the Office of the Coordinator for Reconstruction and Stabilization, U.S. Department of State; Dawn Calabia, former deputy director of the UN Information Center; Roy Williams, director of the Center for Humanitarian Cooperation; and Karen Guttieri, U.S. Naval Postgraduate School. Robert M. Perito chaired the steering committee and edited the publication.

This publication is the work of the steering committee and many other talented hands. The views expressed are those of the contributors alone, and do not necessarily represent the positions of their respective organizations. The views expressed are not those of the United States Institute of Peace, which does not advocate specific policies.

Acknowledgments

THE GUIDE is a revised and updated version of the Institute's best-seller, the *Guide to IGOs, NGOs, and the Military in Peace and Relief Operations*, conceived of and designed by Dr. Judith Stiehm of Florida International University and Pamela Aall. The steering committee owes a deep debt of gratitude to the authors of the original version of the guide, which has served a generation of workers in peace and stability operations. The authors of the first edition were Pamela Aall, vice president for education of the United States Institute of Peace and a specialist on NGOs in conflict; Thomas G. Weiss, Presidential Professor of Political Science at the Graduate Center at City University of New York and a leading expert on the role of the United Nations in responding to conflict; and Lt. Col. Daniel Miltenberger, formerly of the U.S. Army Peacekeeping Institute and a professor of military science at Pennsylvania State University. The steering committee would like to recognize these authors' contributions.

The new edition is also the product of many talented people who assisted the steering committee. Pride of place goes to William Owens, who served as research assistant for the project. Will was a full partner with the steering committee in this enterprise. He contributed to all aspects of the work: researching, writing, editing, and generating ideas. Will's enthusiasm, dedication, and good judgment kept everyone engaged and on track. Special appreciation is also due to Michael Dziedzic and Beth Cole of the Institute; and to Nigel Quinney and Amy Benavides, our editors.

In addition to members of the steering committee, several people contributed by helping to draft sections of the text. Special thanks are due to Mike Esper (U.S. Army Peacekeeping and Stability Operations Institute) for insights on the military; Ambassador Gary Matthews (United States Institute of Peace) for his contribution on international organizations; and Victor Marsh (U.S. Department of State) for the operational scenarios.

Appreciation is also due to a group of volunteers who read the initial draft and offered insights that strengthened the text. These contributors were Eric Schwartz (United Nations); Stephen Tomlin (International Medical Corps); George Devendorf (Mercy Corps); Paul Leonovich and Larry McDonald (U.S. Department of the Treasury); James McAtamney (U.S. Department of Justice); William Garvelink (U.S. Agency for International Development); and Theodore Tanoue (U.S. Department of State).

Finally, this project would not have been possible without the leadership and practical support of Richard Solomon, president of the United States Institute of Peace; Patricia Thomson, executive vice president; Mike Lekson, vice president for professional training; Dan Serwer, vice president for post-conflict peace and stability operations; and the Institute's wonderful publications staff, who took our raw manuscript and handed back a book. To all of these very good people, we are very grateful.

Robert M. Perito
Editor
March 2007

Abbreviations and Acronyms

USIP	United States Institute of Peace

Intergovernmental Organizations

ASEAN	Association of Southeast Asian Nations
AU	African Union
CARICOM	Caribbean Community and Common Market
DPA	United Nations Department of Political Affairs
DPKO	United Nations Department of Peacekeeping Operations
ECOSOC	Economic and Social Council
ECOWAS	Economic Community of West African States
EU	European Union
FAO	Food and Agriculture Organization
GCC	Gulf Cooperation Council
HABITAT	United Nations Human Settlements Program
IBRD	International Bank for Reconstruction and Development (component institution of the World Bank)
ICC	International Criminal Court

ICJ	International Court of Justice
ICRC	International Committee of the Red Cross
ICTR	International Criminal Tribunal for Rwanda
ICTY	International Criminal Tribunal for the former Yugoslavia
IDA	International Development Association (component institution of the World Bank)
IFAD	International Fund for Agricultural Development
IFC	International Finance Corporation
IMF	International Monetary Fund
IOM	International Organization for Migration
MIGA	Multilateral Investment Guarantee Agency
NATO	North Atlantic Treaty Organization
OAS	Organization of American States
OCHA	United Nations Office for the Coordination of Humanitarian Affairs
OECS	Organization of East Caribbean States
OHCHR	United Nations High Commissioner for Human Rights
OIC	Organization of the Islamic Conference
OSCE	Organization for Security and Co-operation in Europe
SADC	Southern African Development Community
UNDP	United Nations Development Program
UNESCO	United Nations Education, Scientific, and Cultural Organization
UNHCR	United Nations High Commissioner for Refugees
UNICEF	United Nations Children's Fund
UNODC	United Nations Office for Drugs and Crime

| WFP | World Food Program |
| WHO | World Health Organization |

Non-Governmental Organizations

AED	Academy for Educational Development
AFSC	American Friends Service Committee
ARC	American Red Cross
CARE	Cooperative for Assistance and Relief Everywhere
CEELI	European and Eurasia Division of the Rule of Law Initiative
CMG	Conflict Management Group
CRS	Catholic Relief Services
ICG	International Crisis Group
IRC	International Rescue Committee
IRI	International Republican Institute
LWR	Lutheran World Relief
MCC	Mennonite Central Committee
MCI	Mercy Corps International
MSF	Médecins Sans Frontières USA
NDI	National Democratic Institute for International Affairs
NED	National Endowment for Democracy
SAWSO	Salvation Army World Service Office
USCRI	U.S. Committee for Refugees and Immigrants

U.S. Government Agencies

CDC	Centers for Disease Control and Prevention
DEA	Drug Enforcement Administration
DRL	Bureau of Democracy, Human Rights, and Labor
FAS	Foreign Agriculture Service
FBI	Federal Bureau of Investigation
ICITAP	International Criminal Investigative Training Assistance Program
INL	Bureau of International Narcotics and Law Enforcement Affairs
OFDA	Office of U.S. Foreign Disaster Assistance
OIA	Office of International Affairs
OPDAT	Office of Overseas Prosecutorial Development, Assistance, and Training
PRM	Bureau of Population, Refugees, and Migration
S/CRS	Office of the Coordinator for Reconstruction and Stabilization
USAID	U.S. Agency for International Development

United States Institute of Peace Framework for Societies Emerging from Conflict

THE UNITED STATES INSTITUTE OF PEACE has developed a framework for success for societies emerging from conflict designed to be shared by intervention leaders from the international community (military, government, NGO, IO, and private sector), as well as by domestic leaders in such societies. The framework is designed to promote unity of purpose and interoperability, a first step to giving peacebuilding the kind of shared doctrine that warfighting has long enjoyed. The framework, first presented by Daniel Serwer and Patricia Thomson in *Leashing the Dogs of War* (Aall, Crocker, Hampson 2006) builds on the research and expertise of the Institute. It also draws upon the work of the Center for Strategic and International Studies (CSIS), the Association of the U.S. Army (AUSA), and RAND. In addition, it incorporates the input of leaders of international interventions collected during discussions at the Institute, as well as concepts from the *U.S. Government Draft Planning Framework for Reconstruction, Stabilization, and Conflict Transformation* (developed by the U.S. State Department's Office of the Coordinator for Reconstruction and Stabilization and the Joint Warfighting Center of the Joint Forces Command, with assistance from the Institute).

Focus on End-States, Objectives, and Leadership Responsibilities

End-states. While the particular circumstances of interventions vary dramatically, there is a remarkable degree of consensus in the post–Cold War period on the end-states sought. While they may be listed in a different order—or combined in different ways—we believe all recent international interventions can be described as having explicitly or implicitly five desired end-states: a safe and secure environment, the rule of law, a stable democracy, a sustainable economy, and social well-being. In this framework, the end-states describe the place a society emerging from conflict ultimately wishes to be. For those familiar with strategic planning, they are the strategic goals—the ultimate ambitions that anchor a plan.

The five end-states are not mutually exclusive. One of the challenges when developing a framework of this sort is to ensure that it is useful and substantive, but not burdensomely complicated. When balancing these demands, it is necessary to divide interrelated components. For example, a safe and secure environment is important in and of itself, but it is also an important condition for a sustainable economy. Similarly, rule of law is an important goal on its own, but it is also important to social well-being, a stable democracy, and a sustainable economy. The end-states of this framework should be treated, not as distinct and independent pillars, but rather as interconnected components that impact and influence one another.

Objectives. Within each end-state is a series of objectives. These represent some of the key things that need to be accomplished in order to achieve the desired end-state and serve as an added level of specificity that further defines the end-state. We have tried to focus on ends, not means, but in some cases this distinction is a tenuous one—a matter of definition, not substance. Moreover, like the end-states, the objectives within each end-state are often related. For example, conducting free and fair elections leads to the creation of a legitimate legislature, which contributes to democratic governance. Or consider economic development: Establishing effective patent laws contributes to a regulatory and legal framework that promotes business development, which contributes to a sustainable economy. We have chosen objectives that are (1) relatively easy to define, (2) at least partially within the control of those engaged in international intervention, and (3) measurable (i.e., corresponding metrics can be identified and used to gauge success).

Leadership responsibilities. This framework also includes critical leadership responsibilities, which are essential to success. Earlier frameworks tended to embed these types of responsibilities within mission activities, which disguised or even entirely hid them. By highlighting critical leadership responsibilities, which cut across all five end-states, the Institute's framework presents a more accurate picture of the elements required for mission success.

In sum, the framework presented herein has several important features. First, it is crafted to be useful to (and ideally shared by) all the actors, civilian and military, involved in post-conflict situations. Second, it is organized around end-states, ensuring a focus on the ultimate goals of societies emerging from conflict. Third, it recognizes that there are critical leadership responsibilities that have a cross-cutting impact crucial to mission success. Fourth, it is designed to allow for easy customization, recognizing that each post-conflict mission will be unique. Finally, we believe this framework is most valuable in planning and operations,

Table 1.1. Framework for Success: Societies Emerging from Conflict

	Safe and Secure Environment	Rule of Law	Stable Democracy	Sustainable Economy	Social Well-Being
DESIRED END-STATES	Prevent renewal of fighting (e.g., enforce cease-fire; secure weapons/stockpiles; disarm, demobilize, and reintegrate former fighters)	Establish coherent, legitimate, and just legal frameworks (e.g., constitution, criminal and civil frameworks)	Develop legitimate systems of political representation at national, regional, and local levels (e.g., legislatures)	Reconstruct infrastructure (e.g., electricity, communications, transportation) • Promote sound fiscal/economic policy	Ensure population is fed • Ensure population has water • Ensure population has shelter
CRITICAL LEADERSHIP RESPONSIBILITIES	Build unity of purpose among the military, NGOs, IOs, government authorities, and private sector • Develop and execute integrated plans that are based on the peace agreement or mission mandate • Ensure involved players have the authority they need to succeed and adequate financial and staff resources • Build and maintain legitimacy • Engage the international community; establish peaceful relations with neighboring countries • Build constituencies for peace; deploy effective strategic communications and public awareness campaigns • Identify and address original and emerging drivers of conflict; manage spoilers • Collect and use intelligence/manage information effectively • Manage transitions from military to civilian and from international to local control				

KEY OBJECTIVES

- Protect civilians (e.g., counter organized crime, de-mine) - Ensure freedom of movement (e.g., for civilians, relief workers, peace monitors) - Protect key historical, cultural, and religious sites, as well as important buildings, property, and infrastructure - Protect witnesses and evidence of atrocities - Protect international borders/airspace/ports of entry - Build effective security forces, under civilian control	- Build effective and independent courts - Build effective police, customs, immigration, and border control forces - Build effective corrections system - Build effective legal profession/bar - Protect human rights - Ensure equal access to justice and equal application of the law - Promote public awareness and legal empowerment	- Build effective and legitimate executive institutions—national, regional, and local levels (e.g., ministries, civil service) - Promote free and responsible media - Promote the creation of political parties - Promote robust civil society and civic participation (including minorities and marginalized groups)	- Build effective and predictable regulatory and legal environment - Build effective financial and economic institutions (e.g., banks) - Create viable workforce - Promote business development; increase access to capital and sustainable employment - Protect, manage, and equitably distribute natural resources/revenues - Limit/contain corruption and illicit economy	- Meet basic sanitation needs - Meet basic health needs - Build effective education system - Enable displaced persons and refugees to return or relocate - Address legacy of past abuses (e.g., truth commissions) - Promote peaceful coexistence (e.g., interethnic, interfaith)

- The end-states, leadership responsibilities, and objectives included above are not presented in any particular order—neither in terms of priority nor sequencing. There is no "one-size-fits-all" solution, and the above framework will need to be tailored as circumstances warrant.
- This framework was first presented by Daniel Serwer and Patricia Thomson in *Leashing the Dogs of War*. It draws upon the expertise of USIP staff and external advisors. It also draws upon the *Post-Conflict Reconstruction Task Framework* developed by the Association of the U.S. Army and CSIS, as well as the U.S. Government's draft *Planning Framework for Reconstruction, Stabilization, and Conflict Transformation*, prepared by S/CRS and the Joint Warfighting Center of JFCOM, with support from USIP. In addition, it incorporates input from leaders of international intervention (collected during discussions at USIP on March 22 and 23, 2005).

but it also has great value as an underlying structure from which training programs, monitoring efforts, and coordination mechanisms should cascade.

Scenarios

THIS SECTION contains three scenarios that illustrate how the United States and the international community may conduct peace, stability, and relief operations. Veterans of such operations know that each situation is unique and that it is impossible to predict how an actual operation might be conducted. Those with field experience are also aware that commonalities do exist between operations and that a predictable cast of characters is likely to appear in a specific type of operation. They also know that operations tend to follow a somewhat predictable pattern in terms of the behavior of international organizations, governments, and private agencies and of the sequencing of the arrival of first responders and organizations that arrive later, but remain for the long term.

The following scenarios describe three situations in which the United States and the international community are likely to intervene with a significant presence: a major natural disaster such as the Asian tsunami; a major threat to international peace and security requiring a U.S.-led military response; and a traditional peace operation where the United Nations is invited to oversee implementation of a comprehensive peace agreement. The descriptions of these situations are indicative of the types of challenges that might be expected. They are not intended to be prescriptive, nor can they be inclusive in terms of the events that might transpire. Instead, they are meant to be instructive in the sense that the reader will be able to see how organizations are likely to respond to crisis and the problems they may encounter.

Scenario: Major Natural Disaster

A major earthquake has leveled entire communities in a remote province of an Asian country. CNN begins broadcasting photographs of the disaster. There is initial confusion and reporting errors about events and the number of people affected. NGOs that specialize in conducting emergency relief operations are the first to arrive, followed closely by locally based representatives of the relevant UN agencies. Although the United Nations and NGOs normally work in cooperation with local government authorities, the extent of the devastation and the government's lack of capacity for emergency response make this impossible. Instead, NGOs move in alone, sending uncoordinated appeals for donations and carrying out direct relief efforts.

In the capital, the government reacts defensively to news of the disaster and the uncontrolled influx of foreigners. The government feels threatened and seeks to restrict the movements of foreign aid workers. The presence of outsiders reinforces the impression locally and abroad that the government is weak and cannot care for its citizens. The government deploys its army—its only logistical arm —with instructions to build temporary shelters, organize clinics, clear transportation arteries, expand air traffic control, and prevent looting. However, the arrival of troops inflames long-standing ethnic and sectarian animosities, prompting clashes between soldiers and local citizens that result in charges of brutality and human rights violations. Growing political tensions necessitate a U.S.-led diplomatic effort to encourage the government to accept international relief, which is providing services the government cannot afford. Representatives from the UN Office for the Coordination of Humanitarian Affairs (OCHA) arrive to assist in coordinating international relief activities, improve the flow of information, and provide a buffer between the government and the NGOs. An expanding IO presence in the affected areas lowers the political temperature and provides a brake on the army's use of excessive force.

In Washington, the president issues a statement of concern and pledges U.S. assistance to the victims. State Department and U.S. Agency for International Development (USAID) officials attempt to assess the situation, weighing options for funding assistance but carefully avoiding specific numbers until needs are defined and Congress is consulted. Utilizing its emergency response mechanisms for natural disasters, USAID sends a Disaster Assistance Response Team (DART) to assess needs, identify priorities, and establish a base for follow-on aid. Additional DART members arrive and the team quickly grows in size and expands its operations. Local officials express frustration with repeatedly being asked the same questions by multiple disaster assessment teams without seeing help materialize.

Meanwhile, the U.S. military combatant commander for the region arranges the deployment of a hospital ship and flies in a medical assessment team. With roads and rail lines into the interior destroyed, finding a way to transport material from the rapidly filling port to areas damaged by the quake becomes a priority. The host government and NGOs seek U.S. military assistance to obtain air and ground mobility. After some discussion, the combatant commander deploys U.S. military assets, including cargo aircraft, helicopters, and ground transport. Logistical support for the air transport of supplies and the medical evacuation of severely injured victims is also provided.

A health crisis looms, exacerbated by the destruction of public utilities, including electric power stations, water treatment plants, and sewage disposal facilities. International medical NGOs request that the U.S. military assist by airlifting in water purification units operated by American NGOs. The U.S. military responds by delivering water-processing units and working with NGOs to deliver water.

As public appeals produce private donations, NGO officials vie for access to television cameras and media representatives to dramatize the crisis and advertise their efforts to relieve suffering. Contributions reach levels at which questions are raised about whether additional funds can be used. The U.S. embassy arranges for a senior American official to tour the affected province to highlight the assistance provided by the United States and other international donors. The host government, however, insists that high-level visits must be restricted to the capital and praises indigenous efforts. International patience grows thin, as the host government seems more interested in protecting its image than in assisting those affected by the earthquake.

The chaos of the first weeks subsides and efforts shift from providing emergency medical treatment, food, and shelter to beginning the process of rehabilitation. The host government in the capital, the provincial governor, the United Nations, and the larger NGOs all seek to establish separate forums to coordinate this effort. However, tense relations between the provincial governor and the army commander mean international agencies and NGOs must receive approvals from each to conduct operations. In response to bureaucratic obstructions, a de facto division of labor is established, with some agencies focused on the north and others on the south, and with the World Health Organization (WHO) and European donors concentrating on health services while USAID takes the lead in restoring the electric grid.

NGOs organize a coordinating council that meets weekly. They choose three rotating representatives to attend the governor's assistance coordination forum, in which multilateral and bilateral donors also participate. With the assistance of OCHA, this forum becomes the main vehicle for sharing information on the situation, explaining what various organizations plan to do, and identifying needs that remain unaddressed. When most of the international media have left and the initial rescue operations are over, the international relief and development community begins amending long-term development plans and projects to address the problems of rebuilding and reestablishing the local economy.

Scenario: Heavy U.S. Military Engagement

After years of ignoring UN sanctions and international appeals for restraint, the extremist government of a Middle Eastern country appears poised to use its newly developed nuclear arsenal against a neighboring state. The UN Security Council (UNSC) votes to authorize the creation of a U.S.-led "coalition of the willing" to enter this country and establish a safe and secure environment. Time is critical, as the U.S.-led coalition must act before the country can finish modifying a weapons delivery system. In a television address from the Oval Office, the president alerts the world to the impending danger and calls upon our allies to rally to the cause.

The U.S. military has already engaged in extensive strategic planning and conducted exercises for the engagement, with its relevant geographic combatant command taking the lead. Immediately after UNSC authorization, the first task is to harmonize those plans with the international nature of the intervention. Though the United States is expected to handle the bulk of the military action, military forces from the Arab League and other nations will also participate in certain phases of the operation. The military capabilities of coalition partners are starkly different, and U.S. military planners have to join with their civilian, diplomatic, and foreign military counterparts to develop coherent joint plans and strategic coordination.

Coalition military forces swiftly establish a presence within the conflict country and effectively subdue local military forces, whose resistance is halfhearted. Long pent-up popular tensions explode in a frenzy of revenge-taking and interethnic violence. Local police, who are identified with the country's leader, go into hiding. Civilian crowds surge into the streets celebrating the fall of the regime and begin looting the commercial district and government ministries. Only when crowds attack hospitals and universities do coalition military forces respond and attempt to reestablish public order.

Military efforts to control civil disorder are exacerbated by the challenge from paramilitary "Dignity Brigades" made up of personnel loyal to the former regime leader. These loyalists engage in hit-and-run attacks before blending into the civilian population. Sensing a climate of impunity, criminal organizations begin the systematic looting of industrial areas and engage in home invasion robbery, carjacking, rape, and murder.

The U.S.-led coalition establishes effective civil administration and begins to provide public services. It also provides for the welfare of the local population. The coalition establishes a Provisional Authority, which assumes responsibility for governing the country. Meanwhile, military Civil Affairs (CA) teams start to restore electric power, water, and sanitation services. They also begin to organize local councils and invite the indigenous police to return to duty. These efforts are often frustrated, however, by continued civil disturbance and criminal activity.

Detention of lawbreakers by coalition forces quickly creates a large population of detainees. Unfortunately, there is no local judicial system, so many are released after spending several uncomfortable weeks in improvised holding facilities. Absence of international police in the coalition force means that responsibility for law enforcement falls on military units that are already stretched to perform other duties. NGOs are highly critical of the interim rule of law measures, especially on the issues of transparency and due process of law. The international press and particularly Arab television provide extensive coverage of protests, which degenerate into violence, outside of the correctional facilities.

To avert growing criticism and alleviate concerns about coalition intentions, the United States announces the creation of an appointed, indigenous, interim governing council. The Provisional Authority also expands its outreach to religious leaders, tribal elders, women's groups, and other representatives of civil society. In Washington, the U.S. government determines that a prestigious civilian administrator should be named to replace the military leadership of the Provisional Authority. There is a diplomatic effort to engage the United Nations and to encourage the appointment of a special representative of the UN secretary-general (SRSG) to lead an expanded UN mission.

The United Nations is wary, however, of close association with the coalition and delays its response. The United States attempts to apply pressure through its representative on the UNSC, but Council politics prevent productive lobbying of the UN Secretariat. The United Nations does agree, however, to organize a UN Police Force to assist the coalition in maintaining order and retraining local police. The United Nations also agrees to extend its humanitarian assistance efforts and to organize local and provincial elections.

The Provisional Administrator arrives, but the Provisional Authority experiences logistical delays and growing dissatisfaction. Under growing pressure, its overworked and thinly stretched staff fails to ensure that public services are restored to citizens residing outside the capital. In the countryside, increasing distrust results in civil disorder. Under the charismatic leadership of a small-town mayor, there are numerous protests.

The Provisional Administrator observes the shifting political climate and responds by traveling throughout the country to explain the coalition's intention to establish democracy and promote economic prosperity. The administrator urges the coalition military commander to have his CA teams emphasize quick-start village improvement projects to create employment in rural areas. The coalition commander agrees but requests assistance from USAID personnel who have greater expertise and cultural competence in delivering crucial services.

The arrival of the Headquarters Unit of the UN Police Force begins the process of shifting responsibility for rule of law. UN Police begin retraining former regime police, who are still distrusted by local citizens. Criminal groups test the resolve of the reorganized police units, committing violent crimes that shake public confidence in the international community. Continued deterioration in the security situation prompts the United States to assist the UN Police mission by organizing an accelerated police training and development program. The U.S. military starts recruiting former soldiers into new police commando units to deal with street gangs and bandits.

To stem growing discontent, the Provisional Administrator and the interim governing council announce that national elections for a new president and parliament will be held in six months, coincident with local and provincial elections already planned. The prospect of national elections produces an immediate spike in sectarian violence, resulting in the need for additional coalition forces and for greater determination to stay the course.

Elections are held on schedule with heavy security and a large turnout. The chairman of the Interim Governing Council wins a plurality of the votes for president, with the charismatic small-town mayor coming in second. Old regime sympathizers are chastened by their poor showing in parliamentary elections, even though the new government seems likely to be weak and unstable. Although a small hard core continues to cause trouble, particularly in the border areas, the coalition prepares to withdraw troops and turn over security to the new government and its re-formed police force.

Scenario: International Peacekeeping Force

Climaxing a successful mediation by the African Union (AU), rival militia leaders engage in a five-person hand-shake, ending a civil conflict that has decimated their nation. The peace agreement includes an interim power-sharing arrangement, a disarmament schedule, and elections for president and parliament. Although peace seems at hand, a faction that refused to participate in the peace negotia-tions remains in control of a rich border region. AU nego-tiators fear the parties will not honor the agreement unless the international community supports the peace process and forces the recalcitrant faction to accept the settlement. Tensions that produced the civil war did not evaporate during the peace negotiations. Therefore, the parties, with AU support, request the UNSC to approve creation of a peacekeeping force that will operate under Chapter VII (peace enforcement) provisions of the UN Charter. Such action, they believe, will make clear the international com-munity's intention to hold the parties to their bargain and deal aggressively with spoilers.

In New York City, the UNSC meets to review the peace settlement and listen to a report from its observer at the peace talks. The UNSC endorses the agreement and au-thorizes an integrated UN peace operation that includes a military peacekeeping force, UN Police, other civilian peacekeeping staff (for example, civil affairs and public information), as well as a range of UN agencies all led in the field by a special representative of the secretary-general. However, the Security Council approves only a Chapter VI mandate to "monitor compliance of all parties with the peace agreement, provide technical assistance for implementation of the agreement, and assist the new government in coordinating a reconstruction program." The UN Department of Peacekeeping Operations (DPKO) extends invitations for member states to contribute military units and police. Unfortunately, the response from contributing nations is slow in coming and pledges of troops, police, and material are well below the levels that UN planners believe are optimal. A number of prominent human rights organizations protest, claiming the UN mandate and small UN force are insufficient to restore stability and protect civilians traumatized by a decade of war.

In country, delays in deploying the peacekeeping force, police, and other elements of the UN mission lead to a widening security gap. The peace agreement provides for demobilization of the warring armies, but the country remains awash in weapons, and there has been a proliferation of criminal gangs, militias, and other illegally armed groups. Press and humanitarian NGOs warn that organized criminal networks are filling the security gap by forcing communities to pay for protection. Looting is sporadic in the capital, and interclan violence continues in the countryside. Thousands of villagers join the flood of internally displaced people into the capital and other large cities. Due to the poor quality of local police and the absence of functioning courts and prisons, these cities become increasingly dangerous. At an international pledging conference organized hastily by the United Nations, donors offer to fund new training of judicial and security personnel and to provide economic aid to jump-start the economy, but international assistance is slow to materialize.

In time, the arrival of the UN military force and police monitors begins to restore stability. UN peacekeeping units arrive with weapons, armored vehicles, and training to restore public order. Intimidated by the UN show of force, disruptive elements pull back and crime and disorder temporarily subside. Irregular militia forces nevertheless harass the peacekeepers, whose limited mandate restricts their ability to disarm combatants. The United States proposes to the UNSC that the peacekeeping force be given more robust rules of engagement and full responsibility for security. The parties oppose the idea at first, but relent when the SRSG offers to accept militia members for training for the new national army. The UN mission establishes a police academy (funded with additional voluntary contributions from member states) and begins recruiting from those who did not take part in the conflict. Again, the parties object, insisting that a percentage of their fighters be guaranteed admission to the new police force. The SRSG agrees, noting that the UN mission's mandate gives him no alternative.

To reduce the threat of renewed violence, the SRSG announces a UN-sponsored program for the disarming, demobilization, and rehabilitation (DDR) of former combatants, many of whom are child soldiers. Many UN agencies assist the peacekeepers in this multifaceted program, including the UN Development Program (UNDP), the International Bank for Reconstruction and Development (IBRD) of the World Bank, and the UN Children's Fund (UNICEF). On the first day, the turnout overwhelms UN representatives, who are unprepared for the thousands of former fighters who want to exchange their weapons for cash and a certificate to a training program. Violence flares when the cash runs out and the United Nations is unable to accept more weapons. A month later, the United Nations reopens the program, but realizes that paying cash for guns has created a market for old guns, while modern arms are hidden away. Former fighters discover that the United Nations is ill prepared to meet the huge demand for training, and the reintegration program suffers from a significant no-show rate.

In the capital, the conflict has shifted from the battle-field to the political stage, with wartime military leaders organizing political parties. Unfortunately, the transitional power-sharing arrangement is based on strict ethnic quotas for senior government positions and natural resource assets, lending a zero-sum dynamic to political issues. Establishing accountability for war crimes is hampered by the fact that former-wartime-commanders-turned-politicians were complicit in widespread atrocities. The SRSG announces a strategy for presidential and parliamentary elections, but preelection polling anticipate that voters will split along ethnic lines.

Meanwhile, economic growth is sporadic and skewed, leaving many average families behind. Hastily drafted, the UN mandate does not provide authority for the UN mission to restore essential services, and the rapacious interim government is not interested in spending on water and electricity. The arrival of hundreds of NGOs and UN personnel bids up rents and skews the salary scale, so local professionals leave their positions to work as drivers and interpreters. The arrival of free-spending contractors brings not only new restaurants and hotels but also prostitution and accusations of the involvement of international personnel.

The security situation is at times tenuous, because the group that refused to sign the peace agreement remains a source of attacks and anxiety. Observers believe the United Nations will hold successful elections but that new leaders will not be able to push forward the needed economic and political reforms. They fear that without economic progress the country will return to civil conflict within five years. Citizens fatigued by the long years of war are hoping that the elections will mark the beginning, rather than the end, of international engagement in the country.

Slowly, donor governments come to recognize that the extraordinary international presence in the country will not be short term. They begin to extend their timetables for progress and drawdown, while working to build local coalitions in support of reform and an increased local sense of responsibility for the country's long-term future.

SECTION

I

International Organizations

An Overview of International Organizations

THE TERM "international organization (IO)" generally refers to international governmental organizations or organizations with a universal membership of sovereign states. The most prominent IO is the United Nations, with 191 members. Other organizations whose membership is global include the World Trade Organization, the Universal Postal Union, and the International Hydrographic Organization. International organizations are established by treaties that provide legal status. International organizations are subjects of international law and are capable of entering into agreements among themselves and with member states.

Universal membership distinguishes international organizations from similar institutions that are open only to member states from a particular region. Examples of regional organizations include the European Union, the African Union, and the Organization of American States. These organizations are established by treaties among their members, enjoy international legal status, and can enter into agreements. There are still other organizations composed of member states that are based on particular criteria, such as historic association (the Commonwealth of Nations), economic development (the Organization for Security and Co-operation in Europe), and religion (Organization of the Islamic Conference).

Among international organizations, the United Nations has the longest and most significant experience with peace operations. International peacekeeping forces wearing blue helmets were first seen in the late 1940s. With a continuing surge in the demand for new peace operations, UN peacekeepers are now deployed in record numbers. In September 2006, the UNSC authorized a 40 percent increase in peacekeeping forces with the addition of 1,600 UN Police for East Timor and 13,000 new troops for southern Lebanon. The UNSC also authorized a 22,000-member peacekeeping force for Darfur, pending Sudanese government approval for the United Nations to replace the existing peacekeeping force of the African Union. The United States contributes police, but not troops, to UN peace operations.

This section of the guide describes the United Nations and its affiliated agencies, such as the World Health Organization, that compose the UN system. It describes a number of regional organizations that have played an important role in recent peace and stability operations. The section also describes a unique organization, the International Committee of the Red Cross (ICRC). ICRC is headquartered in Switzerland and staffed largely by Swiss nationals, but it has international legal status as a result of its responsibilities under the Geneva Conventions.

The United Nations

The United States was instrumental in the creation of the United Nations in 1945, at the end of World War II. According to the UN Charter, its purpose as a global institution is to save succeeding generations from the scourge of war by promoting peace and international security; fostering respect for fundamental human rights, justice, and the rule of law; and promoting social progress and better standards of life, so that all might live "in larger freedom."

Its major structures are the General Assembly, the Security Council, the Economic and Social Council, the International Court of Justice, and the Secretariat. The United Nations faces enormous challenges in adapting its bureaucracy, structure, and operations to the demands of the twenty-first century to transition from being "a convener of meetings to a coordinator of action" (United States Institute of Peace 2005, 4).

In the General Assembly (GA), which bears some resemblance to a world parliament, each of the 191 member states has one vote. Important matters require a two-thirds majority. The budget is adopted by consensus. The president of the General Assembly is elected to preside over an annual session that runs from September to August.

The Security Council (UNSC) has fifteen members. The five permanent members (P-5)—China, France, Russia, the United Kingdom, and the United States—have the power to veto resolutions. The GA elects the remaining ten members for two-year rotating terms. The presidency of the UNSC is held for one month and rotates among all its members. The UNSC recommends candidates for appointment to the post of secretary-general to the GA. The UNSC has primary responsibility for international peace and security, determines the existence of threats or aggression, and can recommend actions that are binding on member states.

Passage of a Security Council resolution requires nine votes with no negative votes (vetoes) from the P-5. The UNSC under Chapter VI can dispatch military observers or a peacekeeping force to reduce tensions, separate warring forces, or create conditions conducive to concluding a peace agreement. Under Chapter VII of the UN Charter, the UNSC can exercise "peace enforcement powers" to impose its decisions on member states through mandatory economic or financial sanctions, armed embargoes, travel bans, or the use of international military forces to create a safe and secure environment.

The UN Secretariat staff of 14,000 is headed by the secretary-general (SG), who is appointed by the General Assembly on the recommendation of the Security Council. The SG may serve multiple five-year terms. The SG is the personification of the United Nations, and his personal stature and impartiality are requisites for his role as a mediator or peacemaker. The SG can use his position as a pulpit for moral suasion, and his views on international issues carry great weight. He cannot, however, require member states to heed his advice. The SG must be particularly attentive to the views of the P-5, whose governments play a major role in setting the priorities and determining the policies of the world organization.

The UN budget is based on progressive assessments, with the United States and other wealthy states paying the largest portion of the organization's operating expenses. The eight largest contributors (Canada, China, France, Germany, Italy, Japan, the United Kingdom, and the United

States) account for more than 70 percent of the assessed contributions to the United Nations' general budget. The United Nations operates on a two-year budget cycle, with the general operating budget approved by the General Assembly. The general budget covers expenses for the Secretariat in New York, Geneva, Vienna, and Nairobi; regional commissions; political missions; and smaller UN offices in many countries. In 2004–05, the United Nations had a budget of $3.16 billion.

While the UN Charter requires member states to pay assessed contributions to support the work of the organization, it is often difficult to collect assessed dues. Nothing reflects more the fact that the United Nations is the servant and not the master of member states than that one-third are usually in arrears in payment of their assessed obligations. Such arrearages often result from member states' internal politics, budget shortfalls, disagreements with specific UN actions, or some combination thereof. As a consequence, the United Nations increasingly resorts to voluntary or extrabudgetary contributions versus mandatory dues to finance specific activities. Peacekeeping expenses are assessed annually for a separate budget that is now larger than the general UN budget. Peacekeeping budgets are annual (July to June) and are funded through a formula that places a higher assessment rate on the P-5. In 2000, UN members agreed to lower U.S. dues for the regular budget from 25 percent to 22 percent and reduced U.S. peacekeeping assessments from 30 percent to 27.1 percent. For July 2005 to June 2006, the combined budget for peacekeeping operations and political missions was about $3.8 billion, which funded 17 peacekeeping missions, troop salaries, and equipment; the UN Logistics base at Brindisi, Italy; and three special political missions in Iraq, East Timor, and Afghanistan.

UN agencies such as the UN Development Program and the UN Children's Fund have separate budgets funded by voluntary contributions. Voluntary funding is also sought for humanitarian assistance where appeals can capitalize on public concern over natural or human-made disasters. Voluntary funding means that crises that attract significant public attention or enjoy a high political profile receive adequate resources, while less-publicized tragedies are underfunded. The Asian tsunami of December 2004 attracted such large donations (80 percent of the total amount required in ten days) that aid organizations began returning money or requesting that donors permit their contributions to be used for other purposes. In contrast, Niger's food crisis in 2004–05 was virtually ignored until the media began reporting on deaths from widespread starvation.

The term "UN system" is something of a misnomer, because no single official has executive authority over the entire collection of agencies. In New York City, the GA has given the SG only limited authority over the staff and budget of the Secretariat. UN reform discussions at the 60th Anniversary World Summit recognized the need for the GA to revisit this and other management issues, but member states remain wary of increasing the SG's authority. Outside of UN headquarters, chief executives of UN specialized agencies, humanitarian funds, and other programs have direct authority over their own staff and budgets. They report to autonomous governing boards with their own priorities, which do not necessarily coincide with those at UN headquarters. Some have larger budgets than the assessed general budget that funds the Secretariat.

Culture and Staff of the United Nations

The UN Charter states that UN staff should have "the highest standards of efficiency, competence and integrity" and should be recruited "on as wide a geographical basis as possible." The founders believed UN staff should mirror the diverse political, ethnic, social, and cultural systems of the member states and operate in a non-partisan, neutral manner. The United Nations today has staff from 176 countries who average 16.5 years of service. Regrettably, some have not lived up to the organization's standards of integrity and excellence, and a few have even committed crimes. Member states have insisted on the development of new financial oversight mechanisms, an ethics office, new codes of conduct, conflict-of-interest rules, and whistleblower protection to improve performance and oversight. The GA is considering giving the SG more authority over staff, while the SG wants to fix the internal structures that are outmoded, cumbersome, and ineffective and conduct a buyout of redundant staff.

In 2004, the United Nations had 37,600 staff recruited globally. The United Nations is a small organization with global responsibilities, offices in more than 133 countries, and a budget that has experienced little real growth over the past decade. The United Nations has international professional and general service civil servants along with locally hired national staff. Overseas, UN national staff (paid at salary scales based on local costs of living) far outnumber internationals and can manage programs in the absence of international staff, as in Afghanistan during the war. Most of the United Nations' professional staff are from the developing world, and 40.5 percent are female (although the percentage at senior ranks is much lower). Geographical distribution formulas now cover less than half of the regular (assessed budget) positions in the Secretariat, yet member states still press for broad geographic diversity and gender parity among UN personnel and ask each year for a report on "under-represented UN members" in staffing. The United States is one of six countries with more than 400 nationals in the Secretariat. (The others are Ethiopia, France, Kenya, the Philippines, and the United Kingdom.)

As part of a multicultural hierarchical bureaucracy, UN employees are sensitive to the importance of an individual's rank and grade, years of service, diplomatic skills, language ability, and adherence to regular processes and norms. They are accustomed to dealing with diversity and accommodating different views and approaches. The personnel system traditionally has rewarded age and years of service in promoting and recruiting. The Secretariat and agency senior managers are older and more diverse than those found in the average corporation or NGO. UN under- and assistant secretary-generals average sixty years of age, while program or office directors (D-1 and D-2) average fifty-five years of age with 13 years of UN service. Senior professionals average 10.7 years of experience within the system. Staff turnover, particularly in the general service category, has been very low. Diversity, loyalty, and years of service remain important in most of the UN system.

The United Nations and its agencies, funds, and programs have a unified personnel, benefit, and pension system —which generally requires the same education and professional experience and similar job titles and pay grades. Employees should speak at least two UN languages (Arabic, Chinese, English, French, Spanish, or Russian) and must retire at age sixty (sixty-two if recruited after 1989). The GA has all but abolished new permanent staff positions, limited contracts to two years, and required Secretariat staff to rotate every five years.

Only core junior and midlevel professional staff (P-2-3) recruited after rigorous academic and linguistic requirements and passage of a competitive internationally offered exam can receive permanent employment. All staff vacancies are posted on the UN Web site (along with all UN documents), and applications are accepted online. Because thousands now apply, the crush of applicants can add more than six months to the time required to hire a new employee.

Member states once wanted salaries and benefits comparable to those of the highest-paid civil service. UN international salaries now are well below that standard. UN staff pay a flat tax to the United Nations, which is credited to their country's dues. Staff are responsible for their own housing and maintenance. Senior UN staff are afforded certain privileges and immunities in the performance of their work, but all staff are subject to the laws of the country in which they work. When serious crimes are involved, and where a fair trial is possible, the SG can waive diplomatic immunity. Member states are reluctant to fund staff training or education. Some say this reluctance hampers the development of staff resources and the United Nations' ability to utilize new technology or management approaches. In 2005, member states agreed to fund a one-time buyout of staff with redundant skills and to consider some additional authority for the SG to manage staff and budget resources.

New requirements for emergency response, disaster relief, and complex peace operations require personnel profiles different from traditional UN staffing. New missions are politically sensitive, urgent operations that require staff who have planning skills; who are highly adaptable; who are problem solvers; and who are experienced with outreach, negotiation, and mediation. Such field staff must be able to produce regular updates and analyses of needs, gauge their operational climate, and make the modifications needed to build and sustain local and international support for their evolving operations. Program managers must also be sensitive to diversity and gender issues in both their staffing and programming. The United Nations is working to develop more flexible administrative rules and procedures to permit rapid start-ups. It is working to integrate peacekeeping with humanitarian and development country operations.

UN staff normally rely on the host government and the parties to a conflict for protection and security. More than 1,900 UN staff have died in the line of duty, and thousands more voluntarily work in difficult and dangerous circumstances, relying on host governments for security. UN neutrality once protected its staff, but deliberate attacks against staff in Timor and UN headquarters in Baghdad disproved this notion, as have other kidnappings and attacks on UN civilian personnel.

The United Nations in the Field

The UN system is present in more than 133 countries and provides more than $13 billion annually in humanitarian and development programs. The United Nations has developed a multiplicity of offices, agencies, funds, and programs with different mandates, management structures, personnel systems, and donor bases. Many of these programs are implemented in partnership with NGOs, civil society groups, and governments. The SG and the GA have sought a greater harmonization of policy and operations in order to achieve a more coherent and effective UN approach, particularly at the country level. The 2005 World Summit supported the SG's efforts to develop greater use of common approaches and improved system-wide coordination. While situations vary, participants in peace and stability operations are likely to encounter the following UN representatives in the field.

The resident representative. The UN Development Program (UNDP), funded by voluntary contributions from governments, operates in 166 countries. It works to reduce poverty, improve governance, eliminate corruption, and connect countries to information and resources that will help local people improve their lives. The head of the UNDP in country is called the resident representative. The resident representative serves as the resident coordinator of UN activities and leader of the UN country team.

Resident coordinator. As the head of the United Nation's operations in country, the resident coordinator (RC) works to promote interagency collaboration, to develop common services, to improve security and communications, and to harmonize approaches and resource utilization to ensure that the UN country team's efforts fit within the parameters the host government agreed to in its UN Development Action Framework (UNDAF) or Poverty Reduction Strategy Policy (PRSP). The RC seeks to develop collaborative planning, assessment, and implementation of humanitarian programs, particularly those related to OCHA's annual Consolidated Appeal or a Flash Appeal for an Emergency. The RC also seeks to manage relations with the host government as well as civil society, NGOs, and bilateral donors.

The UN country team. Representatives from all UN offices, programs, and agencies, as well as the World Bank, and International Monetary Fund (IMF), are members of the UN country team. The RC regularly convenes the country team to collaborate on policy issues and to develop priority programs for implementation under the UNDAF or PRSP, and/or the OCHA annual Consolidated Appeal for humanitarian programs. The RC seeks to harmonize the country team's relations with the host government, NGOs, civil society, and donors and to work collaboratively on political, economic, security, humanitarian, or other issues.

The humanitarian coordinator. Where the United Nations has large relief and humanitarian programs, a humanitarian coordinator (HC) is appointed under the resident coordinator, or the resident coordinator may serve as both the RC and HC. The function of the HC is to oversee the collaborative assessment, planning, implementation, and operation of humanitarian efforts and to liaise with head-quarters, donors, and the host government.

UN field agencies. The UN development and humanitarian agencies often have a long-established presence in country. Staff are often knowledgeable about the local economic, political, social, religious, and cultural conditions. Agencies have developed contacts with government officials, as well as with civil society and NGOs. Some agencies will have multiple subordinate offices, headed by international or national staff, depending on the level of programming and security conditions. These agencies may include UNDP, UNICEF, the World Food Program (WFP), the UN Family Planning Agency (UNFPA), and OCHA, plus the independent specialized agencies like the Food and Agriculture Organization (FAO), WHO, and the International Labor Organization (ILO). If there are refugees, the UN High Commissioner for Refugees (UNHCR) will be present. For a human rights situation, the Office of the UN High Commissioner for Human Rights (OHCHR) may be there.

The United Nations' Tool Kit for Humanitarian Emergency Response

Flash Appeals. For an emergency, OCHA conducts a rapid interagency assessment of the disaster situation and gathers input from the UN country team, agency headquarters, relevant government officials, and NGOs to determine levels of need and the range of participating partners. OCHA and its partners develop a time frame for assistance (often six months) and identify sector needs and the entities prepared to meet them. It consults with providers, donors, and affected governments and determines any efficiencies of scale in procurement. It details funding needs and a plan for humanitarian response by agency and sector, ranging from sanitation to health, shelter, education, protection, human rights, food, water, and agriculture. A Flash Appeal describes both the context of the situation and the planned response. These appeals and related materials are on OCHA's Web site, which also tracks contributions received by donor and by sector. Appeals are updated and modified based on response and need.

OCHA's Emergencies Services Branch (ESB). Based in Geneva, ESB can deploy the following institutions as part of an emergency humanitarian response or as part of a complex peace mission.

Disaster Assessment and Coordination Team (UNDAC). The UNDAC is a standby group nominated and funded by member governments, OCHA, UNDP, and operational UN agencies such as WFP, UNICEF, or WHO. Upon the request of a disaster-stricken country, the team can deploy within hours to provide rapid assessment of priority needs and support for national authorities and UN resident coordinators.

International Search and Rescue Advisory Group (INSARAG). This intergovernmental network provides urban search and rescue (USAR) and related disaster response. It serves as a platform for information exchange, defines standards for international USAR, and develops a methodology for international cooperation and coordination in earthquake response.

The Humanitarian Information Centre (HIC). The HIC is a common service and space (sometimes virtual) accessible to all humanitarian actors and supported by OCHA or UN mission staff. It encourages coordination through the creation of a common framework for information management for assessing, planning, implementing, and monitoring humanitarian assistance. It provides orientation to a situation, develops and promotes data standards and sets, and promotes data sharing among all humanitarian actors. HIC tracks "who is doing what and where" in country.

The Military and Civil Defense Unit (MCDU). MCDU provides support by military and/or civil defense assets (MCDA). It conducts the United Nations' Civil–Military Coordination courses and coordinates UN participation in major exercises with humanitarian scenarios.

UN Central Register of Disaster Management Capacities. This is a database of noncommercial governmental and other resources for humanitarian use, including experts, equipment, and supplies, maintained by MCDU.

Logistics Support Unit (LSU). LSU manages stocks of basic relief items that can be dispatched immediately from the UN Humanitarian Response Depot (UNHRD) in Brindisi. The LSU maintains contingency plans for rapid deployment of supplies for relief and provides interface on logistics with other humanitarian agencies, including WFP, WHO, UNHCR, International Federation of Red Cross and Red Crescent Societies (IFRC), and ICRC.

Geographic Information Support Team (GIST). GIST is an interagency effort to promote the use of geographic data standards and geospatial information in support of humanitarian relief operations. Members are technical experts and information specialists from the UN and donor government agencies involved in disaster management or humanitarian aid. USAID, European Community Humanitarian Aid (ECHO), and the UK Department for International Development (DFID) are members, along with UN agencies.

World Food Program and Emergencies

In addition to providing food aid, WFP administers the UN Joint Logistics Centre (UNJLC)—an interagency facility to coordinate and optimize the logistics capabilities of humanitarian organizations involved in large-scale emergencies. The UNJLC reports to the Humanitarian Coordinator and to the Inter-Agency Standing Committee, UNHCR, UNICEF, and International Organization of Migration partner with the UNJLC and provides staff for the Rome-based core unit, which maintains the Field Operation Manual (FOM) and conducts logistics training for UN and donor government staff. To maximize logistics planning and management, the UNJLC provides pipeline, commodity, and logistics tracking information on the status of border crossings, customs, and infrastructure. It maintains a generic Web site to house general reference and deployment-specific materials.

UN Peacekeeping

There has been an unprecedented surge in the number and size of UN peacekeeping operations. In November 2006, 77,740 UN soldiers and police were serving in 18 missions. These personnel came from 108 UN member states. Anticipated operations in Lebanon, East Timor, and Sudan are expected to bring the number of military, police, and civilian staff to 140,000 in 2007. The cost of running so many large operations will boost the annual UN peacekeeping budget to $6 billion. Most of these operations will have robust mandates authorizing UN forces to impose peace and maintain stability.

Historically, peacekeeping operations were authorized under Chapter VI of the UN Charter, which provides for "The Pacific Settlement of Disputes" and seeks to resolve conflicts through "negotiation, enquiry, mediation, conciliation, arbitration, judicial settlement, resort to regional agencies or arrangements, or other peaceful means of their own choice" (Article 33). Traditional peacekeeping operations such as those in Cyprus and the Golan Heights provided UN military observers to monitor cease-fire or peace agreements with the consent of the parties to the conflict. Their purpose was to prevent outbreaks of conflict and peacefully resolve disputes. UN personnel were generally unarmed and were stationed along a line of demarcation, such as a national border. Their role was to report any infractions of the peace agreement, not to intervene to prevent violations.

More recently, peace enforcement missions have been authorized under Chapter VII, which provides for "Action with Respect to Threats to the Peace, Breaches of the Peace, and Acts of Aggression" and authorizes the Security Council to "take such action by air, sea, or land forces as may be necessary to maintain or restore international peace and security" (Article 42). These operations, such as those in Bosnia, Kosovo, and Somalia, were undertaken without the consent of the parties to the conflict and involved armed forces that imposed order in the country. Actually, neither Chapters VI nor VII mentions the words "peacekeeping" or "peace enforcement."

In the midst of the Congo Crisis in 1960, Secretary-General Dag Hammarskjöld famously coined the term "Chapter VI $1/2$" to describe peacekeeping operations that have functions that reside somewhere between those covered in Chapters VI and VII of the UN Charter.

Modern peace enforcement missions involve simultaneous political, military, and humanitarian activities in contrast to traditional UN peacekeeping, which involved only military tasks—such as monitoring cease-fires, separating hostile forces, and maintaining buffer zones. UN Police officers, electoral observers, human rights monitors, and other civilians have joined military peacekeepers. These civilians are responsible for a range of tasks, from protecting and delivering humanitarian assistance to helping former opponents carry out complicated peace agreements. UN personnel have been called upon to help disarm and demobilize former fighters, to train and monitor civilian police, and to organize and observe elections. Working with UN agencies and other humanitarian organizations, UN representatives have assisted with refugee return, monitored respect for human rights, cleared land mines, and begun reconstruction.

Not all UN peace operations have been successful. A high-level panel on UN peace operations chaired by Ambassador Lakhdar Brahimi (www.un.org/peace/reports/ peace_operations/) found that peacekeeping missions had not achieved their objectives because UN Secretariat staff lacked sufficient expertise and had not given the Security Council the hard truth about the size of forces and financial resources needed to conduct successful operations. The Secretariat had also failed to counsel against unachievable UNSC mandates. The Brahimi report called upon the Security Council to provide clear and achievable peacekeeping mandates and supply adequate resources for UN missions. The report found that the Department of Peacekeeping Operations needed additional experienced military and police personnel to develop and support missions, as well as standby reserves of equipment and forces and added logistics capacity to reduce delays in mission deployments. The report urged the United Nations to develop doctrine and establish a best-practices unit. The Brahimi report was approved by the Millennium Summit held at UN headquarters on September 6–8, 2000. The summit called on all relevant UN bodies to consider its recommendations. Subsequently, some of the report's recommendations were adopted, but many of its more far-reaching suggestions remain on the United Nations' agenda for future action.

Despite the failure to fully implement the reforms recommended in the Brahimi report, a RAND Corporation

Table 1.2. Ongoing UN Peacekeeping Missions

Name	Abbreviation	Location	Strength	2005 Gross Appropriations	Implementation Date
United Nations Truce Supervision Organization	UNTSO	Middle East region	150 military, 98 int'l civilian, 122 local civilian	$29.04 million	May 1948
United Nations Military Observer Group in India and Pakistan	UNMOGIP	Pakistan, India, the State of Jammu and Kashmir	44 military, 24 int'l civilian, 46 local civilian	$8.37 million	January 1949
United Nations Peacekeeping Force in Cyprus	UNFICYP	Cyprus	870 military, 50 civilian police, 39 int'l civilian, 109 local civilian	$50.69 million	March 1964
United Nations Disengagement Observer Force	UNDOF	Golan Heights	1,028 military, 36 int'l civilian, 109 local civilian	$40.90 million	June 1974
United Nations Interim Force in Lebanon	UNIFIL	Lebanon	1,996 military, 101 int'l civilian, 289 local civilian	$92.96 million	March 1978

United Nations Mission for the Referendum in Western Sahara	MINURSO	Morocco	225 military, 6 civilian police, 123 int'l civilian, 114 local civilian	$44 million	April 1991
United Nations Observer Mission in Georgia	UNOMIG	Georgia	119 military, 11 civilian police, 99 int'l civilian, 181 local civilian	$31.93 million	August 1993
United Nations Interim Administration Mission in Kosovo	UNMIK	Kosovo	37 military, 2,992 civilian police, 699 int'l civilian, 2,660 local civilian, 214 UN volunteer	$294.63 million	June 1999
United Nations Mission in Sierra Leone	UNAMSIL	Sierra Leone	3,368 military, 79 civilian police, 234 int'l civilian, 4,501 local civilian, 91 UN volunteer	$291.60 million	October 1999
United Nations Mission in the Democratic Republic of the Congo	MONUC	Democratic Republic of the Congo	16,336 military, 175 civilian police, 751 int'l civilian, 1,211 local civilian, 458 UN volunteer	$957.83 million	November 1999
United Nations Mission in Ethiopia and Eritrea	UNMEE	Ethiopia and Eritrea	3,330 military, 245 int'l civilian, 250 local civilian, 78 UN volunteer	$205.33 million	July 2000

continued

SOI

21

Table 1.2. Ongoing UN Peacekeeping Missions (*cont.*)

Name	Abbreviation	Location	Strength	2005 Gross Appropriations	Implementation Date
United Nations Mission in Liberia	UNMIL	Liberia	14,726 military, 1,060 civilian police, 493 int'l civilian, 717 local civilian, 437 UN volunteer	$822.11 million	September 2003
United Nations Operation in Cote d'Ivoire	UNOCI	Cote d'Ivoire	6,038 military, 218 civilian police, 280 int'l civilian, 234 local civilian, 98 UN volunteer	$378.47 million	April 2004
United Nations Stabilization Mission in Haiti	MINUSTAH	Haiti	6,207 military, 1,288 civilian police, 408 int'l civilian, 800 local civilian, 134 UN volunteer	$379.05 million	June 2004
United Nations Mission in the Sudan	UNMIS	Sudan	10,000 military, 715 civilian police, 1,018 int'l civilian, 2,632 local civilian, 214 UN volunteer	$279.5 million	March 2005

Figure 1.1. Liberia Organizational Chart

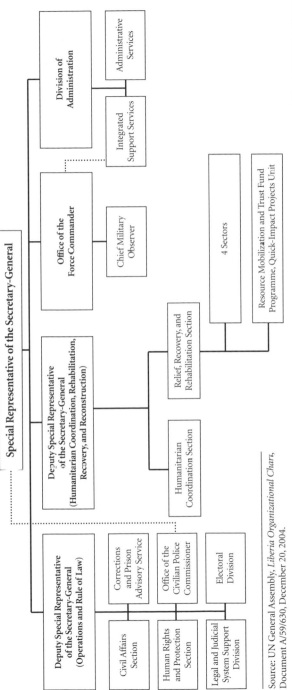

Source: UN General Assembly, *Liberia Organizational Chart*, Document A/59/630, December 20, 2004.

study found that UN peacekeeping efforts generally have been successful, despite the frequent mismatch between ambitious mandates and modest means. "UN missions are nearly always undermanned and underfunded, with uneven troop quality and late-arriving components. But despite these handicaps, the UN success rate among missions studied (seven out of eight societies left peaceful, six out of eight left democratic) substantiates the view that UN-led nation-building can be an effective means of terminating conflicts, insuring against their reoccurrence, and promoting democracy." (Dobbins 2005, 234–236) The study concluded that the United Nations was most suitable for nation-building missions requiring fewer than 20,000 troops, given its comparatively low cost structure and the greater degree of international legitimacy such missions enjoy.

Security Council Mandate and Establishing a Peacekeeping Mission

The Department of Peacekeeping Operations (DPKO) is responsible for managing peacekeeping and political missions for the United Nations. Its *Handbook on UN Multi-Dimensional Peacekeeping Operations* (available at www.un.org) describes the different generic components of a mission, gives background on the roles of senior managers, and explains how the various mission functions fit together. Specific mission information can be gathered from the detailed Web page that each UN peacekeeping mission maintains, which includes its specific UNSC mandate, its structure, senior management, functions, operations, and developments since the start of the mission. The *Handbook* notes that UN peacekeeping operations are multidimensional. Some carry out mandates alongside a regional or multinational peacekeeping force (such as the UN

Assistance Mission in Afghanistan). Peacekeeping provides transitional security and bridges the gap between the cessation of hostilities and durable peace, but only if the parties to the conflict have the political will to sustain peace.

Developing a mandate. The UNSC considers the recommendations of the SG that come from field assessments and consultations with the parties to the conflict and potential troop and police contributors. The UNSC must reach agreement on a broad range of subjects, including mission leadership and objectives, rules of engagement, size of military and police forces, civilian staffing, funding, public information, gender programming, and demobilization of combatants. It must also muster nine positive votes and no P-5 objections (vetoes) in support of a UNSC resolution. Once the UNSC resolution is adopted, the GA must approve the mission's budget. (A mechanism now exists to pay for "pre-mandate" preparations until a mission budget is approved.)

The peacekeeping mandate. The UNSC determines the objectives, size, and resources of the peacekeeping mission for a defined period, usually no longer than a year. The mandate must be renewed by the UNSC, which can modify its components (for example, the mix of forces, logistics, equipment, staff, and rules of engagement) to meet new conditions. The GA must approve any increased budget. When UN military involvement is not feasible or appropriate, the UNSC may authorize a regional force or a coalition to conduct peacekeeping or peace enforcement operations, as the North Atlantic Treaty Organization (NATO) did for Afghanistan. Such missions are funded by the participants or through voluntary trust funds established for this purpose to aid troop contributors that otherwise would be unable to participate. Such UNSC-mandated operations can later be "rehatted" by the UNSC to become traditional blue-helmet, UN-commanded and -operated missions financed by standard, mandatory peacekeeping assessments.

Types of mandates. The mission objectives can include monitoring a cease-fire, establishing a buffer zone, protecting the delivery of humanitarian aid, assisting demobilization of former fighters, clearing mines, protecting civilians, conducting elections, training civilian police, monitoring respect for human rights, and assuming administrative authority, as in Kosovo and East Timor. Given more difficult security climates, the UNSC is increasingly giving missions Chapter VII mandates with rules of engagement calling for robust forces able "to use all necessary means" to protect civilians and prevent attacks on UN personnel. The SG has emphasized repeatedly, however, that the United Nations should use force only as a last resort.

Assembling the mission. The United Nations has a cadre of experienced civilian staff who go from mission to mission, bringing their knowledge of a region, of different forms of government, of different cultures, of NGOs and contractors, and of the realities of working in a war-torn country. These personnel are augmented by temporary UN employees and contractors. The entire mission staff should reflect the United Nations' diversity as well as its concern for gender parity. The United Nations must assemble a staff with experience in justice, civil administration, economic development, engineering, gender issues, public information, and elections. DPKO has developed standby rosters and training programs to speed up deployments. UN volunteers are often used to fill out mission rosters, because UN recruitment can be a lengthy process. The use of short-term deployments (three months) can get personnel into the job, but it can hamper team building as well as winning the confidence and cooperation of wary local actors and donors. The United Nations utilizes private contractors for various administrative functions. Member states voluntarily may make additional personnel available on a nonreimbursable basis to support a peacekeeping mission.

The United Nations cannot maintain standing military and police forces, but must rely on member states to contribute personnel, equipment, and supplies. Agreed-upon rates determine the level of UN reimbursements to contributors. DPKO has to find the correct mix of troops and police for a particular mission while being sensitive to political, historic, or other issues that may make personnel from a given nation unacceptable. The United Nations must also acquire tactical air support, field medical facilities, and lift capacity from member states. The United Nations must conclude a status of forces agreement (SOFA) with the country receiving a mission. This SOFA covers the rights, privileges, and immunities of the mission and its personnel, plus the obligations of the mission to the host government.

More than one hundred member states have contributed troops to UN peacekeeping operations. Overwhelmingly, these member states have been developing nations, with Pakistan, India, and Bangladesh the three largest troop contributors. UNSC resolutions inviting "coalitions of the willing" (such as the NATO-led forces in Bosnia, Kosovo, and Afghanistan) have attracted forces from developed nations to undertake more dangerous peace enforcement missions.

The Key Players in UN Peace Operations

Special envoy. A civilian mediator appointed by the SG to help resolve a conflict, broker a peace agreement, or draw attention to an issue, the special envoy is not usually a resident in the area.

Special representative of the secretary-general. Once the UNSC approves the peacekeeping mission, the SG appoints, with the consent of the UNSC, his special representative (SRSG), a civilian diplomat with the rank of under-secretary-general. The SRSG is the head of the UN mission, serving as the resident director for political, humanitarian, and peacekeeping operations. The SRSG reports to the SG, who in turn reports to the UNSC on the mission's progress. The SRSG has to facilitate the political process by engaging the parties to the conflict in implementing the peace agreement. The SRSG must build a unified UN team that will work together for common goals, while managing relations with bilateral donors, the media, and UN headquarters.

Deputy special representative of the secretary-general (DSRSG). In large missions, the SG may appoint deputy SRSGs who manage selected aspects of the operation, such as political, humanitarian, or judicial affairs. Deputies report to the SRSG.

Chief administrative officer. The UN comptroller appoints the chief administrative officer, who reports to the comptroller.

Military force commander (MFC) or chief military observer. The senior military commander is selected by the SG with the consent of the UNSC. The MFC is a UN employee and serves under the authority of the SRSG. The MFC is responsible for the planning, conduct, and oversight of all activities of UN forces in country.

Police commissioner. The SG selects the commissioner of the UN Police Force with the consent of the UNSC. The commissioner is a UN employee who reports to the SRSG. UN policing may include a mandate for monitoring and training indigenous police, conducting joint operations, or, in executive missions, directly performing police functions such as criminal investigation, arrest, and traffic control until an indigenous force can be trained and deployed.

Blue helmets. These are troops volunteered by member states for a UN peacekeeping mission. National contingents remain under the authority of their government, which is responsible for pay, discipline, and personnel matters. Troops serve under their own officers, wear national uniforms and a blue helmet, or beret, and a UN badge. They take no oath of allegiance to the United Nations. More than one hundred countries contribute troops; fewer than 10 percent of the forces provided are from the developed world.

Military observer. Military observers (MOs) are unarmed military officers. Under a cease-fire or peace agreement, they are deployed to monitor military activities of the parties to the conflict, such as the withdrawal of forces or the cantonment of weapons. MOs serve as military experts to the United Nations and depend on the cooperation of the parties for their security and effectiveness.

Police. UN Police are proposed by their respective member states but individuals must qualify for UN service by passing examinations and satisfying specific requirements for health, physical fitness, professional experience, mission language proficiency, and driving ability. Police officers who pass the UN screening process serve as civilian experts in law enforcement for periods of six months or one year. They work as police trainers, technical advisers, or actual law enforcement officers, depending on the mission mandate.

Spokesperson. Each mission has a public information program to ensure that the United Nations' messages are clear and direct. Good communications are key to building public support for the mission and for highlighting obstacles and celebrating successes.

Types of Mission Organization

PEACEKEEPING LITE: UN ASSISTANCE MISSION IN AFGHANISTAN (UNAMA)

The UN model for intervention in Afghanistan was vastly different from those in Kosovo and East Timor. In those missions, the United Nations established an interim governing authority, while helping the local populace to create the institutions of democratic self-government. In Afghanistan, the United Nations sought to limit international involvement and to encourage the Afghans to assume responsibility for their own political reconciliation and economic reconstruction. Under the leadership of the SRSG, Ambassador Lakhdar Brahimi, the United Nations advocated a light footprint, an approach that minimized the number of international staff and consultants on the ground. This approach was based on the belief that the Afghans' historic intolerance for foreign intervention would not allow a large international presence and foreign administration. It was also based on the practical difficulties of maintaining staff in a challenging and sometimes dangerous environment.

The United Nations brought in a limited cadre of foreign experts and relied heavily on Afghan personnel. A small, NATO-led International Security Assistance Force (ISAF) initially operated only in Kabul. Over time, ISAF expanded its operations throughout the country. U.S.-led coalition forces participating in Operation Enduring Freedom remained in conflicted areas close to the Pakistan border, where they pursued al Qaeda and Taliban insurgents. Civil–Military Provincial Reconstruction Teams (PRTs) led by U.S. or NATO forces were deployed in provincial capitals to promote improved governance, increased security, and economic reconstruction. The United States established the PRTs, which were handed off to NATO countries. In fall 2006, a resurgence of Taliban activity required an increase in U.S. and NATO forces and the conduct of combat operations in the south and east of Afghanistan.

OVER THE HORIZON: UN ASSISTANCE MISSION IN IRAQ (UNAMI)

On August 19, 2003, a suicide truck bomb exploded outside the UN Assistance Mission in Iraq headquarters in

Baghdad, killing the SRSG, Sergio Vieira de Mello, and twenty-two others—the deadliest attack ever on a UN facility. The deliberate targeting of a UN headquarters signaled a dramatic escalation in the Islamist terrorist campaign against the international community. The attack caused the evacuation of nearly all of the UN international staff from Baghdad and triggered an exodus of non-governmental humanitarian and development agencies. In the aftermath, the United Nations created a core UNAMI forward planning team to support UN operations in Iraq and provide information sharing and coordination for the relocated NGO community in Amman, Jordan. During the next two years, UNAMI located its primary base of operations outside of Iraq, sending in teams to engage in activities in support of Iraq's political process, economic reconstruction, and humanitarian requirements.

In the fall of 2005, UNAMI maintained offices in Baghdad, Kuwait, and Amman, with small liaison detachments in Basra and Eribil. From these locations, UNAMI provided technical assistance to the Constitutional Drafting Committee of the Transitional National Assembly on the preparation of the Iraqi constitution. This effort included the printing and authentication of the final draft. In cooperation with IFES and the European Union, UNAMI provided technical assistance to the Iraqi Electoral Commission in organizing and conducting the December 2005 parliamentary elections. This effort included helping to establish 32,000 polling stations across Iraq. In addition, UNAMI provided technical advice to various Iraqi government ministries and through various UN agencies contributed to the construction of schools and the provision of humanitarian and development assistance. In November 2005, the secretary-general visited Baghdad to meet with Iraqi leaders and to honor the memory of the UN staff members who were killed in the August 19, 2003, attack.

INTEGRATED MISSIONS

Many observers find it difficult to understand the complex nature of the UN universe. Some idea of the scale of the coordination challenge can be gleaned from responses to a UN survey: fourteen UN organizations claimed a role in a range of emergency and post-conflict reconstruction activities; the same number claimed to have capacities both in emergency relief and in the protection of refugees and displaced persons; ten had responsibilities in human rights, fourteen in peacebuilding, five in the analysis of post-conflict recovery, twelve in demobilization, nine in demining and mine awareness, and four in peacemaking.

This institutional diversity and overlapping of functions is encouraged by the nature of funding for UN offices and agencies. Humanitarian work is funded by voluntary contributions that generally are spent in the same year they are provided. Agencies have to advertise their needs and attract donor support. Humanitarian and development agencies have similar yet different mandates, and, while part of the UN system, they value their individual identities and approaches. Agencies work to develop loyalty among donor governments, media, and the public and to build recognition of their particular services and accomplishments in order to obtain financial and public support for their programs. The UN system, like most government systems, has many individual actors who channel (stovepipe) their reporting back to their headquarters rather than across agencies in a coordinated manner.

The secretary-general has worked to develop more coordinated and cohesive UN field operations. In 1997, SRSGs were given expanded authority over the in-country operations of all UN agencies to ensure "that humanitarian strategies as well as longer-term development aims were fully integrated into the peacekeeping effort" (United Nations Office of the Secretary-General 1997). In 2000, the

SG further directed SRSGs to provide political guidance to the UN resident coordinators and humanitarian coordinators and clarified their roles and responsibilities. That same year, the Brahimi report recommended forming Integrated Mission Task Forces at UN headquarters to bring together all of the participating offices and agencies to improve planning and support for UN field missions. These task forces had some success.

Developing integrated field missions was the next step. In countries where there is a peace operation, the United Nations now seeks to develop integrated missions that bring the peace operation and the United Nations' pre-existing country program together under the leadership of the SRSG. This means the UN resident coordinator (usually the UNDP resident representative), who headed the UN country team before the peacekeepers arrived, must begin reporting to the SRSG. To ease this transition, the RC is often double-hatted and asked to serve as the senior deputy SRSG as well as the humanitarian coordinator for the peace operation. Ideally, this brings UNDP's expertise and programs into the new peacekeeping mission and provides additional resources and services, offering local civilians immediate benefits at the end of the conflict.

Communication is key to an integrated mission. Members of the former UN country team must understand and embrace the plans and strategic vision of the SRSG. The SRSG's team needs to become acquainted with the resident UN agency representatives and understand their concerns, strategic advantages, information, and human and program resources. It is important that the SRSG and staff make use of their UN colleagues' knowledge of local history, politics, personalities, and social and cultural practices and take advantage of their networks with civil society. The end of armed conflict may require rethinking or realigning humanitarian assistance programs to take advantage of the new political and security climate, to reach once-inaccessible regions or populations, or to aid once-avoided government institutions. This may require not only field and headquarters agreement but donor coordination as well. The SRSG must be sensitive to the agencies' needs for ongoing relations with donors, local authorities, the media, and overseas communities that have traditionally supported their programs. UN agencies may be more responsive to their governing boards back at headquarters or to major donors than to the SRSG in the field.

Integrated missions can bring additional resources to an SRSG, but they also can create friction between UN agencies. The SRSG wants the entire UN family to work together in support of the Security Council mandate. The SRSG's responsibility is to manage relations with all external agencies and local parties so that the host government can resume full responsibility for security and the well-being of its citizens. The sooner that happens, the sooner the peacekeepers can leave.

The dilemma for various UN agencies is that they will be staying. Resident UN agencies may enjoy the protection provided by UN peacekeepers but may also be uncomfortable if they are perceived as part of an armed occupation. During the conflict, UN humanitarian agencies may have provided aid impartially to all parties to maintain a neutral humanitarian space for their work. In the immediate aftermath, they may worry about being closely identified with UN military forces. Integrated missions may experience internal tensions given the UN humanitarian agencies' desire for impartiality and the peacekeeping mission's responsibility to implement the UNSC mandate and strengthen government institutions. Modern UN peacekeeping missions are charged, not just with ending the fighting, but with restoring public order and the rule of law and establishing foundations for long-term economic development and democratic governance. However, maintaining neutral humanitarian space is also important for the UN assistance agencies and must be given appropriate consideration.

Integrated missions are difficult to implement effectively because the UN system contains a multiplicity of offices and agencies with different mandates, funding sources, personnel systems, project cycles, and governing structures. To improve coordination, the secretary-general has established an Executive Board that brings together the twenty-seven chief executives of UN agencies for regular consultations, joint planning, and policy discussions. In addition, OCHA has assumed the task of developing country and regional humanitarian action plans in an established joint planning and appeal process that involves host governments, NGOs, and other UN agencies. Donor response for these appeals averaged 64 percent in 2003–04 ($6.47 billion of $10.8 billion requested). The SG is seeking an enlarged humanitarian emergency fund to address initial funding needs and to permit a more predictable, cohesive, and early response to emergencies.

UN Police

UN Police have become an essential element in peace operations. The UN Police Division is now an independent unit within the UN Department of Peacekeeping Operations, with a staff of twenty-five. In May 2006, 7,500 UN Police were engaged in seventeen UN operations, an increase from one mission with thirty-five officers twenty years ago. The largest deployment was in Kosovo (2,086 as of May 2006). The longest-serving mission is in Cyprus, where UN Police have assisted in security arrangements in the "Green Line" since 1964. The United States has been a major contributor of police personnel. U.S. police officers have served in Haiti, Bosnia, Kosovo, East Timor, and

Liberia. As of May 2006, 284 U.S. police officers were serving in UN missions.

UN Police officers were first included in UN peace operations in 1960 in the Congo, when a Ghanaian unit was attached to the UN military force to help the Congolese police maintain order. The term "CIVPOL," for "United Nations Civilian Police," originated at the start of the UN peacekeeping mission in Cyprus. The SGRC suggested including a military police unit in the peacekeeping force. The UN military commander proposed adding a civilian police unit instead; thus the term CIVPOL to differentiate civilian from military police. The official name was changed to UN Police in 2005.

The growth in the number of UN Police missions results from the ability of police to restore public order in the short term, while building law enforcement agencies that are critical for long-term stability. In crisis states, national law enforcement personnel either are unavailable, unwilling, or unable to provide security. UN Police have demonstrated the ability to assist the national law enforcement agencies or, in some cases, replace them entirely. UN Police missions are less expensive than military operations. The presence of UN Police is often more acceptable to host governments and citizens than that of foreign military forces.

Along with increased missions, there has been an expansion of the tasks UN Police are asked to perform. Their core duties are usually to assist in the reform, restructuring, and rebuilding of national law enforcement agencies as well as provide security support to such bodies through the deployment of formed police units. Initially, their role was limited to monitoring national law enforcement agencies to ensure that they respected international criminal justice norms and standards. The UN Police's responsibility was to "observe and report" infringements to higher levels in the UN mission. Over time, UN Police were assigned additional responsibilities, such as training and advising national law enforcement officials, identifying weapons caches, protecting refugees, and assisting with elections. The goal was to strengthen national law enforcement agencies, not to replace them.

This changed in 1999, when the Security Council authorized UN Police in Kosovo and East Timor to exercise a full array of executive law enforcement authority, including arrest, detention, and searches. The assumption of such far-reaching authority was necessitated by the withdrawal of Yugoslav security personnel from Kosovo and Indonesian police from East Timor under the terms of the respective peace agreements.

UN Police deployed in Kosovo and East Timor included formed police units. These units were armed and specially trained and equipped to perform crowd-management functions and other critical public order and law enforcement functions. In Kosovo, they carried out high-risk arrests of organized crime figures, provided close protection for UN officials, protected candidates and election rallies, manned border crossing points and patrolled the border, guarded the airport and prisons, and handled crowds at sports events and public gatherings. These units proved so versatile that they now make up nearly half of the UN Police deployed in peace operations.

While their number and authority have increased, UN Police missions have been troubled by problems with recruiting, training, logistics, and timely deployment. These problems result from the nature of policing worldwide. There is an international shortage of police, particularly those with special expertise. There are also wide differences among nations in the way police are trained and the duties they perform. Unlike military forces that are trained and kept in a state of "readiness" to deploy abroad, police are usually fully occupied serving their communities. Individuals must usually qualify as UN Police by passing a UN-administered examination. The United Nations must provide their facilities and equipment, including vehicles and communication. Recruiting and equipping a large police force drawn from dozens of countries takes time. Normally, UN Police forces require six months to one year to reach their authorized strength and become fully operational.

To address these problems, the UN Police Division has undertaken a number of important initiatives and reforms. It has developed policies for the conduct of police missions, improved criteria and procedures for selection of personnel, and enhanced the United Nations' ability to provide logistic support. The division has created an initial standing police capacity to deploy twenty-five trained and equipped police experts to provide rapid start-up for new police missions. This rapid response headquarters unit can quickly establish a UN presence and begin preparations for the arrival of a UN Police force. The Police Division has also added specialists in the two other elements of the justice system: legal and judicial systems and prisons. These experts advise the UN Police and are available to work with national institutions during peace operations.

Disarmament, Demobilization, Rehabilitation, and Reintegration (DDRR)

Every peacekeeping mission must deal with reducing the number of armed units and returning former combatants to civilian life. Assessed UN peacekeeping contributions cover the costs of UN peacekeepers, police, and civilian staff; conduct of the mission; and the disarmament and demobilization (DD) of former combatants. The SG's High-Level Panel on Threats found demobilization a key component of future stability. "Demobilizing combatants is the single most important factor determining the success of peace operations. Without demobilization, civil wars cannot be brought to an end and other critical goals such as democratization, justice and development—have little chance for success. These programs will be ineffective without the provision of resources for reintegration and rehabilitation" (United Nations Office of the Secretary-General 2004, 64).

The final stages in the process—rehabilitation and re-integration (RR) of former combatants—are achieved through programs that provide education, skills training, and access to land, seeds, tools, micro credit, or cash grants. Unlike disarmament and demobilization, these equally important activities are funded by voluntary contributions from donors and are provided either by UN agencies or through NGOs. A review of OCHA's 2003–04 appeal for RR programs showed that voluntary donor contributions often arrived late, if at all. Donors voluntarily contributed only 30 percent of the funds requested for rehabilitation, versus 100 percent of those accessed for peacekeeping. Fortunately, the 2005 World Summit directed the SG to establish a peacebuilding fund of $250 million to provide these services and to help restart local economies and institutions.

Programs to educate, retrain, and equip demobilized soldiers to return to civilian life are important stability investments. Without a means of livelihood, ex-combatants are prone to take up arms and turn to mercenary or criminal activity. Paid employment and business development opportunities can offer hope and a sense of personal security to populations disrupted by conflict. Reintegration programs are an integral part of the work of peacebuilding. It is important that the United Nations provide "assessed funding for first-year, quick impact projects in peace operations, as well as the full range of early disarmament, demobilization, and reintegration assistance when those have been identified in pre-mission assessments as critical for success"(United States Institute of Peace 2005, 97).

Peacebuilding Commission

On December 20, 2005, the UN General Assembly and the Security Council acted in concert to establish the UN Peacebuilding Commission (www.un.org/peace/peacebuilding), a new institution that aims to prevent countries emerging from conflict from falling back into chaos. After an initial period of post-conflict recovery, international attention often shifts elsewhere, leaving nascent governments and traumatized societies to cope on their own. The dropoff in external support for political reconciliation and economic development can have tragic consequences, including a rekindling of violent conflict. Developing rule of law institutions and local capacity for the protection of human rights and delivery of public services takes time. The new commission will bring together relevant actors to marshal resources, propose integrated strategies, develop best practices, and ensure predictable financing for recovery activities.

The commission will focus attention on reconstruction and institution building, provide leadership within the UN system, coordinate donor support, ensure predictable funding, and help sustain international efforts in countries emerging from conflict. Its thirty-one member states will include the five permanent members of the Security Council, seven members of the Economic and Social Council (ECOSOC), five countries that are leading contributors to UN budgets, and five top providers of military and police personnel to UN missions. Creation of the commission implements a proposal made in the report of the High-Level Panel on Peace and Security, which was endorsed by the 2005 World Summit. In establishing the commission, the United Nations recognized the importance of creating an institution that was dedicated to preventing conflict and building peace and stability.

Promise and Problems

For more than sixty years, the United Nations has served as a neutral convening body, dealing with issues as diverse as human rights, refugees, crime and drug control, food safety, maritime and airline safety, and disease control. The United Nations assisted Kosovo and East Timor in establishing democratic institutions and organizing elections for self-governance. In Afghanistan, the United Nations assisted with returning refugees, rebuilding government institutions, and drafting a new constitution. The United Nations has helped rally the world to fight the scourges of terrorism, to coordinate responses to natural disasters like the 2004 tsunami, and to deal with deadly pandemics like HIV/AIDS. But the United Nations' machinery for personnel management, program implementation, and decision making by member states is problematic. Following are brief descriptions of a number of problems that have confronted the world body.

RWANDA AND BOSNIA

In 1994, a UN peacekeeping force of 2,500 troops failed to prevent the death of 800,000 Tutsi and Hutu moderates in the Rwandan genocide. In July 1995, a small force of 110 armed UN peacekeepers failed to prevent Bosnian Serb militias from killing 8,000 defenseless Muslim men and boys who had sought refuge in a UN safe area at Srebrenica, Bosnia. At the request of the secretary-general, these two tragedies were analyzed in separate objective and self-critical UN reports. The UN report *The Actions of the UN During the 1994 Genocide in Rwanda* concluded that UN troops did not take appropriate actions and that member states lacked the political will to stop the massacre (www.un.org/News/dh/latest/rwanda.htm). The *UN*

Report on Srebrenica admitted UN complicity in the massacre, noting that the Security Council had allowed political considerations and the UN's tradition of neutrality and nonviolence to influence military decisions that were wholly inappropriate to the conflict in Bosnia (www.haverford.edu/relg/sells/reports/UNsrebrenicareport.htm).

THE OIL FOR FOOD PROGRAM IN IRAQ

In 2003, the United Nations faced a serious crisis regarding Iraq, which had been under UN sanctions since the first Gulf War. The United States sought agreement on an armed intervention in Iraq but was unable to convince the Security Council of the need for such action. After the U.S.-led "coalition of the willing" toppled Saddam Hussein, serious allegations surfaced regarding the United Nations' previous conduct of the Oil for Food Program (OfFP), a massive Security Council–approved project intended to protect Iraqi civilians from the ill effects of sanctions following the first Gulf War. Concerned about the seriousness of the charges, the SG asked Paul Volcker, former chairman of the U.S. Federal Reserve System, to head a UN-sponsored Independent Inquiry Committee (IIC) to investigate the allegations of kickbacks, official corruption, and other improprieties in the administration of the program. The SG pledged full UN cooperation with the probe.

After an extensive investigation, Volcker's panel found that the United Nations had failed to live up to the high standards of integrity and competence member states expected of its management of the program and that some of its staff had accepted bribes. Volcker found that the United Nations lacked effective audit and oversight of OfFP, which permitted corruption, inflated contracts, and kickbacks; sales of shoddy goods; and bribery of officials. The U.S. Congress demanded prosecution of anyone responsible for these crimes. Volcker reported that the United

Nations' operation of the program under the Security Council and the Secretariat was "a recipe for confusion and administrative evasion of responsibility" and a serious blow to the UN's credibility. He also noted that petroleum smuggling and other activities undertaken in violation of UN sanctions brought in additional illicit earnings for Saddam's regime. The final Volcker report on OfFP was completed in October 2005 with added calls for management reform.

The SG agreed on the need for management reforms. The United Nations would discipline any staff engaged in wrongdoing, waive immunity for anyone involved in criminal activity, and cooperate fully with national judicial authorities, since prosecutions could be conducted only by member states. At the September 2005 UN World Summit, world leaders endorsed most of the SG's recommendations for reform. New ethics, conflict-of-interest prohibitions, and whistle-blower protections were approved, as well as agreement for expansion of the Office of Internal Oversight Services (OIOS) and creation of an independent audit body.

PREVENTING SEXUAL EXPLOITATION AND ABUSE

In 2004, the United Nations discovered that peacekeepers and UN civilian staff had sexually abused and exploited some of the people they were sent to aid. Despite a UN policy of "zero tolerance of sexual exploitation and abuse," some peacekeepers and civilian staff had ignored local laws and UN restrictions and had raped and abused children and adults in UN missions in Congo, Liberia, and Haiti. The news produced a storm of outrage, statements that such serious crimes were totally unacceptable, and demands for action. The United Nations needed to develop effective deterrent measures to prevent such abuse, find ways to bring those committing such crimes to justice, and to force the abusers or their governments to provide assistance and compensation to the victims.

In 2003, the SG reminded staff that they were prohibited from visiting brothels (even where prostitution is legal). They were also discouraged from engaging in consensual sex with local citizens (United Nations Office for the Coordination of Humaninitarian Affairs 2003). At the same time, the Inter-Agency Standing Committee (a group of UN agencies and NGOs) adopted policies to prevent sexual abuse by UN staff and others working in post-conflict societies. In 2005, the U.S. Congress made this policy mandatory for any IO or NGO receiving U.S. funds.

In 2004–05, the discovery of new incidents of sexual exploitation and abuse (SEA) by UN peacekeepers and staff in the Democratic Republic of the Congo indicated that additional action was needed. The SG asked Prince Zeid Ra'ad Zeid Al-Hussein, Jordan's permanent representative to the United Nations and a former peacekeeper, to recommend actions that would end the tolerance for such crimes, increase reporting of such abuses, and produce appropriately severe punishments for UN personnel.

Prince Zeid presented recommendations to the United Nations in March 2005 (United Nations General Assembly 2005). He urged that all UN military and civilian personnel receive training on a mandatory UN Code of Conduct, which clearly prohibited SEA, and gave concrete advice on how to prevent and report incidents. Civilian violators would be subject to immediate dismissal and local prosecution. If the host country could not prosecute, offenders would be sent home with recommendations for disciplining and/or criminal prosecution. Prince Zeid urged all countries contributing troops to court-martial military perpetrators in the field (which has not yet been agreed to) and to seek restitution for victims from the responsible soldier or accept their government's liability to provide assistance. He noted that efforts to raise public awareness of the problem would lead to a rise in incident reports. Zeid emphasized the need for public and private pressure on member states for enforcement of zero tolerance of sexual abuse and for punishment of offenders.

The SG urged member states to immediately adopt Zeid's recommendations and provide the resources to implement them. The World Summit agreed to create a mandatory victim restitution mechanism by the end of 2005 and urged further GA consideration of Zeid's recommendations. As a result, DPKO is developing a training program on ethics, codes of conduct, and the prevention of sexual exploitation and abuse for all UN staff in peacekeeping missions. Several countries have initiated prosecutions of suspected offenders. UN mission heads have sent home a number of individuals and units that have engaged in misconduct. Some UN missions have issued additional restrictions to curb abusive behavior, forbidding fraternization, establishing curfews, and requiring uniforms to be worn at all times.

Darfur, Sudan

Darfur province in western Sudan has been wracked by ethnic violence. UN mediation failed to end the conflict between the Sudanese government, which is supported by Arab militias, and African rebel groups. The UNSC was divided on the issue of military intervention. Instead, the United Nations deferred to the African Union, a regional organization, which sent a small force of military observers and police to monitor events in the region. Despite the presence of the AU force, government-sponsored violence against civilians continued. In 2004, the United States described the government's campaign of killing Africans and destroying their villages as genocide. A subsequent UN Commission of Inquiry found massive human rights abuses by the government of Sudan but declined to describe the situation as genocide.

The AU agreed to expand its force to 7,000 troops and police and to aid victims and facilitate humanitarian aid. AU deployments were slow, however, despite efforts of the United States and European Union (EU) to provide logistic support. Diplomatic efforts by the United Nations, the United States, and other governments failed to produce a political settlement. Violence continued in what the SG described as "hell on earth" for the victims. To end the continuing violence, on August 31, 2006, the UNSC adopted a resolution authorizing a 20,000-member UN military force for Darfur. The Sudan government strongly opposed creation of such a force and urged UN member states not to contribute troops or police. In the ensuing standoff between the UNSC and the Sudanese, there was reluctance among member states to contribute forces, and the humanitarian crisis continued to worsen, with no resolution in sight.

In its study of UN reform, the U.S. Institute of Peace Task Force on the United Nations focused on Darfur and what the United Nations should do collectively to prevent genocide. Its findings speak to one of the realities of the United Nations: "the UN is a body composed of individual nation-states. Regretfully, too often member-states have found it convenient to lay the blame for failures solely on the UN in cases where they themselves have blocked intervention or opposed action by the UN. On stopping genocide, all too often the statement that the 'UN failed' should actually read 'members of the UN blocked or undermined action by the UN'" (United States Institute of Peace 2005, 4).

Reforming the United Nations

The failure of UN peacekeeping forces to prevent the massacre of Muslims in Srebrenica, Bosnia, and the genocide in

Rwanda prompted the secretary-general to call for a review
of the manner in which the United Nations conducted
peace operations. This appeal was given added urgency by
the initial failure of the UN peacekeeping mission in Sierra
Leone, where large numbers of UN troops surrendered
their weapons and uniforms without a fight and were taken
hostage by irregular forces.

On March 7, 2000, UN Secretary-General Kofi Annan
convened an expert Panel on United Nations Peace Operations to review UN peace and security activities and make
recommendations for improving the future conduct of
such UN peace operations. Former Algerian Foreign Min-
ister Lakhdar Brahimi chaired the panel, whose report was
submitted to the Security Council and the General Assembly on August 21, 2000. Release of the Brahimi Commission
Report (www.un.org/peace/reports/peace_operations/)
was timed to make it available for consideration by world
leaders at the Millennium Summit held at UN Headquarters on September 6–8, 2000. The report was approved in principle and all relevant UN bodies were requested to give it every consideration.

In December 2003, the growing scandal surrounding the
UN Oil for Food Program in Iraq encouraged the secretary-
general to renew his campaign for reform. The SG sought
to replace ineffective UN institutions, such as the discredited
Human Rights Commission; to refocus the organization's
work on peace, security, human rights, and development;
and to increase members' confidence. He commissioned
two groups of international experts to look at the challenges facing the world organization. The first group's report, *A More Secure World: Our Shared Responsibility,* contained recommendations for improving the United Nations'
work on global security (www.un.org/secureworld/). The
second group made recommendations on how member
states could meet the United Nations' target of halving the
worst incidences of poverty and underdevelopment by

2015 (the Millennium Development Goals, available at www.unmillenniumproject.org/).

In September 2005, the SG invited heads of state to a Special World Summit to consider adopting structural and management reforms, including the expansion of UNSC membership, a new Human Rights Council, and other measures covered in his report *In Larger Freedom: Towards Development, Security, and Human Rights for All* (United Nations General Assembly 2005). At the World Summit, government leaders agreed in the Summit Declaration to endorse for the first time a collective international responsibility to protect populations from genocide, war crimes, ethnic cleansing, and crimes against humanity. They also endorsed creation of a Human Rights Council and a new UN Commission on Peacebuilding, but deferred action on expanding the Security Council.

United States Institute of Peace Study on UN Reform

Concerns about the United Nations' performance led Congress in 2004 to direct the U.S. Institute of Peace to undertake a bipartisan study of U.S. interests in the United Nations and to recommend changes that would make the United Nations more effective. The study was undertaken by a bipartisan task force cochaired by Newt Gingrich, former speaker of the House of Representatives, and Senator George Mitchell, former majority leader of the Senate. The task force's report, *American Interests and UN Reform* (United States Institute of Peace 2005), was critical of UN administrative practices and recommended reforms to improve oversight of UN management and finances. These recommendations included creating an independent oversight body; a strengthened and independent Office of UN Inspection and Oversight Services; the appointment of a chief operating officer; and the tightening of UN conflict-of-interest, ethics, and whistle-blower-protection rules.

IOs

Profiles of Major International Organizations

T HIS SECTION OFFERS profiles of international organizations that may be involved in peace, stability, and relief operations. The contact information and descriptions in the profiles are based on information provided by the organizations themselves. The profiles are divided into two broad categories: global organizations and regional organizations.

Global Organizations

UNITED NATIONS (UN)
UN Headquarters
First Avenue at 46th Street
New York, NY 10017

Phone: 212-963-1234
Fax: 212-693-4416
Internet: www.un.org

When people speak of the United Nations, they usually refer to the UN headquarters in New York City. The United Nations was established in 1945 when 51 countries signed the UN Charter. Today, the United Nations has 191 members. The United Nations serves many purposes,

Figure 1.2. The United Nations
as a Series of Concentric Rings

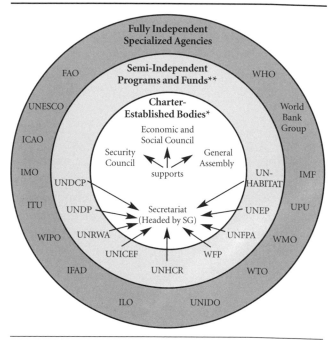

*Most funded by regular budget through assessed contributions
**Funded primarily by voluntary contributions but generally bound by
rules of the Secretariat

Source: United States Institute of Peace, *American Interests and UN Reform:
Report of the Task Force on the United Nations,* designed for the UN Task Force
by Branka, Jikich, www.usip.org/un/report/index.htm.

including promoting international peace and security, promoting human rights and justice, promoting political and
economic development, and coordinating humanitarian,
technical, and economic operations. The UN Secretariat,
the Security Council, the General Assembly, and the Economic and Social Council are located at UN headquarters.

The Secretariat

The Secretariat is composed of the international administrative staff of the United Nations led by the secretary-
general, the United Nations' most prominent official. The

Secretariat is responsible for daily operations of UN bodies, arranging their meetings and implementing their decisions. It also supports a broad range of UN-sponsored activities, including UN peace operations. Members of the Secretariat staff are recruited on the basis of merit from all member states. The largest concentration of Secretariat personnel is at UN headquarters in New York, but they also staff UN offices around the world.

The Security Council

Under the UN Charter, the Security Council has primary responsibility for maintaining international peace and security. The Security Council has fifteen members. The five major Allies in World War II—China, France, Russia, the United Kingdom, and the United States—are permanent members. The remaining ten members are elected by the General Assembly for two-year terms. Each member of the UNSC has one vote. Decisions require nine votes in favor, with none of the five permanent members casting a veto. Collecting nine votes in favor of a controversial resolution can be difficult because members are allowed to abstain. Unlike the GA, decisions taken by the Security Council are considered to be binding on member states. The Security Council decides on UN participation in peace operations. Security Council resolutions provide the mandate (authority) for the conduct of peacekeeping missions and authorize the organization of UN military and police forces and their deployment to crisis states.

The General Assembly

The General Assembly is the primary deliberative body of the United Nations. With every member state represented and having one vote, it is often likened to a world parliament. Unlike national parliaments, however, the General Assembly can adopt only resolutions that are not binding on member states. Its primary power lies in its authority to approve the UN budget and direct the Secretariat. The GA has authority to consider any matter within the scope of the UN Charter. Decisions on important matters such as the admission of new members require a two-thirds majority; decisions on routine matters require only a simple majority. The General Assembly meets in September for its annual session, which lasts until the end of the year. Given the growing number of issues brought before it each year, the GA assigns initial consideration of complex issues to its six Main Committees, which deal with the following issues: First Committee (international security), Second Committee (economic), Third Committee (social and cultural), Fourth Committee (political), Fifth Committee (budget and administration), and Sixth Committee (legal).

The following offices are located in the Secretariat:

UN OFFICE FOR THE COORDINATION OF HUMANITARIAN AFFAIRS (OCHA)
UN Headquarters
First Avenue at 46th Street
New York, NY 10017

Phone: 212-963-1234
Fax: 212-963-1312
E-mail: ochany@un.org
Internet: http://ochaonline.un.org

Established in January 1998, OCHA focuses on three core areas: (1) policy development and coordination in support of the secretary-general, ensuring that all humanitarian issues are addressed; (2) advocacy of humanitarian issues with the Security Council and General Assembly; and (3) coordination of humanitarian emergency response by ensuring that an appropriate response mechanism is established, through Inter-Agency Standing Committee (IASC) consultations on the ground. OCHA is the UN steward of Humanitarian Information Centres established in UN missions to support the coordination of humanitarian assistance through the management and provision of information. HICs were established in Kosovo, Eritrea, Afghanistan, and Iraq and then in Jordan and Liberia.

OCHA, with a staff of 860, maintains field coordination arrangements in sixteen countries and one region. Coordination is managed primarily through the IASC, chaired by OCHA's head, the emergency relief coordinator, with participation from all humanitarian partners, including the Red Cross and Red Crescent Movement. The IASC fosters interagency decision making in natural disasters and complex emergencies through joint needs assessments, consolidated appeals, field coordination arrangements, and the development and dissemination of humanitarian policy. The Consolidated Appeal issued at the end of 2004 was an inclusive, coordinated planning document for 2005 that analyzed context and needs and planned a prioritized joint humanitarian response, under the leadership of field humanitarian coordinators. OCHA maintains a database tracking donor contributions to Consolidated Appeals and Emergency Appeals.

UN DEPARTMENT OF PEACEKEEPING OPERATIONS (DPKO)

UN Headquarters
First Avenue at 46th Street
New York, NY 10017

Phone: 212-963-1234
Fax: 212-963-4879
Internet: www.un.org/depts/dpko/dpko

DPKO's mission is to plan, prepare, manage, and direct UN peace operations. Headed by an under-secretary-general, DPKO has a relatively small staff of military and police officers. DPKO is responsible for maintaining liaison with the member states that provide military and police personnel; maintaining logistics depots; providing vehicles, communications gear, and other equipment; and informing the UNSC on the status of peace operations.

INTERNATIONAL COURT OF JUSTICE (ICJ)

Peace Palace
2517 KJ, The Hague
The Netherlands

Phone: 31-(0)70-302-2323
Fax: 31-(0)70-364-9928
E-mail: information@icj-cij.org
Internet: www.icj-cij.org

The ICJ, also known as the World Court, was established in 1954 and consists of fifteen judges elected by the General Assembly and the Security Council. It adjudicates disputes between states. Only countries may be parties in a case before the ICJ. If a country does not wish to take part in a proceeding, it cannot be forced to participate. If it accepts the court's jurisdiction, it is obligated to comply with the court's decision.

INTERNATIONAL CRIMINAL COURT (ICC)

PO Box 19519
2500 CM, The Hague
The Netherlands

Phone: 31-(0)70-515-8515
Fax: 31-(0)70-515-8555
E-mail: pio@icc-cpi.int
Internet: www.icc-cpi.int/

The Rome Statute of the International Criminal Court was adopted on July 17, 1998, by 120 states attending the United Nations Diplomatic Conference of Plenipotentiaries on the Establishment of an International Criminal Court. The statute entered into force on July 1, 2002. Unlike the ICJ, the ICC can try individuals. National courts have primary jurisdiction, but persons who commit any of the crimes listed in the statute are liable for prosecution by the ICC. Such crimes include genocide, war crimes, and crimes against humanity. Though the United States is a signatory to the Rome Statute, the U.S. government has raised several objections concerning the ICC, and Congress has not ratified the implementing treaty. The U.S. government's primary concern is that the ICC will have jurisdiction over the nationals of nonparty states to the agreement, which would put U.S. military personnel at risk. Additionally, the U.S. government is concerned that the Office of the Prosecutor is unchecked in its authority and could engage in politically motivated prosecutions.

INTERNATIONAL CRIMINAL TRIBUNAL FOR THE FORMER YUGOSLAVIA (ICTY)

PO Box 13888
2501 EW, The Hague
The Netherlands

Phone: 31-(0)70-512-5493 (Outreach Program)
Fax: 31-(0)70-512-8953 (Outreach Program)
Internet: www.un.org/icty/

ICTY was established by UNSC Resolution 827 on May 25, 1993, to deal with serious violations of international humanitarian law committed during the wars in Bosnia, Croatia, and Kosovo. The objectives of the ICTY are to bring to justice persons responsible for serious violations of international humanitarian law; to render justice to the victims; to deter further crimes; and to contribute to the restoration of peace by promoting reconciliation in the former Yugoslavia.

INTERNATIONAL CRIMINAL TRIBUNAL FOR RWANDA (ICTR)

Arusha International Conference Centre
PO Box 6016
Arusha, Tanzania

Phone: 255-27-250-4207 or 212-963-2850
(UN Headquarters office)
Fax: 255-27-250-4000 or 212-963-2848
(UN Headquarters office)
E-mail: ictr-press@un.org
Internet: www.ictr.org

UN Security Council Resolution 955 created ICTR on November 8, 1994. ICTR was established for the prosecution of persons responsible for genocide and other serious violations of international humanitarian law committed in Rwanda between January 1, 1994, and December 31, 1994. ICTR may also deal with the prosecution of Rwandan citizens responsible for genocide and other violations of international law committed in neighboring countries during the same period.

SPECIAL COURT FOR SIERRA LEONE (SCSL)

Jomo Kenyatta Road
New England, Freetown
Sierra Leone

Phone: 232-22-297-000
Fax: 232-22-297-001
E-mail: scsl-mail@un.org
Internet: www.sc-sl.org

The Special Court for Sierra Leone was established in 2000 by the United Nations and the government of Sierra Leone. The court is mandated to try those responsible for war crimes, crimes against humanity, and other serious violations of international humanitarian law and Sierra Leonean law committed in Sierra Leone since November 30, 1996. Specifically, the charges include murder, rape, extermination, acts of terror, enslavement, looting and burning, sexual slavery, conscription of children into an armed force, and attacks on UN peacekeepers and humanitarian workers.

Other UN and UN-Affiliated Entities

The UN system is composed of numerous affiliated organizations and agencies. The following profiles spotlight UN agencies that may be involved in peace, stability, and relief operations.

UNITED NATIONS DEPARTMENT OF POLITICAL AFFAIRS (DPA)

UN Headquarters
First Avenue at 46th Street
New York, NY 10017

Phone: 212-963-1234
Fax: 212-963-1312
Internet: www.un.org/Depts/dpa/

The mission of DPA is to advise the secretary-general on all political matters related to the SG's responsibilities under the UN Charter concerned with international peace and security. This includes analyzing and assessing political developments throughout the world; identifying potential or actual conflicts where the United Nations could play a useful role; recommending to the SG appropriate actions in such cases and executing the approved policy; and advising the SG on requests for electoral assistance and coordinating programs established in response.

DPA has primary responsibility within the United Nations for conflict prevention, peacebuilding, and peacemaking. To accomplish this mandate, DPA has five thematic divisions:

- Electoral Assistance Division, which assists with the formation of governments through the conduct of free and fair elections
- Security Council Affairs Division, which provides advice and services to the Security Council and its subsidiary organs
- Decolonization Unit, which helps implement the Declaration on the Granting of Independence to Colonial Countries and Peoples and assists the General Assembly regarding the remaining Non-Self-Governing Territories
- Division for Palestinian Rights, which is responsible for generating heightened international awareness on the question of Palestine
- Office of the United Nations Special Coordinator for the Middle East Peace Process, which serves as the United Nations' focal point for the Middle East Peace Process

FOOD AND AGRICULTURE ORGANIZATION (FAO)

Viale delle Terme di Caracalla
00100 Rome
Italy

Phone: 39-06-57051
Fax: 39-06-570-53152

E-mail: FAO-HQ@fao.org
Internet: www.fao.org

FAO was founded in October 1945 with a mandate to raise levels of nutrition and standards of living, to improve agricultural productivity, and to better the living conditions of rural populations. Today, FAO is the largest autonomous agency within the UN system, with 180 member states plus the European Union and more than 4,300 professional staff. Since its inception, FAO has worked to alleviate poverty and hunger by promoting agricultural development, improved nutrition, and the pursuit of food security. The organization offers direct development assistance; collects, analyzes, and disseminates information; provides policy and planning advice to governments; and acts as an international forum for debate on food and agriculture issues. FAO is active in land and water development; plant and animal production; forestry and fisheries; economic and social policy; investment; nutrition; food standards and commodities; and trade. It also plays a major role in dealing with food and agriculture emergencies.

INTERNATIONAL FUND FOR AGRICULTURAL DEVELOPMENT (IFAD)

Via del Serafico, 107
00142 Rome
Italy

Phone: 39-065-4591
Fax: 39-065-043-463
E-mail: ifad@ifad.org
Internet: www.ifad.org

IFAD was established as an international financial institution in 1977 as one of the major outcomes of the 1974 World Food Conference. IFAD's mission is to finance agricultural development projects in developing countries to increase food production. One of the most important insights emerging from the conference was that the causes of food insecurity and famine were not so much failures in food production, but structural problems relating to poverty and to the fact that the majority of the developing world's poor populations were concentrated in rural areas. Through low-interest loans and grants, IFAD works with governments to develop and finance programs that enable the rural poor to overcome poverty themselves by improving access to natural resources, appropriate technologies, financial services, and markets.

INTERNATIONAL MONETARY FUND (IMF)

700 19th Street NW
Washington, DC 20431

Phone: 202-623-7000
Fax: 202-623-4661
E-mail: publicaffairs@imf.org
Internet: www.imf.org

The IMF was established at a conference held in Bretton Woods, New Hampshire, in July 1944. It came into official existence on December 27, 1945, when 29 countries signed its Articles of Agreement. Now with 182 member states, the organization is open to any country that is willing to adhere to the IMF charter of rights and obligations. The IMF's statutory purposes include promoting the balanced expansion of world trade, the stability of exchange rates, the avoidance of competitive currency devaluations, and the orderly correction of a country's balance of payments problems. The IMF makes its financial resources temporarily available to member states experiencing balance of payments difficulties under adequate safeguards so as to shorten the duration and lessen the degree of disequilibrium in the international balances of payments of members. The IMF has a staff of 2,700 from 23 countries.

UNITED NATIONS CHILDREN'S FUND (UNICEF)
333 East 38th Street
(Mail Code: GC-6)
New York, NY 10016

Phone: 212-686-5522
Fax: 212-779-1679
E-mail: information@unicefusa.org
Internet: www.unicef.org

The UN General Assembly established UNICEF in 1946 to assist children in Europe following World War II. In 1953, UNICEF became a permanent organization of the UN system and had its mission expanded to include meeting the needs of children throughout the world. UNICEF advocates and works for the protection of children's rights so that young people can meet their basic needs and reach their full potential. It works with other UN bodies and with governments and NGOs to promote community-based services in primary health care, basic education, and safe water and sanitation in more than 140 developing countries. Some of UNICEF's largest and best-known projects include immunization, salt iodization, oral rehydration, sanitation, prenatal care, and vitamin and other nutritional supplement programs. In humanitarian crises, UNICEF organizes tranquility programs, which supply suffering children and their families with temporary shelter, bedding material, and food. UNICEF maintains programs in 161 countries, with 8 regional offices, 126 country offices, and a staff of more than 5,500. Internationally recognized celebrities often serve as goodwill ambassadors for UNICEF.

UNITED NATIONS DEVELOPMENT PROGRAM (UNDP)

One United Nations Plaza
New York, NY 10017

Phone: 212-906-5295
Fax: 212-906-5364
Internet: www.undp.org

UNDP is the world's largest multilateral source of grant funding for economic development. It was founded in 1965 through a merger of two predecessor programs: the UN Expanded Program of Technical Assistance and the UN Special Fund. UNDP is supported by voluntary contributions of UN member states and UN-affiliated agencies, which together provide approximately $1 billion annually. Its mission is to help countries build national capacity to achieve sustainable human development, giving top priority to eliminating poverty and building equity. Through a unique network of 132 country offices and a staff of 5,300 personnel, UNDP works in more than 170 countries and territories, providing programs on environmental regeneration, job creation, and the advancement of women. UNDP also promotes sound governance and market development and assists in rebuilding societies in the aftermath of war and humanitarian emergencies. UNDP draws on the expertise of developing country nationals and NGOs, the other specialized agencies of the UN system, and research institutes in every field.

UNITED NATIONS EDUCATION, SCIENTIFIC, AND CULTURAL ORGANIZATION (UNESCO)

7 place de Fontenoy
75352 Paris SP
France

Phone: 33-(0)1-45-68-1000
Fax: 33-(0)1-45-67-1690
Internet: www.unesco.org

UNESCO was created in 1945 to restore European education systems following World War II. Today, UNESCO has expanded to function as a laboratory of ideas and a standard-setter on emerging ethical issues. UNESCO promotes international cooperation among its 192 member states and six associate members in the fields of education, science, culture, and communication. These efforts encompass three main strategic thrusts: (1) developing and promoting universal principles and norms in education, science, culture, and communication; (2) promoting pluralism through safeguarding diversity and respecting human rights; and (3) promoting empowerment and participation in the emerging knowledge society through equitable access, capacity building, and sharing of information.

UNITED NATIONS HUMAN SETTLEMENTS PROGRAM (HABITAT)

UN-HABITAT
Room DC2-0943, Two UN Plaza
New York, NY 10017

Phone: 212-963-4200
Fax: 212-963-8721
E-mail: habitatny@un.org
Internet: www.unchs.org

Since its inception in 1978, HABITAT has promoted socially and environmentally sustainable towns and cities through programs that provide adequate shelter; reduce poverty; and promote sustainable development, social inclusion, access to safe water and sanitation, and environmental protection. To advance its mandate, HABITAT uses

IOs

information management to expand the global understanding of urban development and creates strategic partnerships to leverage resources and coordinate international program activities that work toward similar ends.

UNITED NATIONS HIGH COMMISSIONER FOR HUMAN RIGHTS (OHCHR)

Palais des Nations
CH-1211 Geneva 10
Switzerland

Phone: 41-22-917-9434
Fax: 41-22-917-9024
E-mail: InfoDesk@ohchr.org
Internet: www.ohchr.org

The High Commissioner for Human Rights is the principal UN official responsible for promoting respect for internationally recognized human rights and fundamental freedoms. The post was created in 1993. The Office of the High Commissioner for Human Rights (OHCHR) leads the international human rights movement by acting as a spokesperson with moral authority and as the main voice of support for victims. OHCHR encourages links between regional, national, and international groups and organizations to ensure practical implementation of the findings and recommendations of international human rights bodies. To foster those links, OHCHR has working agreements with many organizations, has appointed regional representatives and advisers, and has set up field offices worldwide.

UNITED NATIONS HIGH COMMISSIONER FOR REFUGEES (UNHCR)

Case Postale 2500
CH-1211 Geneva 2
Switzerland

Phone: 41-22-739-8111
Internet: www.unhcr.ch

The UN General Assembly created UNHCR in 1950 to assist World War II refugees in Europe. Today, UNHCR's mission is to protect refugees worldwide by providing protection, food, shelter, medical care, and other types of assistance. It has also assumed responsibility for asylum seekers and internally displaced people in addition to those who have crossed international borders. UNHCR has offices in 116 countries. Its 6,689 staff members care for a total of 20.8 million people of concern. UNHCR works with nearly a thousand NGOs that assist refugees as implementing partners.

UNITED NATIONS MINE ACTION SERVICE (UNMAS)

Department of Peacekeeping Operations
Two UN Plaza, 6th Floor
New York, NY 10017

Phone: 212-963-1875
Fax: 212-963-4879
Internet: www.mineaction.org

Mine action entails more than removing land mines from the ground. It also includes a range of efforts aimed at protecting people from danger, helping victims become self-sufficient, and advocating for a mine-free world. In many countries, unexploded ordnance, or UXO, poses a threat to people's safety. Bombs, mortars, grenades, missiles, or other devices that fail to detonate on impact, but remain volatile and can kill if touched or moved, are UXO.

There are five aspects (or pillars) of mine action: (1) removing and destroying land mines and UXO and marking or fencing off contaminated areas; (2) educating people to help them understand the risks, identify mines and UXO, and learn how to avoid them; (3) providing medical assistance and rehabilitation services to victims, including job skills training; (4) encouraging countries to participate in international treaties and conventions designed to end the production, trade, shipment, or use of mines; and (5) helping countries destroy their stockpiles of mines, as required by international agreements, such as the 1999 Anti-Personnel Mine-Ban Convention.

UNITED NATIONS OFFICE ON DRUGS AND CRIME (UNODC)

Vienna International Centre
PO Box 500
A-1400 Vienna
Austria

Phone: 43-1-26060-0
Fax: 43-1-26060-5866
Internet: www.unodc.org

Established in 1997, UNODC has approximately 500 staff members worldwide. UNODC is mandated to assist member states in their struggle against illicit drugs, crime, and terrorism. The three key activities of UNODC are (1) increasing international understanding of threats posed by international organized crime, particularly trafficking in narcotics; (2) assisting states to implement international treaties and develop domestic legislation on drugs, crime, and terrorism; and (3) enhancing the capacity of member states to counteract drugs, crime, and terrorism. UNODC has assisted the Afghan government in surveying opium production; publishing annual reports on cultivation and production; and developing new laws, regulations, and enforcement programs.

WORLD BANK GROUP

1818 H Street NW
Washington, DC 20433

Phone: 202-473-1000
Fax: 202-477-6391
Internet: www.worldbank.org

The World Bank Group is composed of four organizations: the International Bank for Reconstruction and Development (IBRD), the International Development Association (IDA), the International Finance Corporation (IFC), and the Multilateral Investment Guarantee Agency (MIGA). The IBRD and the IDA, combined, make up the World Bank. Established in 1945, the IBRD is owned by 180 governments, which share responsibility for how the organization is financed and how its money is spent. Under its Articles of Agreement, only countries that are members of the International Monetary Fund (IMF) may be members of the IBRD. The IDA was established in 1960 to assist poorer developing countries on terms that would bear less heavily on their balance of payments than IBRD loans.

The World Bank offers loans, advice, and an array of customized resources to more than a hundred developing countries. It does this in a way that maximizes the benefits and cushions the shock to poorer countries of participation in the global economy. The World Bank uses its money and staff, and coordinates with other organizations to help developing countries achieve stable, sustainable, and equitable growth. The bank emphasizes the need for investing in people, particularly through basic health and education. It also encourages environmental protection, private sector development, and delivering government services to create a stable macroeconomic environment conducive to investment and long-term planning. The World Bank is the largest provider of development assistance, committing about $30 billion in new loans each year. The World Bank also coordinates with other organizations to ensure that resources are used to full effect in supporting a country's development agenda.

WORLD FOOD PROGRAM (WFP)

Via C. G. Viola 68, Parco dei Medici
00148 Rome
Italy

Phone: 39-06-65131
Fax: 39-06-6513-2840
E-mail: wfpinfo@wfp.org
Internet: www.wfp.org

The UN General Assembly and the Food and Agriculture Organization established WFP in 1963. It is the world's largest food aid organization and is at the forefront of eradicating world hunger. WFP's mission is to provide food aid to save lives in refugee and other emergency situations; to improve the nutrition and quality of life of the most vulnerable people; and to promote the self-reliance of poor people and communities through labor-intensive work programs. WFP uses food aid to support economic and social development; meet refugee and other emergency food needs; and promote world food security. WFP's 8,000 staff members work in food aid emergency and development operations that benefit 104 million people in more than eighty countries. WFP provided 4.2 million metric tons of food aid around the world in 2005, primarily to the least developed and most food-deficit countries.

WORLD HEALTH ORGANIZATION (WHO)

Avenue Appia 20
1211 Geneva 27
Switzerland

Phone: 41-22-791-2111
Fax: 41-22-791-3111
E-mail: info@who.int
Internet: www.who.int/en/

WHO provides worldwide guidance in the field of health; cooperates with governments to strengthen the planning, management, and evaluation of national health programs; and develops and transfers appropriate health technology, information, and standards for health care. Since its creation in 1948, WHO has led the fight against infectious diseases by providing health services and essential medicine. The agency's global immunization programs have saved millions of children each year from death and disability. WHO was at the forefront of the eradication of smallpox in 1980 and is playing a significant role in trying to eliminate other major diseases, such as poliomyelitis, guinea-worm disease, and leprosy. WHO has a staff of 3,800.

Outside the UN System

Although most international organizations are part of the United Nations system, several are not. Within the fields of humanitarian assistance, human rights, and refugee resettlement, two of the most prominent are the International

Committee of the Red Cross and the International Organization for Migration (IOM).

INTERNATIONAL COMMITTEE OF THE RED CROSS (ICRC)

19 Avenue de la Paix
CH 1202 Geneva
Switzerland

Phone: 41-22-734-6001
Fax: 41-22-733-2057
E-mail: webmaster.gva@icrc.org
Internet: www.icrc.org

The ICRC was established in 1863 by an international
conference. Originally named the International Committee for Relief to the Wounded, the ICRC draws its legal status from the four Geneva Conventions (1864, 1907, 1929,
and 1949) and the two Additional Protocols of 1977. Thus,
it is an independent international organization with a
basis in international law. The ICRC is subject to the Swiss
Civil Code and, until recently, all representatives of the
ICRC were Swiss nationals.

The ICRC, the International Federation of Red Cross
and Red Crescent Societies, and the National Red Cross and
Red Crescent Societies make up the International Red Cross
and Red Crescent Movement. (Red Crescent societies are
the Red Cross' counterparts in Islamic countries.) In August 2005, the International Red Cross and Red Crescent
Movement accepted the decision of a diplomatic conference held in Geneva to create a third emblem for the organization alongside the red cross and red crescent. The
new emblem, a red square frame balancing on one corner
on a white background, meets the demand for an organizational symbol that is free of religious, political, or other
connotations.

Under the Geneva Conventions and the 1977 Protocols, the ICRC provides protection and relief to members of the armed forces wounded in conflict or at sea, prisoners of war, and civilians in occupied or hostile territory. The ICRC visits prisoners of war and internal conflicts; exchanges letters and correspondence; traces missing persons; and facilitates family reunions. It provides emergency medical assistance in certain conflict zones and food and shelter in humanitarian emergencies. The ICRC has a staff of more than 10,000, of whom 9,000 work in the field. ICRC staff members visited more than half a million detainees a year throughout the world. The ICRC works closely with the 176 National Red Cross and Red Crescent organizations. According to the movement's charter of 1965, all component organizations are subject to seven fundamental principles: humanity, impartiality, neutrality, independence, voluntary service, unity, and universality.

INTERNATIONAL ORGANIZATION FOR MIGRATION (IOM)

17 Route des Morillons
CH-1211 Geneva 19
Switzerland

Phone: 41-22-717-9111
Fax: 41-22-798-6150
E-mail: info@iom.int
Internet: www.iom.int

IOM was created in 1951 at the initiative of Belgium and the United States. IOM organizes the safe movement of people for temporary and permanent resettlement or return to their countries of origin. It provides predeparture medical screening and cultural orientation programs. Activities include the movement of refugees resettling in new countries, medical evacuation of war victims, and aid to irregular and trafficked migrants returning voluntarily to their country of origin. In emergency and postcrisis situations, such as in Afghanistan, East Timor, and Kosovo, IOM has organized the movement of people in need of international assistance, stabilized populations through the provision of emergency relief and short-term community and microenterprise development programs, returned and reintegrated both internally displaced persons and demobilized combatants, and organized out-of-country voting. IOM has a staff of 1,000 spread among its 72 field offices. IOM has 109 member countries; another 24 countries have observer status.

Regional International Organizations

Many of the world's international organizations are regional in nature—that is, they serve a limited geographic area and/or are composed of member states that are located in a certain region. Under Chapter VIII of the UN Charter, the Security Council can assign regional organizations responsibility for conflict resolution in their geographic area. Since the end of the Cold War, regional organizations have played a prominent role in peace operations. Given the immediacy of the problem, regional organizations have both a substantial interest in preventing the reigniting of conflict and more relevant expertise in regional affairs than does the United Nations. In Liberia, the Economic Community of West African States (ECOWAS) provided a force of armed peacekeepers that augmented a UN mission of unarmed observers. In the Balkans, the Organization for Security and Co-operation in Europe and the European Union took over from the United Nations and managed the final stage of the peace implementation process. UN peacekeeping gave way to EU tutoring to prepare countries for eventual membership in a variety of European institutions.

Following are descriptions of regional organizations that have played a role in meeting humanitarian emergencies and participating in peace and stability operations.

AFRICA AND THE MIDDLE EAST

AFRICAN UNION (AU)
PO Box 3243
Addis Ababa
Ethiopia

Phone: 251-11-551-7700
Fax: 251-11-551-7844
E-mail: webmaster@africa-union.org
Internet: www.africa-union.org

Founded in 1963 as the Organization of African Unity, the African Union is the continent's primary political body and guarantor of African security. Its secretariat serves as the organization's bureaucratic organ. Heads of state and government of its fifty-three member countries meet once a year for a summit. More than 500 people from the member states staff the AU. The purpose of the African Union is to promote the political and socioeconomic integration of African states, improve living conditions, and promote international cooperation with Africa.

In 2002, the AU created the Peace and Security Council, which is composed of the Panel of the Wise, an Early Warning System, the African Standby Force, and the Peace Fund. The protocol establishing the council authorizes the AU to intervene in the internal affairs of member states to protect civilians, a first for an intergovernmental organization. The protocol also requests that each African region establish a rapidly deployable brigade for peace operations.

The AU deployed its first peacekeeping mission to Burundi in 2003. South Africa provided leadership and most
of the funding for the 3,400-member AU force, which was
replaced by a UN mission after fourteen months. In October 2004, the AU authorized deployment of 3,320 military,
police, and political personnel to the western Sudan region
of Darfur to protect civilians in response to mounting evidence of genocide. Even after doubling the size of its force,
the AU was unable to protect civilians in Darfur owing to
the size of the territory, a lack of cooperation from Sudan's
government, and the organization's inability to provide
adequate logistics and other types of support. Following
action by the UNSC in August 2006, expectations were
raised that the AU eventually would hand off to a larger
and more capable UN force.

ECONOMIC COMMUNITY OF WEST AFRICAN STATES (ECOWAS)

101, Yakubu Gowon Crescent
Asokoro District P.M.B.
Abuja 401
Nigeria

Phone: 234-(9)31-47-647-9
Fax: 234-(9)31-43-005
E-mail: webmaster@ecowas.int
Internet: www.ecowas.int

ECOWAS was established on May 28, 1975, in Lagos,
Nigeria. ECOWAS is an economic union, composed of fifteen West African countries, established to raise living
standards, enhance economic stability, foster relations
among members, and contribute to the development of

West Africa. The organization's fundamental principles are equality and interdependence of member states; solidarity and collective self-reliance; mutual nonaggression; maintenance of regional peace, stability, and security; peaceful settlement of disputes; promotion and protection of human rights; and promotion and consolidation of democracy. ECOWAS formed a Standing Mediation Committee in 1990 and created a West African peacekeeping force known as the ECOWAS Cease-Fire Monitoring Group (ECOMOG), which conducted peace operations in Liberia and Sierra Leone.

GULF COOPERATION COUNCIL (GCC)
PO Box 7153
Riyadh 11462
Saudi Arabia

Phone: 966-1-482-7777
Fax: 966-1-482-9089
Internet: www.gcc-sg.org

The GCC was founded in Abu Dhabi in response to the Iran-Iraq war. Its aims are to coordinate resistance to outside intervention in the Gulf and to strengthen cooperation in areas such as agriculture, industry, investment, security, and trade among its six members. Its main bodies include the Supreme Council, the Conciliation Committee (which serves as a mediator in cases of conflict between members), and the Council of Ministers. The GCC has a permanent secretariat and standing committees that deal with economic, social, and cultural cooperation as well as internal and external security.

INTERGOVERNMENTAL AUTHORITY ON DEVELOPMENT (IGAD)
IGAD Secretariat
PO Box 2653
Djibouti
Republic of Djibouti

Phone: 253-354-050
Fax: 253-356-994
E-mail: igad@intnet.dj
Internet: www.igad.org

The Intergovernmental Authority on Drought and Development (IGAD) was founded in 1986 to coordinate efforts to combat drought and desertification. In 1996, its name was shortened, but its priorities remained environmental protection, food security, conflict resolution, and regional economic cooperation. IGAD played a peacemaking role in the north-south Sudanese conflict when the Sudan government accepted the IGAD Declaration of Principles as an agenda for discussions that ultimately resulted in a Comprehensive Peace Agreement.

LEAGUE OF ARAB STATES
1100 17th Street NW, Suite 602
Washington, DC 20036

Phone: 202-265-3210
Fax: 202-331-1525
E-mail: Arableague@aol.com
Internet: www.arableagueonline.org

When established in 1945, the League of Arab States aimed to promote Arab unity and independence from colonial rule. Since then, the League's objectives have expanded to include advancing the collective interests of the Arab community; handling disputes arising between member states;

promoting regional security by providing a mechanism for collective Arab security; promoting economic and political development of Africa and the Middle East; and strengthening ties between the Arab world and the West.

The League, which has twenty-two members, is composed of several primary bodies. Its highest body is the Council of the League, the unanimous decisions of which are binding on all members. Its Joint Defense Council coordinates military policy, and its Economic and Social Council promotes cooperation in economic and social fields. Its main bureaucratic arm is the General-Secretariat, which carries out the day-to-day decisions of the League. The League is also composed of ministerial committees and specialized agencies. Among these specialized agencies are the Arab Monetary Fund; the Arab Bank for Economic Development in Africa; the Arab Agricultural Development Organization; the Arab Fund for Economic and Social Development; the Arab Atomic Energy Board; and the Arab League Educational, Cultural, Scientific Organization.

ORGANIZATION OF THE ISLAMIC CONFERENCE (OIC)
PO Box 178
Jeddah – 21411
Saudi Arabia

Phone: 966-1-690-0001
Fax: 966-1-275-1953
E-mail: oiccabinet@arab.net.sa
Internet: www.oic-oci.org

The OIC was established in Rabat, Morocco, in September 1969. It is a regional organization grouping fifty-seven member states and three observer states that have decided to pool their resources and speak with one voice to safeguard the interests and well-being of their peoples and of all Muslims in the world. The structure of the OIC is similar to that of the Arab League, featuring summits, a Conference of Foreign Ministers, a secretary general, and subsidiary organizations. The conference of Kings and Heads of State and Governments—the Islamic Summit— meets every three years; the Council of Foreign Ministers holds biannual meetings with regular sessions. OIC's aims are to promote solidarity among its members, adopt measures to foster international peace and security, coordinate efforts to protect the Holy Places of Islam, and support the struggle of the Palestinian people. OIC has been involved in humanitarian efforts in Afghanistan, Sierra Leone, Somalia, the former Yugoslavia, and Kashmir.

SOUTHERN AFRICAN DEVELOPMENT COMMUNITY (SADC)

SADC House
Private Bag 0095
Gaborone
Botswana

Phone: 267-3951-863
Fax: 267-3972-848
E-mail: registry@sadc.int
Internet: www.sadc.int

The thirteen-member SADC was established in 1980 to harmonize economic development among the countries in Southern Africa. Originally created to coordinate opposition to South Africa's apartheid regime, SADC now has South Africa as its most prominent member. SADC's objectives are to achieve development and economic growth, alleviate poverty, enhance the standard and quality of life of the people of Southern Africa, and support the socially disadvantaged through regional integration. SADC member states hope to evolve common political values, systems, and institutions; promote self-sustaining development on the basis of collective self-reliance; and achieve complementarities between national and regional strategies.

ASIA AND THE PACIFIC

ASSOCIATION OF SOUTHEAST ASIAN NATIONS (ASEAN)

70A Jalan Sisingamangaraja
Jakarta 12110
Indonesia

Phone: 6221-726-2991
Fax: 6221-739-8234
E-mail: public@aseansec.org
Internet: www.aseansec.org

ASEAN was established in Bangkok, Thailand, in 1967 with the signing of the Bangkok Declaration. Today, ASEAN is composed of ten Southeast Asian nations. The Bangkok Declaration set out guidelines for ASEAN's activities and defined the aims of the organization. The ASEAN nations came together with three main objectives in mind: to promote the economic, social, and cultural development of the region through cooperative programs; to safeguard the political and economic stability of the region against big-power rivalry; and to serve as a forum for the resolution of intraregional differences. ASEAN is not a security organization and has never conducted peace operations, leaving that role to the United Nations. Of all the major regional organizations, ASEAN is furthest from embracing a security role.

While ASEAN has not acted collectively to deal with threats to regional security, individual members have responded to bilateral appeals from other members to provide monitors. In 2004, Malaysia deployed a military monitoring group to the Philippines, which was engaged in a struggle against separatist forces. Individual members have also contributed to UN peacekeeping forces. Indonesia and the Philippines have been the leading ASEAN contributors to missions in Africa and Haiti. Thailand has contributed forces to the UN mission in Burundi, while Singapore played an important role in the deployment of the UN mission to East Timor.

EUROPE AND EURASIA

COMMONWEALTH OF INDEPENDENT STATES (CIS)

Building 1
39 Myasnitskaya Street
Moscow 107450
Russian Federation

Phone: (7-095) 207-4237
Fax: (7-095) 207-4592
E-mail: info@cisstat.com
Internet: www.cis.minsk.by

The CIS was founded in 1991 by former Soviet republics. Its components are the Council of CIS Heads of State, the Council of CIS Heads of Government, the Coordination and Consultative Committee, the Executive Secretariat, the Parliamentary Assembly, the Council of Ministers for Foreign Affairs, the Council of Ministers for Defense, the Economic Court of the CIS, the Interstate Economic Committee of the Economic Union of CIS, and the Interstate Monetary Committee.

COUNCIL OF EUROPE (COE)

Avenue de l'Europe
67075 Strasbourg Cedex
France

Phone: 33-(0)3-8841-2033
Fax: 33-(0)3-8841-2745
E-mail: infopoint@coe.int
Internet: www.coe.int

Founded in 1949, the Council of Europe was the first regional IO to be established in Europe after World War II. Today it has a membership of forty-six countries. The organization's principal bodies are the Committee of Ministers (the Council's primary decision maker), the Parliamentary Assembly, and the Secretariat. Resolutions and conventions of the Council are advisory and become binding on member states only upon ratification.

The Council's main purposes are to promote democracy; to advance the rule of law; to protect human rights; to encourage Europe's political, economic, and social development; to assess Europe's problems and propose solutions; and to assist former members of the Warsaw Pact with the transition to democracy. The Council has been instrumental in promoting and protecting human rights in Europe, especially in the former Soviet Union and the former Yugoslavia. The council has also played an important role in monitoring elections in central Europe. Under the provisions of the European Convention on Human Rights (passed by the Council of Europe in 1950), individuals may bring claims of human rights violations to the European Commission of Human Rights and the European Court of Human Rights.

IOs

European Union (EU)

Rue de la Loi 200
B-1049 Brussels
Belgium

Phone: 32-2-299-9696
Internet: http://europa.eu

In 1957, the Treaty of Rome created the European Economic Community (EEC) with twelve member states. As of May 2005, twenty-five countries, many of them former members of the Soviet Bloc, have become members of the renamed European Union (EU). The EU is a family of democratic countries that are committed to working together for peace and prosperity. Its member states have set up common institutions to which they delegate some of their sovereignty so that decisions on specific matters of joint interest can be made democratically at the European level. In recent years, the EU has assumed a high-profile role in international affairs. Acting in consort through the EU, European nations have assumed responsibility for guiding the constituent republics of the former Yugoslavia to independence and integration into European institutions. The EU also has developed the capacity to conduct peace and stability operations and has sent peacekeeping forces outside of Europe.

The Council of the European Union represents the governments of the member states and is the major policy-making organ of the EU. The Presidency of the Council is held for six months by each member state on a rotating basis. The Council meets in Brussels, which increasingly is regarded as the capital of Europe. The European Parliament meets in Strasbourg and is tasked with passing resolutions and approving certain decisions of the EU. Parliamentarians are elected directly by voters from member states. The European Court of Justice, in Luxembourg, ensures compliance with EU law and settles disputes among member states relating to the EU. Finally, the Court of Auditors, in Luxembourg, manages the EU's budget.

Under the European Security and Defense Policy, the EU has created the capacity to rapidly deploy 60,000 troops and 5,000 police for peace operations. In 2004, the EU began its largest military mission by deploying 7,000 soldiers (EUROFOR) to replace NATO peacekeepers in Bosnia. A similar mission was sent to Macedonia. This followed the 2003 deployment to Bosnia of the EU Police Mission that replaced the UN International Police Task Force. Also in 2003, the EU undertook its first deployment outside Europe by sending a French-led EU military force to the Democratic Republic of the Congo. EU military and police forces are expected to replace NATO and UN peacekeepers in Kosovo once a decision is reached on the territory's final status. Currently, the EU is working to create a 3,000-member European Gendarmerie Force that would be available for rapid deployment in post-conflict interventions. EU capacity to provide military forces for peace operations is expanding; it is still less than that of NATO.

EUROPEAN COMMISSION (EC)

Berlaymont
Rue de la Loi 200
B-1040 Brussels
Belgium

E-mail: sg-web-president@cec.eu.int
Internet: http://europa.eu.int/comm/index_en.htm

The Commission is the executive body of the EU. The primary humanitarian aid entity within the Commission is the European Community Humanitarian Office department (ECHO). ECHO's task is to ensure that goods and services get to crisis zones as quickly as possible. Goods may include essential supplies, specific foodstuffs, medical equipment, medicines, and fuel. Services may include medical teams, water purification teams, and logistical support. Goods and services reach disaster areas via ECHO partners. Since 1992, ECHO has funded humanitarian aid in more than eighty-five countries. Its grants cover emergency aid, food aid, and aid to refugees and displaced persons for a total of more than €500 million per year. Recent significant aid operations by ECHO have been in Afghanistan, the Democratic Republic of the Congo, Burundi, Iraq, and multiple nations in Africa. ECHO currently has operations in over twenty-five nations.

The Directorate General for Development (DG DEV) within the European Commission of the EU works on policy formulation at the global and regional level. The DG DEV formulates the development policy applicable to all developing countries and conducts forward studies to this end. The main areas covered are those on which the development policy focuses: linking trade with development; fostering regional integration and cooperation; supporting macroeconomic policies; and promoting equitable access to social services in coherence with the macroeconomic framework, supporting transport, promoting food security and sustainable rural development, and supporting institutional capacity building.

Through the European Union Common Foreign and Security Policy (CFSP), a Rapid Reaction Mechanism (RRM) allows the Community to respond urgently to the needs of countries threatened with or undergoing severe political instability or suffering from the effects of a technological or natural disaster. Its purpose is to support measures aimed at safeguarding or reestablishing the conditions under which the partner countries of the EC can pursue their long-term development goals. The main added value of the RRM is its ability to provide support to the political strategy of the Commission when faced with a crisis in a third country. The total budget for 2005 was

€30 million. Recent deployments of the RRM have been in support of mediation efforts and monitoring of implementation of peace or cease-fire agreements (Liberia, Ivory Coast, Aceh, Sri Lanka); reestablishment of rule of law and civilian administration (Democratic Republic of the Congo, Afghanistan); confidence-building measures, including reconstruction and mine action directly linked to the promotion of ongoing peace processes (Macedonia, Sri Lanka, Horn of Africa); civil-society development (Bolivia, Indonesia); development of an independent media (Afghanistan); emergency electoral support (Georgia); high-level policy advice, including the planning of economic reconstruction (Afghanistan, Macedonia, Iraq, Lebanon); and demobilization and reintegration of combatants (Democratic Republic of the Congo).

NORTH ATLANTIC TREATY ORGANIZATION (NATO)

NATO Headquarters
Boulevard Leopold III
1110 Brussels
Belgium

E-mail: natodoc@hr.nato.int
Internet: www.nato.int

NATO is a twenty-six-member military alliance of countries from North America and Europe. The North Atlantic Treaty was signed in Washington on April 4, 1949, creating an alliance of twelve independent nations committed to one another's defense. Today, the alliance has grown to twenty-six member states and has continued to guarantee the security of its members. Following the end of the Cold War and of the division of Europe, the alliance has been restructured to enable it to participate in the development of cooperative security structures for the whole of Europe.

It has also transformed its political and military structures to adapt them to peacekeeping and crisis management tasks undertaken in cooperation with countries that are not members of the Alliance and other international organizations.

NATO forms the core of the international peacekeeping mission in Kosovo and leads the International Security Assistance Force in Afghanistan. NATO also conducts training, military assistance, and counterterrorism exercises in the Middle East, Africa, and the Mediterranean. NATO is the most capable regional organization in terms of its ability to provide military forces and respond to crises. NATO's expansion outside Europe has demonstrated its awareness that transnational threats to its security originate in weak and failing states.

Kosovo Force (KFOR), in which 17,000 troops from thirty-five nations are deployed, seeks to build a secure environment within Kosovo in which all citizens, irrespective of their ethnic origins, can live in peace. NATO forces arrived in Kosovo in June 1999. NATO forces entered Bosnia following the signing of the Dayton Accords in January 1995. They handed over operations to peacekeeping forces of the European Union in 2004.

As the leader of the 31,000-member International Security Assistance Force, NATO is helping establish self-sustaining peace and security in Afghanistan. This is NATO's first mission outside the Euro-Atlantic area. Initially restricted to providing security in Kabul, ISAF has expanded its mission to all of Afghanistan. ISAF expansion from relatively safe areas in the north and west of Afghanistan to heavily contested areas along the border with Pakistan has tested NATO's combat skills and determination against a resourceful and aggressive enemy. NATO's effort to suppress the Taliban-led insurgency will determine whether the new, democratic, government of Afghanistan will survive.

ORGANIZATION FOR SECURITY AND CO-OPERATION IN EUROPE (OSCE)

Kaerntner Ring 5-7
1010 Vienna
Austria

Phone: 43-4-514-36-0
Fax: 43-1-514-36-96
E-mail: info@osce.org
Internet: www.osce.org

In 1975, the Helsinki Final Act created the Conference for Security and Co-operation in Europe (CSCE) as a loose, conference-style organization, composed of members of NATO and the Warsaw Pact, to provide a forum for dealing with the problems of the Cold War. CSCE held a series of meetings and conferences, setting norms and commitments and periodically reviewing their implementation. In 1990, the Charter of Paris for a New Europe called upon the organization to help manage the historic change in Europe and respond to the challenges of the post–Cold War period. In 1994, the name was changed to the Organization for Security and Co-operation in Europe (OSCE) to reflect a growing responsibility for new initiatives related to European security in the broadest sense. Unlike other international organizations, however, OSCE was not created by treaty and had no international legal status.

OSCE is composed of 56 countries with a total staff of 3,500. OSCE operates 18 field missions in 16 countries. The United States and Canada are members; 11 countries in the Mediterranean region and Asia are affiliated as Partners for Cooperation. As a regional arrangement under Chapter VIII of the UN Charter, OSCE is responsible for early warning, conflict prevention, crisis management, and post-conflict rehabilitation in Europe. OSCE takes a cooperative approach to a wide range of security-related issues, including rule of law; arms control; preventive diplomacy;

confidence- and security-building measures; human rights; election monitoring; and economic security.

OSCE is composed of several institutions. The organization's headquarters, Secretariat, and Permanent Council are located in Vienna. The Secretariat is led by the secretary-general, who is appointed for three years. The Permanent Council is the major decision-making body. Member states have equal status. Decisions are made by consensus and are politically, but not legally, binding. OSCE foreign ministers hold an annual Ministerial Council Meeting. Every two years, an OSCE Summit of Heads of State or Government is convened. The Parliamentary Assembly meets once a year to consider declarations, recommendations, and proposals to enhance security and cooperation in the OSCE area. The Parliamentary Assembly's secretariat is located in Copenhagen.

Beginning in 1992 with the breakup of Yugoslavia, OSCE has deployed a growing number of field missions concerned with monitoring human rights violations and promoting the rule of law. OSCE played a key role in democratization, institution building, and media development in Macedonia, Kosovo, Albania, Croatia, Bosnia, and Serbia. OSCE activities in Eastern Europe focused on election monitoring, rule of law, and conflict resolution in Ukraine, Belarus, and Moldova. OSCE supports the Caucasus states of Azerbaijan, Georgia, and Armenia in the areas of economic and environmental development, conflict resolution, and democratization. Since 2002, OSCE has played a leading role in combating human trafficking in Europe. The Kosovo Police School is considered OSCE's greatest achievement and has been emulated in subsequent peace operations. OSCE works closely with the United Nations and NATO. Its role is limited in some operations, however, by the requirement to operate by consensus.

Since one member can veto the organization's budget, there will always be constraints on OSCE's actions.

NORTH AND SOUTH AMERICA

CARIBBEAN COMMUNITY AND COMMON MARKET (CARICOM)

PO Box 10827
Avenue of the Republic
Georgetown
Guyana

Phone: 011-592-226-8353
Fax: 011-592-226-4493
E-mail: carisec3@caricom.org
Internet: www.caricom.org

CARICOM is the result of an effort to foster regional integration that began with the establishment of the British West Indies Federation in 1958. A Caribbean Free Trade Association (CARIFTA) followed in 1968, CARICOM in 1973.

CARICOM has concentrated on promoting economic integration, coordinating the foreign policies of independent member states, and encouraging functional cooperation, especially in areas of social and human endeavor. The principal organs of the community are the Conference of Heads of Government and the Community Council of Ministers. CARICOM formed the Assembly of Caribbean Community Parliamentarians in 1996. It also formed the Regional Negotiating Machinery to coordinate external relations and the Caribbean Disaster Emergency Response Agency in 1991.

In 2001, CARICOM established the Pan Caribbean Partnership Against HIV/AIDS to fight the spread of the disease in the region. Project activities include a Law,

Ethics, and Human Rights Project to encourage member states to promote respect and nondiscrimination for persons infected by HIV/AIDs and a project to promote information sharing among partners. CARICOM is also engaged in a Renewable Energy Development Program to reduce barriers to the use of renewable energy, thus reducing the dependence on fossil fuels while contributing to the reduction of greenhouse gas emissions.

ORGANIZATION OF AMERICAN STATES (OAS)

17th Street and Constitution Avenue NW
Washington, DC 20006

Phone: 202-458-3000
E-mail: pi@oas.org
Internet: www.oas.org

The OAS was established in 1951 and has its headquarters in Washington, D.C. It is composed of all of the countries in the Western Hemisphere, except Cuba, which was excluded in 1962. The organization's primary institutions are the Secretariat, the General Assembly, and the Permanent Council. The General Assembly, which is the supreme organ of the OAS, meets annually. Daily matters are decided by the Permanent Council, which is composed of a permanent representative from each member state. The OAS must act through consensus, which limits its ability to manage conflicts between member states.

The OAS exists to (1) strengthen regional peace and security; (2) promote democracy; (3) ensure the peaceful settlement of disputes; (4) promote regional economic, social, and cultural development; and (5) limit armaments and encourage the use of resources for the economic and social development of the member states. To attain these objectives, the OAS has established the Inter-American Council for Integral Development, the Inter-American Juridical

Committee, the Inter-American Court of Human Rights, the Inter-American Commission on Human Rights; and the Free Trade Area of the Americas. The OAS routinely sends election observers and political advisers to assist member states in achieving democratic government.

In Haiti, the OAS played a leading role in stabilization efforts through the Special Mission for Strengthening Democracy. The OAS provided training and technical assistance to the Haitian National Police and the Haitian judiciary. Through the Electoral Technical Assistance Program, the OAS worked with the United Nations and Haiti's Provisional Electoral Council to conduct a massive voter registration drive for local, legislative, and presidential elections in February 2006. This effort provided identification cards to more than 3.5 million citizens, a first in the nation's history. Elsewhere, OAS conducted successful campaigns in Guatemala and Nicaragua for the removal of landmines and control of small arms. It also launched good-governance initiatives in other Central American countries that were recovering from civil wars.

ORGANIZATION OF EASTERN CARIBBEAN STATES (OECS)

Morne Fortune
PO Box 179
Castries
Saint Lucia

Phone: 758-452-2537
Fax: 758-453-1628
E-mail: oesec@oecs.org
Internet: www.oecs.org

The Organization of Eastern Caribbean States came into being on June 18, 1981, when seven Eastern Caribbean countries signed a cooperation agreement. The mission of

OECS is to contribute to regional development and facilitate intelligent integration with the global economy. OECS also seeks to harmonize the foreign policies of its members and promote good relations with the international community. OECS promotes common trade policies, telecommunications, health sector reforms, and judicial/legal reforms in the Caribbean region through such institutions as the Eastern Caribbean Telecommunications Authority, the Directorate of Civil Aviation, the Eastern Caribbean Central Bank, and the Eastern Caribbean Supreme Court. The OECS Social Development Unit works to strengthen linkages between economic and social development and to provide the OECS Secretariat with the capacity to assess and monitor human and social development–related activities, including poverty reduction, for purposes of supporting the development planning processes in the subregion.

ORGANIZATIONS WITH HISTORIC, LEGAL, OR LINGUISTIC TIES

THE COMMONWEALTH

The Commonwealth Secretariat
Marlborough House, Pall Mall
London SW1Y 5HX
United Kingdom

Phone: 44-(0)20-7747-6500
Fax: 44-(0)20-7930-0827
E-mail: info@commonwealth.int
Internet: www.thecommonwealth.org

The Commonwealth is an association of fifty-three developed and developing nations around the world. The British Commonwealth came into being at the Imperial

Conference of 1926, at which prime ministers adopted the Balfour Report, which was then adopted into British law in 1931 as the Statute of Westminster. The Commonwealth has no charter. Membership is entirely voluntary, but its members are bound by guiding principles, deeply held beliefs in the promotion of international understanding and cooperation, and the belief that their interests are served by working in partnership with one another.

The main body is the Commonwealth Secretariat. Other bodies include the Commonwealth of Learning and the Commonwealth Foundation, the latter supporting more than three hundred Commonwealth NGOs with targeted financial and other assistance. The program Advancing Fundamental Political Values promotes efforts to spur conflict prevention and resolution, strengthen democratic values and electoral processes, assist in the drafting of constitutions, advance the rule of law and human rights, build consensus, and consolidate the transition in South Africa.

SECTION

II

Non-Governmental Organizations

Introduction

URING THE PAST twenty years, the importance of
NGOs in the international arena has grown sig-
nificantly. Working alone or partnered with
governmental and international organizations, NGOs are
essential players in the international response to humanitarian emergencies, natural disasters, and violent conflicts.
NGO involvement with situations of conflict often spans
the life of a conflict, from the first sign of violence through
the eventual reconciliation and beyond.

Committed to long-term grassroots work within communities in developing countries, these organizations are
also capable of rapid action in the face of floods, hurri-
canes, civil unrest, and ethnic and religious conflict. NGOs
may be found in every trouble spot throughout the world
—from Haiti to Afghanistan, Iraq, the Democratic Republic of the Congo, and the tsunami-devastated countries of
Asia. Most international NGOs are headquartered in
Western countries, where many of them also render assistance to local victims of natural disasters. In the United
States, for example, international NGOs delivered services
in the wake of Hurricane Katrina.

Despite the breadth and variety of NGO activities, only
the largest of these organizations, such as CARE or Save

Note: This chapter is an updated, revised, and expanded version of
the chapter "Nongovernmental Organizations," by Pamela Aall,
which appeared on pages 85–180 of *Guide to IGOs, NGOs, and the
Military in Peace and Relief Operations,* by Pamela Aall, Lt. Col.
Daniel Miltenberger, and Thomas G. Weiss (Washington, D.C.:
United States Institute of Peace Press, 2000).

the Children, are well known. Outside of a specialized community that works with NGOs, they and their vital roles are not well understood. This section of the book introduces the NGO world and describes the variety of organizations involved in peace and stability operations. This section begins with a general overview of NGOs, moves on to describe their structure (how they are organized, managed, and staffed), and then examines their work in situations of conflict. Next it outlines the challenges of coordination among civilian organizations and between civilian organizations and the military. It concludes by describing four varieties of activities that NGOs undertake in conflict—rendering humanitarian assistance, promoting human rights, building civil societies and democracy, and resolving conflict—and by providing sketches of the best-known or most representative organizations that undertake these activities.

NGOs

An Overview
of NGOs

What Is an NGO?

A precise definition of NGOs—also known as private voluntary organizations (PVOs), civic associations, nonprofits, and charitable organizations—is difficult to pin down. The common ground of all NGOs is the desire to make the world a better place, a desire that underlies every organization's mission statement. Beyond this, however, NGOs vary enormously.

Here, we define an NGO as a private, self-governing, not-for-profit organization dedicated to alleviating human suffering by promoting education, health care, economic development, environmental protection, human rights, and conflict resolution and encouraging the establishment of democratic institutions and civil society. In essence, NGOs are dedicated to the service and protection of those sectors of society that tend to be unserved or underserved by governments. During and after violent conflicts, NGOs provide lifesaving humanitarian assistance such as food, water, shelter, and medical care.

The number of NGOs is growing rapidly. The Union of International Associations reports, in the 2005–06 edition of its *Yearbook of International Organizations,* that NGOs around the world now total around 38,000, which is more than double the number reported in the 1998–99 edition. The current number of NGOs is almost fifty times greater than the number of NGOs in 1951. Of the 163 members of

InterAction, an umbrella organization for major American relief and development NGOs, more than two-thirds were founded after 1960, a majority after 1975. Some were created to render assistance in specific upheavals—for example, the conflict in Bosnia, the Ethiopian famine of the mid-1980s, and the massive flooding in Bangladesh in the 1990s. Most, however, were formed to offer emergency assistance or long-term development aid throughout the world. NGOs are found throughout society and may operate at the local level with two or three persons or at the international level supporting programs employing hundreds.

A Brief History

The NGO community of today was born in the nineteenth century. One of the first NGOs was the Young Men's Christian Association (YMCA), founded in Britain in 1844 to help young men cope with an industrializing economy. The International Committee of the Red Cross was founded in 1863 to assist wounded soldiers and prisoners of war. The American Red Cross (ARC), which works worldwide as part of the International Federation of Red Cross and Red Crescent Societies, was founded in 1881 by Clara Barton, and today is supported by more than one million volunteers.

The twentieth century saw the creation of a handful of large international agencies, many of which set the foundation for the scope of activities NGOs participate in today. For instance, CARE, originally formed as a cooperative of twenty-two organizations that provided aid to victims of World War II, set the standard for humanitarian relief activities. The field of human rights found expression through Amnesty International, established in 1961. Many NGOs were founded by religious groups, sometimes as the relief arm of a church or other religious institution and sometimes as an outgrowth of the group's activities. Although developed and partly funded by religious organizations, most of these NGOs (for example, Adventist Development and Relief Agency, Mennonite Central Committee, and Catholic Relief Services) deliver help regardless of religion, race, or ethnicity. Finally, numerous NGOs were founded to address a very specific need but have since expanded the scope of their operations. The Center for International Health and Cooperation, for example, was formed in response to the war in Somalia in 1992, reacting primarily to the effects of land mines, but it has expanded its assistance programs to encompass humanitarian needs and human rights. This expansion of effort is common among NGOs as they seek to address the root causes of relief needs while working to alleviate immediate suffering.

Since the 1990s, the need for humanitarian assistance has grown sharply because of a significant rise in the numbers of refugees and displaced persons, most of whom have been caught up in warfare within their nation's borders. The UNHCR estimates that in 2005 there were 11.5 million asylum seekers and refugees and an additional 21.3 million internally displaced persons.

The global political transformation following the Cold War affected the character of international humanitarian activity. The end of superpower rivalry loosened the structures that had constrained sectarian and intrastate rivalries. As ethnic and religious conflicts have proliferated, so has the need for organizations specializing in human rights, refugee protection, humanitarian relief, and conflict resolution. NGOs have also intensified their activities in response to the political opportunities provided by the end of the Cold War. Organizations such as the National Democratic Institute and the International Republican Institute were founded in the United States and Europe to promote democracy, freedom of speech, and civic education in many previously closed societies.

After September 11, 2001, NGOs faced unprecedented dangers at a time when their work was increasingly critical to the lives of the world's most vulnerable people. The Asian tsunami and other natural disasters left a broad path of devastation, while an epidemic of ethnic and sectarian conflicts left a tragic legacy of largely civilian casualties. The rise of international terrorist movements based on religious extremism heightened the risks to NGO personnel. In Afghanistan and Iraq, Islamist insurgents targeted soldiers and relief workers alike. Kidnapping and murder of agency staff forced NGOs to rely exclusively on local personnel or withdraw to nearby countries. In Afghanistan, some NGOs claimed the involvement of coalition military Civil Affairs teams in village improvement projects blurred the distinction between combatants and relief workers, endangering their personnel. In Iraq, NGOs left the country after the unprecedented attack on the UN headquarters in Baghdad. Insurgents' disregard for international norms caused NGOs to rethink their reliance on concepts such as humanitarian space, their methods of operation, and their need for security. An example of the extent of change in the international environment was the advent of NGOs that provide security for other NGOs.

A Broad Assortment of Institutions

The structures and objectives of NGOs are as varied as their origins. Their objectives can range from providing humanitarian assistance, community development, democratization, and construction to delivering relief supplies. NGOs provide emergency assistance following natural or human-made disasters. They also can provide longer-term assistance, tackling the root causes of poverty, hunger, disease, and suffering; advocating for human, racial, gender, economic, and political rights; encouraging democratic institution building, conflict resolution practices, and fair electoral practices; and building sustainable agriculture, a healthy environment, and the infrastructure of a civil society.

Most countries are home to a large number of indigenous NGOs—among them, women's organizations, human rights groups, legal organizations, religious bodies, and neighborhood associations—that focus their efforts on meeting local needs. International NGOs frequently work with and through these indigenous NGOs. This is increasingly true as security, especially for expatriate staff, becomes a growing concern.

In any one setting, many NGOs are likely to be active. Their presence has much to do with the size of the problem, public awareness, and organizational expectations. In 1998, IRC, Mercy Corps, and Oxfam established the NGO Council in Kosovo. Subsequently, more than 150 international NGOs became members. Some 300 NGOs were operating in Sri Lanka within two months of the tsunami on December 26, 2004. The rise of insurgencies in Afghanistan and Iraq, however, has discouraged NGO participation. Following the bombing of the UN headquarters in Baghdad, many NGOs withdrew from Iraq and relocated their missions to Jordan. Similarly, attacks on NGO personnel in Afghanistan have caused many organizations to employ only local staff, withdraw to Kabul, or suspend operations entirely.

The Structure and Organization of NGOs

AN NGO is a private, self-governing, not for-profit organization acting of its own volition on behalf of others. In the United States it usually takes the form of a registered corporation with a board of trustees, an administrative structure, a set of bylaws, a mission statement, a permanent headquarters, and a means of funding. Its size, scope, mission, structure, history, affiliations, activities, and governance determine the character of each NGO.

Because they are self-defining, NGOs are usually quite clear about their values, their goals, and the purpose of their activities, which are set forth in a charter. The NGO's country of origin usually recognizes the charter. Today, all U.S. private service organizations of any size are incorporated as not-for-profit organizations under the Code of the U.S. Internal Revenue Service. This status, awarded to organizations engaged in educational, humanitarian, environmental, or other such activities, exempts those bodies from taxation and allows contributors to take a tax deduction for donations.

Some of the larger NGOs, such as CARE, Oxfam, Save the Children, and Amnesty International, have expanded into autonomous chapters in different countries, sharing name, mission, image, and operating procedures, but with each chapter being self-governing and financially independent. For example, Save the Children USA, in Westport, Connecticut, is a member of the International Save the Children Alliance, headquartered in London, United Kingdom. The U.S. chapter maintains formal affiliations with Save the Children chapters in twenty-six other countries throughout the world.

Formal Structure and Lines of Authority

In U.S. NGOs, a board of trustees governs the organization according to its bylaws. Board members are recruited from various sectors—including the corporate, political, religious, legal, medical, media, and educational sectors—for their diverse skills. Board members, like the staff, usually join because of a strong commitment to charitable work. As board members, they become "trustees"—literally and legally—of the organization. They are legally accountable for its operations and responsible for the fulfillment of its mission and financial obligations. They serve without compensation, hold regular meetings, elect officers, set the mission and direction of the organization, and ensure that the organization has the capacity to meet these directives.

Board decisions typically involve matters of policy, not day-to-day issues. Board action is likely to be needed when an organization considers undertaking an activity outside its current scope or venturing into a new geographic area. The board is responsible for recruiting and hiring the organization's executive director, but not other staff members. Although board members are apprised of ongoing activities and may visit field offices to observe the staff at work, they generally are not involved in operational decisions.

The administrative head of an NGO—the executive director, director, chief executive officer (CEO), or president —is directly accountable to the trustees and usually has a very close and interdependent relationship with the board. Other management staff are recruited and hired by the executive director. These positions typically include directors of finance, government relations, communications and public relations, and programs.

Larger U.S.-based NGOs have a significant staff presence in their headquarters. Staff in field operations is increasingly made up of local nationals. Security and the recognition of the importance of local input are contributing factors to this trend.

Decision Making

Most NGOs are quite decentralized and do not have an elaborate hierarchical structure. In many cases, staff work is largely independent and decisions are often made with little reliance on a structured chain of command and may appear to outsiders as inefficient. However, NGOs are heavily dependent on the individual commitment and initiative of their staff, and, in this situation, the most effective managerial style is characterized by a high degree of personal engagement.

In a tumultuous situation, the decentralized, independent approach to management can be a great asset. The willingness of NGOs to act when speed is essential and detailed planning is impossible makes these organizations among the best equipped to respond to sudden challenges. But this ability to turn on a dime—to change strategies, shift resources, quickly expand or shut down operations—can appear chaotic to organizations such as the military that value detailed planning and preparation.

Field staff are likely to have the authority to design or commit to specific projects, at least at the level of providing seed money. If a new project seems to hold promise, staff members begin designing proposals and seeking funds to permit its fuller implementation. New funds may come from the organization's own resources or from other private sources. Often, proposals respond to funding offers by the United Nations, the USAID, the World Bank, ECHO, and other funding agencies. Increasingly common is a blend of funding sources, which includes private donations from individuals and foundations plus an increasing amount of support from corporate entities.

Budgets and Funding

Senior-level NGO executives and their boards devote much time and attention to securing funding for program activities, staff salaries, and overhead. Raising money is a constant concern; whether an organization's annual budget is less than $100,000 or more than $100 million, much of that sum will have to be raised every year.

Amounts and sources of financial support vary from one NGO to another. For example, in 2004, Catholic Relief Services received 19 percent of its revenues from private, corporate, or foundation donations; 50 percent from in-kind donations; 26 percent from government grants; and 3 percent from other sources. In the same year, Oxfam America received 95 percent of its funding from private, corporate, or foundation donations and 5 percent from other sources.

Solicitations for private donations take many forms—annual appeals, issue-specific campaigns, year-round membership drives—and are delivered in many ways—direct appeals by telephone or mail, telethons, television commercials, newspaper advertisements, through Web sites, and so forth. Celebrities often lend their name and talent to fund-raising activities: Barbara and George Bush and

Greg Norman for AmeriCares; Rosalyn and Jimmy Carter for Habitat for Humanity; and Bono and Chris Tucker for Save the Children. Donations may be in the form of money, securities, bequests, charitable trusts, real estate, or in-kind gifts. In-kind donations can range from medical supplies to seeds, from books to clothing. Although governments provide most of the in-kind food assistance, companies, hospitals, churches, and other bodies also provide many in-kind gifts.

Some NGOs accept money from private sources only, fearing that the acceptance of government funding will lead to a loss of independence and pressure to compromise organizational integrity. Others accept public money but maintain an uneasy relationship with the government that provides those funds. They sometimes complain that governments put economic and political considerations ahead of humanitarian ones. They point out that a government may be giving assistance to victims of officially sanctioned violence while maintaining ties with the offending government through trade relations and sometimes even arms sales. They also claim that some donor governments are reluctant to furnish long-term development aid and instead prefer to concentrate on providing direct relief, such as food, because it benefits their own economies (alternatively, some governments prohibit aid to sectors that might threaten competition to their own exports).

Notwithstanding such complaints and reservations, public funding has become a significant part of the budgets of some U.S. NGOs. According to the 2005 USAID *Report of Voluntary Agencies,* while working in partnership with government organizations or as grantees or private contractors to deliver services during fiscal year 2003, NGOs received $2.2 billion from USAID and $2.1 billion from other U.S. government sources and international organizations. This makes up 26 percent of the $17 billion in total support and revenue that private voluntary organizations received for development and humanitarian relief in 2003. U.S. humanitarian organizations raised some $12.7 billion privately in 2003. It should be noted that to be eligible for USAID funding, an NGO must raise more than 20 percent of its annual budget from non-U.S. government sources. In practice, this percentage is much higher; USAID reported that in 2003 the 563 NGOs registered with its program raised 74 percent of their budgets from sources other than the U.S. government.

A common difficulty facing NGOs is the focus of donors on their service delivery activities. Typically, donors want all of their money to go for relief of victims or other types of direct assistance. This leaves many NGOs with little support for development of core capacities, such as hiring better management and improving administration. NGOs must carefully control overhead growth, which is difficult when they need to provide security.

The visibility of NGOs, including the awarding of two Nobel Peace Prizes, has grown in the past ten years as television coverage of humanitarian crises has spotlighted the vital role of NGOs in relieving suffering. The public's desire to help in these humanitarian emergencies has boosted private funding for some NGOs and sparked the creation of new NGOs dedicated to responding to a particular crisis. Convincing donors that their donations are going to worthwhile causes is one reason why NGOs are conscious of generating and sustaining media attention and why some may seek to paint a bleak picture of conditions in the crisis-torn country. The high profile produced by the media is typically short-lived; thus NGOs may not continue to receive donations when the initial crisis is over. On-and-off public exposure can actually complicate the financial life of these organizations, which must contend with enormous fluctuations in the level of donations they receive from an audience whose interest in a crisis often waxes and wanes according to the degree of media coverage the crisis attracts. The tsunami of December 2004 was an extreme example of this phenomenon. Some NGOs engaged solely in relief activities had to request that no more contributions be made for tsunami relief. Media exposure also has an impact on staffing and technical capabilities of NGOs, which cannot retain highly skilled or experienced staff without the needed financial resources.

The importance of publicity to an NGO's budget can create what may appear to be unseemly competition among NGOs. It can also foster the impression that NGOs focus only on the most dramatic problems. In fact, NGOs often work in obscurity in tense situations long before the television news cameras arrive, and they remain committed to helping solve local problems long after international public interest has faded.

Staff and Their Working Environment

Individuals choose to work for NGOs for a variety of reasons. Some want to devote their skills and energy to an organization whose mission and programs inspire them. Some are committed to a particular field, such as human rights or child protection, and join organizations that allow them to focus on their interest. Some are drawn to international NGOs by the attraction of travel, the excitement of operating in difficult situations, and the adventure of living in a foreign culture and speaking another language. The culture embodied in many NGOs—a culture that values independence, flexibility, and mobility—also appeals to many people.

It is not uncommon for NGO staff to remain within the NGO world throughout their careers. Those who have worked in the fields of relief, development, or human rights may move to UN agencies with similar missions,

such as UNICEF, UNHCR, OHCHR, and WFP. A number
of former NGO employees can be found on the staffs of
funding agencies, such as USAID and the World Bank.

Advanced degrees are common among NGO staff.
Medical doctors become involved in the administration of
health-oriented organizations, and engineers in the operation of agencies that deliver technical aid. University professors of political science, sociology, or psychology may
be active in the field of conflict resolution. Lawyers domi-
nate the staffs of human rights organizations and are well
represented in refugee organizations. Other degrees common among NGO staff include business administration,
public health administration, public affairs, and international affairs.

The skills of the particular staff vary according to the
work of the NGO, the stability of its funding, and its personnel policies and practices: One agency may need a full-
time biomedical equipment technician to inspect heart
monitors, EKG machines, and intravenous pumps, while
another may require an engineer-architect to design a
warehouse for food storage in tropical climates.

The staff of large NGOs needs high levels of administrative and entrepreneurial skills. Whether for profit or not
for profit, a multimillion-dollar operation requires decisive
action in difficult situations, skilled financial management,
and firm control of a geographically extended enterprise.
In addition, NGO managers must be aggressive fund-
raisers, and they must be able to meld together the energy
and commitment of volunteers and paid staff.

When responding to a crisis, an international NGO will
usually dispatch only a small number of its staff from its
home office to the scene and will hire local residents to fill
other essential positions. Local staff members are selected
for their skills, their local knowledge, their command of
languages, and their ability to bridge the gap between international NGO staff and host country nationals. The

professional caliber of such workers can be high, because in a crisis zone there is sometimes a large pool of highly trained but unemployed professionals from which the NGO can select its staff.

However, hiring local staff can pose problems for both the NGO and the employees. Often, local workers will need permission from their government to work for a foreign NGO, and that government may summon workers away for military service or government work at any time. Governments also exercise a more direct influence, granting permission to work for international NGOs only to persons they find politically acceptable or loyal. Local staff may be forced to act as informers about NGO activities. At the same time, NGOs have been criticized for hiring away educated and skilled local personnel to serve as drivers and translators. NGOs can deplete local government and industry of their best workers, including doctors and engineers, by offering salaries in hard currencies that are well above the local pay scale. The benefits of hiring local staff, however, can be high, bringing local expertise to the project and paving the way for its future management by domestic groups rather than foreign NGO staff. Where security is a factor, local nationals may be able to work in areas that are too dangerous for expatriate staff.

NGOs

NGOs in Conflict

NTERNATIONAL NGO field staff, especially relief workers, often experience hardships similar to those of local residents. Coping with the lack of electricity and water was common in Iraq. Dealing with the threat of insurgents' attacks was part of the daily reality of NGO representatives in Afghanistan. In both countries, NGO representatives in some areas had to exercise great caution to avoid being kidnapped or killed by insurgents. NGOs try to identify and ally themselves with groups seeking to resolve political differences, but this may offer little protection in conflicted regions where extremists may target all outsiders. Even in more stable environments typical of peacekeeping operations, NGOs can be snared in a host of political and practical difficulties by unwitting involvement in tribal rivalries, land disputes, or criminal activities. NGOs must carefully evaluate local conditions and local actors to avoid unintended consequences of their actions.

Operating in Conflict: Challenges to Neutrality and Security

NGOs dedicated to humanitarian relief operations generally attempt to maintain a policy that is consistent with the NGO/IFRC Code of Conduct, which has three main guiding principles: the humanitarian imperative, independence, and impartiality in situations of conflict. Their purpose is to relieve human suffering regardless of political, ethnic, religious, or other affiliation. NGOs that focus specifically on conflict resolution also value their neutrality; unless they are seen as impartial, they are unlikely to be able to promote dialogue and establish common ground between the antagonists (individuals and community groups, as well as governments and rebel forces) with whom they work. Most human rights organizations are also careful to limit their advocacy to the rights of individuals or groups, rather than take sides in the conflict.

Operations in Afghanistan and Iraq have increased discussion within the NGO community on what constitutes "humanitarian space." This phrase has been used in the sense of an area protected by the imperatives of neutrality, impartiality, and independence—the cornerstones of NGO work in conflict areas. The term has also been applied in a more pragmatic manner to a permissive area that is not directly protected by military elements. Differences notwithstanding, the humanitarian community has largely accepted the fundamental necessity for humanitarian work to be done in areas not subject to questions of conflicting allegiances or political motivation. Humanitarian space is generally understood to include the following elements:

- Physical access to those with assistance and/or protection needs (geographical dimension)
- The necessary social, political, and military conditions for humanitarians to carry out their work, including security and immunity from attack (physical and institutional dimensions)
- Respect for humanitarian principles, including independence and the humanitarian character (nonmilitary and nonpolitical) of humanitarian work (temporal and categorical dimensions) (ECHO 2004)

In interstate or even intrastate conflicts that are fought between easily distinguishable forces on battlefields with relatively well-defined front lines, there is some clarity about what constitutes neutral behavior—for example, an NGO is more likely to be regarded as impartial if it delivers food and medical supplies to all sides in a conflict if it focuses its efforts solely on innocent populations, such as small children. But in civil conflicts that target civilian populations—especially in cases where particular regions or peoples are denied food and other supplies—it is much harder for NGOs to maintain an appearance of neutrality.

In Iraq and Afghanistan, civilians are often in close proximity to the conflict. NGOs, therefore, are hard pressed to find ways to deliver assistance and maintain some semblance of humanitarian space. The pace of the fighting in Iraq outstripped the miltary's ability to respond to the needs of a population whose well-being was now in its hands. The dilemma for the NGOs was how to assist without being seen as a party to the occupation itself. This issue emerged even before the fighting in Iraq had started, as NGOs entered into extensive internal debates on their potential roles. They pressed the military to understand the importance of humanitarians being perceived by all parties as neutral.

Security is an enormous concern of international NGOs, especially those engaged in relief, refugee, and human rights work in conflict situations. The continuing increase in the number of NGO workers—and in particular, in total number of local workers, who are more likely than foreign workers to be caught in the conflict—has exacerbated the problems raised by inadequate security and a lack of basic security training. Sometimes, partnering with local groups can render an international NGO suspect because of the political affiliations or activities of the local staff.

Security concerns have prompted international NGOs to consider a variety of approaches to ensuring staff safety. InterAction, the U.S. NGO association, has developed a training module to promote security for staff operating in high-risk zones. The training emphasizes personal conflict-handling techniques rather than deterrence and physical protection. It recognizes that, because of their work, NGO staff members are vulnerable to assaults and other violence, and it aims to heighten their sensibility to potentially threatening situations and give them tools to defuse or avoid confrontations. Acceptance of this approach forms the foundation of NGO security management. This involves building and carefully maintaining relationships, positive reputation, and consistent image with local actors. NGO attitudes are based on a combination of principles and pragmatic considerations necessary to ensure their survival in conflict areas.

NGOs are increasingly aware of their potential to be seen as a threat in traditional societies simply because they are associated with external influences coming from Western and secular societies and from globalization. The phrase "blurring of roles" has come to describe this situation. NGOs also find that they are seen as exercising political or social influence simply because they control resources that have an impact. In Iraq and Afghanistan, Islamist terrorists have attacked NGOs as part of their campaign to drive out all Western influence. They also want to prevent NGOs from assisting governments in fulfilling their promises of economic development and a better life.

NGO-Military Coordination

Traditionally, NGOs and the military have perceived their roles to be distinctly different and separate. NGOs have felt uneasy working with military forces, whether from their own country or from the country receiving assistance. NGOs are conscious of the need to preserve their impartiality because of the protection that affords them. Military leaders have tended to regard NGOs as undisciplined and their operations as uncoordinated and disjointed. Yet NGO staff working in complex emergencies often need the help of the military for protection, logistics, and even evacuation. Attitudes on both sides have begun to change. Exposure to each other's strengths and capabilities has increased the military's respect for the innovation and dedication of NGOs and fostered an appreciation among NGOs for the unsurpassed logistical capacity of the military.

In recent years, militaries have sought to improve their relationship with NGOs by creating Civil Military Operations Centers (CMOCs) that allow military, NGO, and IO personnel to meet and work together to advance mutual goals. These centers allow the three groups to share information and views and provide a venue for practical matters, such as briefings by the military on land mines or security conditions. They do not, however, serve as coordinating mechanisms, and they have not always been able to bring the three communities together. NGOs have not always been willing to be engaged with CMOCs, fearing the consequences of the appearance of a too-close association with the military.

In Afghanistan, the involvement of U.S. military-led Provincial Reconstruction Teams in reconstruction provoked extensive and, at times, bitter criticism from NGOs. The United States was a combatant and its forces were engaged in ongoing military operations. NGOs argued that the aura of neutrality that relief workers relied on for their personal safety would be compromised if local people were unable to differentiate between foreign civilian and military actors. If military personnel engaged in relief and reconstruction activities, the boundary between civilian and military efforts would be blurred, if not erased altogether. PRTs were accused of contributing to this ambiguity when troops wearing the same uniforms were seen both fighting insurgents and building clinics.

NGO representatives argued that soldiers were not experts in development and that CA projects often reflected a lack of expertise. Economic development involved more than simply constructing buildings, especially if construction was undertaken in an uncoordinated manner. PRT development projects often competed or conflicted with NGO projects, undermining relationships developed with Afghan communities. Relations with NGOs became strained, and many NGOs refused to have direct contact with PRTs, fearing retaliation from insurgents. Some NGOs argued that PRTs should concentrate on the military's primary duty, which was establishing a safe and secure environment. Over time, the PRTs adjusted their operations in response to these criticisms, increased coordination with NGOs, and concentrated their efforts in areas where it was too dangerous or difficult for NGOs to operate.

The military's initial objective is to achieve stabilization and provide security first for its own forces and then for others; its end-state includes an exit strategy and a defined —and limited—mission. The objective of NGOs is to address the humanitarian needs brought on by the conflict, and their end-state is open-ended. NGOs will seek to continue their activities until the humanitarian crisis is contained and longer-term development work can resume. The military's concern to avoid "mission creep" accentuates the soldiers' previously ingrained desire to go in, fix the problem, and get out quickly. Conversely, the NGOs' perspective during such crises is long term, aimed as much at addressing the root causes of the crisis as at delivering relief. These different goals and parameters inevitably produce different plans, expectations, and timelines.

The recent experiences in Afghanistan and Iraq have called into question the initial planning assumptions of the military. The ongoing conflicts placed the concept of a clear exit strategy with a responsible handover to NGOs and local institutions out of reach. It was clear that the military was unprepared to meet public expectations following the end of major combat operations and that the military's understanding of the roles of the relief community was insufficient.

There are at least two differences in communications between the military and the NGO communities. The first concerns technology. Although international NGOs have access to the Internet and mobile phones, they lack the sophisticated information-gathering and dissemination equipment of the military. This difference is only one indication of the disparity in size and resources between militaries and NGOs. The second concerns information. NGOs that have long-standing relationships with the local community are an excellent source of information, valuable to both the United Nations and peacekeeping forces. For example, they can provide information on such subjects as how best to set up a distribution system within a particular area and the relative dependability of various local groups and individuals. However, NGOs are sensitive about sharing information. They see their long-term success and physical security as dependent on good and open relationships with the indigenous population and are consequently wary of compromising the trust they have established by providing information to the military. They may even be reluctant to be seen with military personnel. One challenge for cooperative action is to find a way for the military and the NGOs to communicate and share information while respecting such inhibitions on full disclosure.

The Defense Department's Directive on *Military Support for Stability, Security, Transition, and Reconstruction Operations* (Department of Defense 2006), established peace and stability operations as core missions for the U.S. Defense Department and the U.S. military. To implement this mission, the directive states that the military should be prepared to engage in planning and operations with a range of civilian agencies, international organizations, and

NGOs. The directive makes clear that coordination should begin before NGOs and the military first interact on the ground. In light of the directive, both groups are gaining a greater understanding of their respective roles, motivations, and responsibilities. They pay increasing attention to joint briefings, participation in training exercises, and the distribution of information such as that in this guide.

NGO/Military Guidelines

Beginning in March 2005, senior representatives of major U.S. humanitarian organizations and U.S. civilian and military leaders met at the United States Institute of Peace to conduct a dialogue on the challenges to civil-military relations posed by operations in combat and other non-permissive environments. The Working Group on Civil-Military Guidelines in Non-Permissive Environments, facilitated by the Institute, was created to focus on doctrine and best practices; information and communication; and training, education, and planning. InterAction, the umbrella organization for many U.S. NGOs, coordinates the non-governmental delegation and is joined in the discussion by representatives from the Department of Defense, the Joint Chiefs of Staff, the State Department Office of the Coordinator for Reconstruction and Stabilization, and the U.S. Agency for International Development.

To address concerns about the roles of NGOs and the military when both are operating in nonpermissive environments, the Working Group began developing guidelines for the NGO-military relationship. After producing the guidelines, the Working Group will continue to act as a forum for implementation of the guidelines and for airing and resolving concerns emanating from various operations. In addition, the Working Group will seek to promote understanding through improved doctrine, training, and education.

Do No Harm

NGOs operating in conflict areas can be dragged into the fight by choosing to work with one group in need rather than with another group, by bringing supplies and resources into the war zone, or by becoming a target of the war effort. In addition, in a number of crises, NGOs have come to assume responsibilities that far exceeded their original missions. For instance, in Haiti and Liberia, NGOs moved into the vacuum caused by the collapse of central authority, undertaking many of the basic public services—food distribution, education, and health services—usually provided by the local governments. In these areas, the NGOs effectively replaced the state. Their ability to swiftly initiate and improvise alternative services certainly benefited the local people, but at a significant cost to the effort to create an effective national government with functioning ministries capable of providing essential services to the population.

The often-conspicuous disparity in the standards of living between NGO field staff and the population of the communities in which they work can make them a target for misunderstanding. In meeting their own needs, NGOs may absorb the best of what is available locally in terms of office and living space, as well as local staff. NGO transportation and communication facilities are likely to be far better than those of the local government. This can cause tension in the best of circumstances. In Afghanistan, government officials accused NGO representatives of misappropriating funds for personal use and thereby slowing the pace of development. These accusations were unfounded and were strongly denied by NGOs and foreign governments, but they reflected local suspicions, and overcoming them took time and effort.

Another set of concerns revolves around the traditional independence of NGOs. It is not the good intentions of the NGOs that are in question. Rather, concern focuses on the unintended consequences of an international NGO's pursuit of its mission to help, protect, or empower. NGOs have no obligation to enter a situation of conflict; no obligation—once in—to remain committed; and no obligation to pull out if other third parties disengage. Therefore, NGOs contribute to the unpredictability of the international community and to its seeming inability to coordinate a unified response to conflict. The abrupt departure of NGOs in response to a terrorist incident can affect popular confidence in a newly established government or undermine efforts by other international actors to create stability.

Concern about the impact of actions by NGOs has led to a debate in the international community over NGO accountability. Are NGOs accountable to the local people, or to the international community, or to the government of the country in which they are headquartered, or to their boards of trustees, or to their funders? In the eyes of the NGOs, the answer probably depends on each group's mandate and organization. U.S. relief NGOs that receive funding from USAID or UN agencies are certainly accountable to them. Most international NGOs also adhere to some formal standards: international humanitarian law (generally accepted or agreed rules of behavior during war), human rights law, and various codes of conduct drawn up and signed by groups of NGOs. In addition, certain standards of performance increasingly figure in the expectations of the NGOs and their supporters alike.

The Sphere Project

The Sphere Project was established in 1997 by a group of humanitarian NGOs and the Red Cross and Red Crescent movement as an effort to improve the quality of assistance provided to people affected by calamity and conflict and to improve the accountability of states and humanitarian agencies to their constituents, their donors, and their beneficiaries. Sphere is based on two core beliefs: first, that all possible steps should be taken to alleviate human suffering arising out of calamity and conflict, and, second, that those affected by disaster have a right to life with dignity and therefore a right to assistance.

The *Sphere Handbook* embodies a Humanitarian Charter as well as a set of minimum standards to be attained in disaster assistance. The cornerstone of the handbook is the Humanitarian Charter, which is based on the principles and provisions of international humanitarian law, international human rights law, refugee law, and the Code of Conduct for the International Red Cross and Red Crescent Movement and Non-Governmental Organizations in Disaster Relief. The Charter describes the core principles that govern humanitarian action and reasserts the right of populations affected by disaster, whether natural or human-made (including armed conflict), to protection and assistance. It also reasserts the right of disaster-affected populations to life with dignity. The Charter points out the legal responsibilities of states and warring parties to guarantee the right to protection and assistance. When the relevant authorities are unable or unwilling to fulfill their responsibilities, they are obliged to allow humanitarian organizations to provide humanitarian assistance and protection.

The handbook also contains a list of minimum standards and key indicators in each of four main sectors: (1) water, sanitation, and hygiene promotion; (2) food security, nutrition, and food aid; (3) shelter, settlement, and non-food aid; and (4) health services. These standards and key indicators were developed by broad networks of practitioners experienced in each of these sectors. Most of the standards, and the indicators that accompany them, are not new, but they consolidate and adapt existing knowledge and practice. Taken as a whole, they represent a remarkable consensus across a broad spectrum, and reflect a continuing determination to ensure that human rights and humanitarian principles are realized in practice. To date, more than 400 organizations in eighty countries around the world have contributed to the development of the minimum standards and key indicators presented in the second (2004) edition of the handbook.

The handbook has been endorsed by several major donor organizations, including the U.S. Department of State and USAID, and the UN Inter-Agency Standing Committee (a unique interagency forum for coordination, policy development, and decision making involving key UN and non-UN humanitarian partners chaired by the United Nations' emergency relief coordinator). The handbook is used in training humanitarian relief personnel from the NGO community, and it has rapidly developed into a guiding standard of performance for the NGOs and many donors.

The *Sphere Handbook* has served both as a document providing guidance on performance standards and as a focal point for NGO cooperation in arriving at shared objectives. In this latter capacity it has performed an unexpected and most valuable service: NGOs have reached a higher standard of coordination in the field, and external entities such as government agencies and national militaries have had clearer expectations during cooperative efforts with NGOs.

The Challenges
of Coordination

COORDINATION HAS BECOME the focus of many critiques of the international response to humanitarian disaster or internal conflict. Criticisms about coordination have been targeted at all the operational institutions: the United Nations, the military, and humanitarian NGOs. Critics claim that the lack of a coordinated response, a refusal to share information and resources, and an unwillingness to subordinate particular national or institutional goals to an overriding peacebuilding agenda have characterized peace and stability operations. Although there may be reasonable explanations for this lack of coordination, it is apparent that disunity weakens peacemaking efforts and that strengthening collaborative efforts must be a priority for all the intervening actors. Here, we look briefly at two types of collaborative activities: within the civilian community (including NGOs and IOs) and between that community and the military.

Coordination within
the Civilian Community

Before the age of complex emergencies, NGOs often acted independently, with little collaboration either among themselves or between themselves and other entities such as military forces. As a result of the many-layered international response to crisis, however, that practice is changing. Although they prize their autonomy, NGOs are increasingly working together in complex emergencies. Inter-NGO relationships allow individual NGOs to pool their knowledge, expertise, and sometimes their resources, or to coordinate their efforts to tackle a multifaceted problem. They are making systematic efforts to reinforce and expand response capacity on all levels. In some cases, donors actively support these efforts. One such example is the Interagency Working Group (IWG), aimed at increasing collaboration among CARE, Catholic Relief Services, International Rescue Committee, Mercy Corps, Oxfam GB, Save the Children USA, and World Vision International. In addition, international relief NGOs often develop close affiliations with indigenous NGOs, first contracting with local organizations for services, then training local staff to take charge of ongoing projects, and finally passing along the governance and management of projects to local entities. NGOs active in the fields of human rights, civil-society building, and conflict resolution also work with local groups where they exist. Where they do not exist, the international NGOs often promote their creation to establish a local capacity to press for political reform or to facilitate dialogue between opposing sides.

In humanitarian crises, UN operational agencies often take the lead in coordinating NGO activities within a given sector by providing funding, setting out the scope of work, and monitoring the results. Even within such an operating framework, however, NGOs retain a great measure of independence, carrying out their own assessments of the problem, its extent, and the needs of the affected population. UNHCR works with some three hundred NGOs to run refugee camps, and the UN World Food Program works through these and other NGOs to transport food and supplies to refugee populations around the globe. NGOs also work regularly with UNICEF. Within the United

Nations itself, OCHA is charged with coordinating UN humanitarian activities. Besides the UN agencies, a number of government funding agencies, such as USAID and the Canadian International Development Agency, have close ties with relief NGOs that bolster their ability to promote coordination. In the United States, the organization Inter-Action also plays an important role among humanitarian NGOs through its ability to convey information among the NGOs and between NGOs and the U.S. government.

UN personnel staff important structures designed to support NGO and UN operations in the field. These include Humanitarian Information Centres located in regions where there are ongoing operations. HICs serve as a repository of current information important to relief workers and others. They provide standard information products useful in joint planning. In addition, Joint Logistic Centers (JLCs), also staffed by UN personnel, frequently facilitate the movements of supplies and staff. These are significant bodies because they also work closely with the NGO community and function as common points for exchanges of information.

A recent phenomenon has been the increased effort of NGOs to work in coordinated groupings, referred to as "clusters," based on breakdown of planning and execution into so-called working sectors, such as water and sanitation or maternal and child care. These clusters bring together different organizations and facilitate expanded joint action.

Profiles of the
NGO Community

Notwithstanding their tremendous variety, the work that NGOs do in conflict zones can be grouped into four major activities:

- Humanitarian assistance
- Human rights
- Civil-society- and democracy-building
- Conflict resolution

To help the reader understand these different activities, this guide has organized the discussion of NGOs around them. Some NGOs specialize in one of these activities, and some undertake all of them. Hence, whereas Catholic Relief Services was founded as a humanitarian organization, it also funds and carries out many human rights, civil-society building, and conflict resolution activities. Although the international relief and development organizations play the most prominent role in humanitarian emergencies, human rights NGOs, civil-society- and democracy-building NGOs, and conflict resolution organizations also make significant contributions to peacemaking.

Humanitarian Relief NGOs

GENERAL INTRODUCTION

Like the military, the NGO community is, in many ways, a direct reflection of the societies from which it comes.

133

NGOs are frequently seen as vehicles for expression of the concerns and aspirations of their society. NGO respective members reflect the values expressed through the group norms. The roles and objectives of the NGO community, writ large, can diverge, but recognizing this aspect of their origins may be the basis for achieving significant levels of understanding and communication. In short, one cannot expect a U.S. NGO to behave like a European or Islamic NGO.

It is important to remember that the NGO community is as diverse as its parent societies, whether Western or non-Western. This diversity is simultaneously a strength and a complicating factor in its effectiveness and its relation to other communities, such as the military. There is no one attitude among NGOs toward working with the military or, indeed, even with each other. Frequently, NGOs are put into seemingly open competition because of their reliance on donor support. When engaged in fund-raising, NGOs may even highlight their differences in order to attract donor support.

Next, we will look at what makes an NGO in the minds of its staff and supporters. It is useful to understand this in order to relate to this family of organizations.

WHAT GUIDES NGOS

A Code of Conduct for disaster relief guides many NGOs and the International Red Cross and Red Crescent Movement (www.ifrc.org/publicat/conduct/). This code commits NGOs to assist victims wherever possible and to operate under guidelines requiring impartiality, independence, and the humanitarian imperative. The code provides ten principles to which all NGOs should adhere in their disaster response work and describes the relationships agencies working in disasters should seek with donor governments, host governments, and the United Nations. The code calls on NGOs to provide assistance on the basis of need, without adverse distinctions or effort to further any political or religious view. NGOs should not act as instruments of governments and should treat victims with dignity and respect.

HUMANITARIAN SPACE AND SECURITY

For NGO workers, humanitarian space, put simply, is that area where they can perform their work without concern over interference from outside political or military influences. It is a physical area where the personal security of NGO workers and the beneficiaries of their aid is maintained. Creating this space is not a matter of setting up a cordon of barbed wire and inviting those who wish to benefit to enter. It is more a matter of recognizing that such space is a prerequisite for humanitarian work and facilitating its existence through avoidance of military presence and overt involvement where possible. The term is not an abstract or idealized concept. For NGOs, it means what it says: We need to be free and secure to help others.

HUMANITARIAN/RELIEF NGOs

These NGOs provide direct assistance in the manner of emergency response teams. They typically wear T-shirts emblazoned with their organizations' names, which serve as uniforms.

These organizations are usually organized to be at the scene of a disaster or a conflict-related situation as quickly as possible. Frequently, they can have an emergency response team on the ground within as little as twenty hours. This initial presence is in the form of an assessment team whose objective is to determine where the organization's particular area of competence and available resources can have the most impact. In many cases, they will already be present maintaining long-term programs that predate the disaster. There are a great many of these agencies of varying size and background. Organizations such as CARE, the International Medical Corps, the International Rescue Committee, and World Vision fall into this category. They are the organizations with which most people are familiar, as they operate during well-reported disasters or conflicts. They also operate in far less well-known situations, as their mission statements require that they attempt to respond to needs wherever they exist to the extent of their resources and abilities.

Among NGOs, there are varying degrees of willingness to work with the military. Many NGOs will tailor their relations to military forces based on the specific mission of those forces (warfighting, peacekeeping, or support to humanitarian operations). In Afghanistan, NGOs have differing policies with regard to their interactions with the International Security Assistance Force, which is engaged in peacekeeping, and the U.S.-led coalition, which is engaged in combat operations. Their unwritten terms of reference frequently include "we don't coordinate directly with the military but, just maybe, we can work together cooperatively." Working together cooperatively assumes recognizing each other's areas of competence and capacity. For example, military logistical capabilities far exceed those of any NGO, and there are times when military assistance makes the difference in meeting the needs of a population. Some NGOs will exchange information on the health status of populations or other concerns within their competence. NGOs will look to the military to share information on security, such as the location of minefields or other dangers.

NGOs will not share "intelligence." It is important to accept the distinction NGOs make here. It is important to their physical security that they not be suspected of spying, which would compromise their relationship with the local population, and hence their security.

Command and Control

Delegating responsibility to the field is very much a part of the NGO approach. This does not mean that NGOs do not plan and worry about allocation of resources and information management at headquarters. NGOs, of necessity, often manage resources and information in a less controlled manner than the military or government agencies precisely because of their limited budgets. NGOs rely on donors, most of whom are looking at the immediate plight of the victims and are little inclined to fund support services.

Asking an NGO field director what the organization is doing will provide a good sense of its mission and of the nature of the organization. A typical plan of action for a humanitarian response agency is based on meeting an observed need. In the field, NGOs have the flexibility to adapt their operations to changing requirements.

Local NGOs

An added strength of the NGO system and an important aspect of its management structure is the close relationship with local NGOs. Frequently, much of the actual work is done by a local organization under the guidance of or by arrangement with an international NGO. These arrangements have been used extensively and provide NGOs with considerable sources of local knowledge and expertise as well as reducing the need to maintain expatriate staff in situations where the threats to local staff are considerably less. So-called national NGOs are formed to reflect local aspirations or needs. Indicators of their competence may be gained from the international NGOs with which they work or a determination of the degree of local acceptance.

Profiles

The following NGOs may engage in long-term development projects and are likely to be operating during a response to a natural or human-made emergency. They usually field emergency teams, which either begin providing immediate assistance or engage in assessments of need. Such NGOs are usually prepared to work closely with local residents and institutions and frequently have specific target groups, such as women and children, as a primary concern.

AMERICAN RED CROSS (ARC)

2025 E Street NW
Washington, DC 20006

Phone: 202-303-4498
Fax: 202-303-0044
E-mail: info@usa.redcross.org
Internet: www.redcross.org

A member of the International Red Cross and Red Crescent Movement, ARC serves as the official representative of the movement in the United States. A humanitarian organization led by volunteers and guided by its Congressional Charter and the Fundamental Principles of the International Red Cross Movement, ARC provides direct relief to disaster victims and refugees and helps people prevent, prepare for, and respond to emergencies. It seeks to enhance its sister national societies in disaster preparedness and response, primary health care and health education, HIV/AIDS education, blood collection and processing, capacity building, and social services. The organization coordinates youth exchange programs between itself and sister national societies; promotes international cooperation through community-based programs in the United States; and also provides development assistance.

The American Red Cross is generally present through its support of members of a local chapter of the International Federation of Red Cross and Red Crescent Societies (IFCR). The member agencies are part of a national society and operate at the grassroots level. This relationship to the local population is an important element in a successful response.

CARE (COOPERATIVE FOR ASSISTANCE AND RELIEF EVERYWHERE)

151 Ellis Street NE
Atlanta, GA 30303-2439

Phone: 800-521-227 or 404-681-2552
Fax: 404-577-5977
E-mail: info@care.org
Internet: www.care.org

CARE, which celebrated its sixtieth anniversary in 2005–06, was founded when twenty-two organizations formed a cooperative to rush lifesaving CARE packages to victims of World War II in Europe and, later, in Asia. In the years that followed, CARE sent food, tools, and other relief assistance to people recovering from natural disasters and conflicts throughout the world. In addition, CARE was an early leader in long-term development projects that enabled impoverished people to become self-sufficient. CARE is one of the largest nonprofit, independent relief and development organizations in the world and now operates in sixty-two nations in Africa, Asia, Eastern Europe, Latin America, and the former Soviet Union, helping the developing world's poor strive for social and economic well-being. CARE programs offer technical assistance, disaster relief, training, food, other material resources, and management in combinations appropriate to local needs and priorities. Whatever the method, the guiding principle is

NGOs

that programs provide people with sustainable means to achieve self-sufficiency. Programs are carried out under partnership agreements among CARE, private and government agencies, and local communities.

CARE is among the largest of the international NGOs, and it has been active in many areas of disaster response, including food delivery in Somalia and public health programs in Iraq. It is a leader in issues concerning NGO security. Its programs sometimes overlap with long-term development activities, so it is not unusual to encounter CARE programs that have been in a region for decades. This presence has frequently given it an advantage when a disaster strikes.

CATHOLIC RELIEF SERVICES (CRS)

209 West Fayette Street
Baltimore, MD 21201-3443

Phone: 800-736-3467 or 410-625-2220
Fax: 410-685-1635
E-mail: WebMaster@CatholicRelief.org
Internet: www.catholicrelief.org

Founded by the Catholic Bishops of the United States in 1943, CRS is the official overseas relief and development agency of the Catholic Church in the United States. CRS assists persons on the basis of need, not creed, race, or nationality. Its first mission provided food and shelter for World War II refugees. In the 1960s, the agency also began to look for ways to help the poor break out of the cycle of poverty. Emphasis has since shifted to the promotion of new farming techniques, loans for small business, and health and water projects. Peacebuilding and reconciliation, gender-responsive programs, and the development and strengthening of civil society are active parts of its promotion of social justice in the countries in which it works.

INTERNATIONAL MEDICAL CORPS (IMC)

1919 Santa Monica Blvd., Suite 300
Santa Monica, CA 90404

Phone: 310-826-7800
Fax: 310-442-6622
Internet: www.imcworldwide.org

IMC is a global humanitarian nonprofit organization dedicated to saving lives and relieving suffering through health care training and relief and development programs. Established in 1984 by volunteer doctors and nurses, IMC is a private, voluntary, nonpolitical, nonsectarian organization. Its mission is to improve the quality of life through health interventions and related activities that build local capacity in areas worldwide where few organizations dare to serve. By offering training and health care to local populations and medical assistance to people at highest risk, and with the flexibility to respond rapidly to emergency situations, IMC rehabilitates devastated health care systems and helps bring them back to self-reliance.

IMC places special emphasis on training local medical personnel in the skills and knowledge needed to rebuild their own health care systems. IMC provides extensive hands-on training in areas including primary health care, maternal/child care, health education, emergency relief, HIV/AIDS, reproductive health care, water and sanitation, reconstructive surgery, nutrition services, microfinance, and managerial skills needed to restore self-reliance. Those who train with IMC, including thousands of female health care workers, go on to teach others in their communities, thus expanding IMC's legacy of care.

INTERNATIONAL RESCUE COMMITTEE (IRC)
122 East 42nd Street
New York, NY 10168

Phone: 212-551-3000
Fax: 212-551-3185
E-mail: info@theirc.org
Internet: www.theirc.org

The IRC was founded in 1933 at the request of Albert Einstein to assist opponents of Hitler. It provides emergency relief, public health, medical, and educational services to refugees and displaced persons in more than two dozen countries. Through reconstruction and rehabilitation projects, the IRC assists in the repatriation of refugees to their home countries, provides resettlement services for refugees in the United States, and advocates on the behalf of refugees, especially women and children.

LUTHERAN WORLD RELIEF (LWR)
700 Light Street
Baltimore, MD 21230

Phone: 800-597-5972
Fax: 410-230-2882
E-mail: lwr@lwr.org
Internet: www.lwr.org

LWR began in 1945 to support Lutherans in Germany and Scandinavia after World War II and soon after moved worldwide. Its mission is to assist people outside the United States in disaster and emergency situations and to support development programs on behalf of the Evangelical Lutheran Church in America, the Lutheran Church-Missouri Synod, and other U.S. Lutherans, usually through counterpart church-related agencies. LWR focuses on long-range integrated community development projects. It operates or supports its programs mainly by providing financial and material support and by working to improve harvests, health, and education.

MERCY CORPS INTERNATIONAL (MCI)
3015 SW First Avenue
Portland, OR 97201

Phone: 800-292-3355 or 503-796-6800
Fax: 503-796-6844
E-mail: info@mercycorps.org
Internet: www.mercycorps.org

Founded in 1979, Mercy Corps exists to alleviate suffering, poverty, and oppression by helping people build secure, productive, and just communities. A nonprofit organization with headquarters in Portland; Seattle; Cambridge; Washington, D.C.; and Edinburgh, Scotland, Mercy Corps has provided over $1 billion in assistance to people in eighty-one nations. In 2005, the agency's programs reached seven million people in more than thirty-five countries, including some of the world's most difficult conflicts and disasters. Mercy Corps pursues its mission through (1) emergency relief services that assist people afflicted by conflict or disaster; (2) sustainable economic development that integrates agriculture, health, housing and infrastructure, economic development, education and environment, and local management; and (3) civil-society initiatives that promote citizen participation, accountability, conflict management and the rule of law.

In 2004, Mercy Corps absorbed the Conflict Management Group (CMG), based in Cambridge, Massachusetts, fusing both organizations' skills and expertise into a formidable international organization. The fusion of the two organizations gives Mercy Corps a wealth of knowledge and experience in defusing crises and in peacebuilding.

CMG's expertise enhances its ongoing commitment to integrate shorter term relief with long-term development programs in countries recovering from conflict, war, and economic despair. CMG is an intellectual leader in conflict resolution with a track record of taking on the toughest peace challenges, from Northern Ireland to the Korean peninsula.

OXFAM AMERICA
26 West Street
Boston, MA 02111

Phone: 800-776-9326 or 617-482-1211
Fax: 617-728-2594
E-mail: info@oxfamamerica.org
Internet: www.oxfamamerica.org or www.oxfam.org

Formed in 1970, Oxfam America is an autonomous, non-profit development agency that collaborates with the eleven other independent Oxfams around the world (the name Oxfam comes from the original Oxford Committee for Famine Relief, founded in England in 1942). Oxfam America funds disaster relief and a variety of self-help development projects carried out by grassroots community groups. It seeks to promote self-reliant, participatory development among poor people through projects that assist their efforts to supply more of their own food. Oxfam helps poor people gain more control over resources and decisions that affect their lives. It provides emergency relief assistance to selected countries. It conducts a development education program for people in the United States about the causes, challenges, and solutions regarding underdevelopment and hunger.

SAVE THE CHILDREN USA

54 Wilton Road
Westport, CT 06880

Phone: 800-728-3843 or 203-221-4030
Fax: 203-454-3914
E-mail: intlprograms@savechildren.org
Internet: www.savethechildren.org

Save the Children was created in 1932 to respond to the needs of children of coal miners in Appalachia. In more than thirty-five countries around the world and in fifteen states across the United States, Save the Children helps people learn to help themselves through projects that address interrelated problems and promote self-sufficiency. Save the Children especially focuses on early childhood education, preventive health care, and economic opportunities, including sustainable agriculture, natural resource management, and family support. Women are a major focus of Save the Children's work. Through their multiple roles as economic producers, primary caregivers, and community managers, women play a leading role in development. Save the Children programs endeavor to increase women's options to break intergenerational cycles of poverty and ensure a better quality of life for future generations.

AFRICARE

440 R Street NW
Washington, DC 20001

Phone: 202-462-3614
Fax: 202-387-1034
E-mail: development@africare.org
Internet: www.africare.org

Africare is a private, nonprofit organization dedicated to improving the quality of life in rural Africa. For more than thirty years, Africare has assisted children, women, and families in countries throughout Africa through self-help programs in agriculture, water resource development, environmental management, health and emergency humanitarian aid, and projects in microenterprise development, democratic governance, and initiatives in Africa to combat the HIV/AIDS epidemic.

In the United States, Africare focuses on building understanding of African development through public education and promotional outreach. Africare's work is supported financially through grants and contributions from corporations, foundations, organizations, the religious community, the U.S. government, international agencies, foreign institutions, and thousands of individual donors.

SALVATION ARMY WORLD SERVICE OFFICE (SAWSO)

615 Slaters Lane, PO Box 269
Alexandria, VA 22313

Phone: 703-684-5528
Fax: 703-684-5536
E-mail: SAWSO@USN.salvationarmy.org
Internet: www.sawso.org

SALVATION ARMY INTERNATIONAL HEADQUARTERS

101 Queen Victoria Street
London EC4P 4EP
United Kingdom

Phone: 44-20-7332-0101
Fax: 44-20-7236-4681
Internet: www2.salvationarmy.org

The Salvation Army was founded by William Booth in London in 1865 as an international movement and an evangelical part of the universal Christian church. SAWSO provides financial and technical assistance to the International Salvation Army in support of its work in a variety of programs, including education, health services, relief and disaster services, and community development. It also assists the Salvation Army in developing community-based initiatives that address the underlying causes of poverty in developing countries.

SAWSO was established in 1976 to find long-term solutions to worldwide poverty. Directed by the world headquarters in London, it focuses on five areas: health, employment, community development, disaster relief, and training of indigenous personnel. Financing comes from private and public sectors.

MÉDECINS SANS FRONTIÈRES USA (MSF USA)

(Doctors Without Borders USA)
333 Seventh Avenue, 2nd Floor
New York, NY 10016

Phone: 212-679-6800
Fax: 212-679-7016
E-mail: doctors@newyork.msf.org
Internet: www.doctorswithoutborders.org

International Headquarters

Rue de Lausanne 78
CP 116 – 1211
Geneva 21
Switzerland

Phone: 41-(0)22-849-8400
Fax: 41-(0)22-849-8404
Internet: www.msf.org

A private, nonprofit humanitarian organization, Doctors Without Borders (DWB) was founded in 1971 by a small group of French doctors determined to respond rapidly and effectively to public health emergencies, with complete independence from political, economic, and religious powers. DWB delivers emergency medical relief to populations threatened by armed conflict, civil strife, epidemics, or natural or human-made disasters. A DWB team provides primary health care, performs surgery, vaccinates children, rehabilitates hospitals, operates emergency nutrition and sanitation programs, and trains local medical staff.

DWB is among the most proactive of all the NGOs. It works in a wide range of countries and has a reputation for principled and courageous work in the field. Its opposition to cooperation with the military has generated a great deal of debate. DWB withdrew from Afghanistan in 2005 after claiming that the location nearby of a U.S. military Provincial Reconstruction Team contributed to a deadly insurgent attack on its personnel.

WORLD VISION
800 West Chestnut Avenue
Monrovia, CA 91016-3198

Phone: 888-511-6598
Fax: 206-815-3442
E-mail: newsvision@wvi.org
Internet: www.wvi.org

World Vision was founded in 1950 in response to the needs of Korean War orphans. It is now a global partnership conducting child-focused emergency relief and sustainable community development in more than 4,500 projects. World Vision is an international partnership of Christians committed to transformational development, emergency relief, the promotion of justice, and strategic initiatives to serve the church. It focuses on clean water, education, health care, agricultural improvements, public hygiene, food, shelter, and medical care to victims of natural or human-made disasters.

A Special Category: The NGO Coalition

This body frequently represents groups of NGOs in discussions and statements of common concerns. Many of the organizations listed here are members.

INTERACTION

1717 Massachusetts Avenue NW, Suite 701
Washington, DC 20036

Phone: 202-667-8227
Fax: 202-667-8236
E-mail: ia@interaction.org
Internet: www.interaction.org

Formed in 1984, InterAction is a coalition of more than 160 U.S.-based relief, development, environmental, and refugee agencies working in more than a hundred countries around the world. InterAction seeks to enhance the identity, autonomy, credibility, and diverse perspectives of each member agency; provide a broadly based participatory forum for professional consultation, coordination, and concerted action; foster the effectiveness and recognition of the private voluntary organization community, both professionally and publicly; and set the highest ethical standards in carrying out its mission.

Member organizations promote economic development and self-reliance, improve health and education, provide relief to victims of disasters and wars, assist refugees, advance human rights, protect the environment, address population concerns, advocate for more-just public policies, and increase understanding and cooperation among people. Women are central to many of these programs, and special efforts are made to promote women's participation and equity. The InterAction consortium has standing committees on humanitarian policy and practice, development policy and practice, public policy, advancement of women, and ethical standards.

InterAction is an umbrella organization serving its members and the NGO community in the United States. It is not the coordinating arm of the NGO community and does not replace the individual decision making of its members. It should not be assumed that InterAction can provide a one-stop shop for dealing with the NGO world.

Human Rights and Advocacy NGOs

Historically, the definition, observance, and enforcement of individual human rights was not written into international law that dealt with the law of nations. Protection of individual rights is a recent issue and not a popular one with repressive regimes or with governments whose religious or cultural values are at odds with the principles of individual rights. Human rights NGOs, together with international organizations such as the United Nations, attempt to define and promote the basic rights of all people regardless of beliefs or background and to prevent political and economic repression. Some NGOs also focus on social and cultural rights. To avoid compromising their work, many human rights organizations do not accept funding from government sources.

It is worth noting that in the past there have been seemingly clear distinctions between the roles of the human rights and humanitarian NGOs. This apparent separation has broken down as humanitarian NGOs find themselves increasingly involved in situations where protection of individual rights and lives is a significant factor. The conditions in Darfur, for example, have placed many NGOs in unaccustomed roles in this regard.

Like humanitarian organizations, human rights NGOs are diverse in size, objectives, mandates, and areas of operation. A fundamental distinction is between those NGOs that operate internationally and those that focus on conditions in their own countries. The human rights NGOs listed here are international bodies, but they all have close ties to groups working at the local level. The basis for their human rights work also differs. Local NGOs that operate in countries with a strong tradition of guarantees of civil or political rights often base their campaigns on domestic law. Local NGOs operating in countries without such guarantees frequently base their work on rights guaranteed by international law and codified in the Universal Declaration of Human Rights and the International Covenant on Civil and Political Rights.

As the result of a campaign by human rights groups, the 1945 UN Charter refers to human rights in its preamble and in later articles. In 1946, the organization also established the UN Commission on Human Rights, which drafted the Universal Declaration of Human Rights, embraced by the UN General Assembly in December 1948. Since then, significant but sporadic efforts have addressed the issue. The United Nations adopted the Convention on the Prevention and Punishment of the Crime of Genocide at the same time as the Universal Declaration, but the United States did not ratify it until 1986. The Supplementary Convention on Slavery—the result of work by the British NGO Anti-Slavery International—passed in 1956.

The important International Covenant on Civil and Political Rights (1966), which established the UN Human Rights Committee, opened a channel of regular communication between the United Nations and NGOs. The Convention on the Rights of the Child was adopted in November 1989 through the efforts of a working group created by the Commission on Human Rights and composed of the UNHCR, UNICEF, the International Labor Organization, WHO, and a number of NGOs. In 1993, after years of lobbying by NGOs and some member states, the United Nations established the Office of the High Commissioner for Human Rights, whose tasks include coordinating human rights throughout the UN system.

ICRC has been a principal source of international humanitarian law, defined by Lawrence Weschler (Gutman and Rieff 1999, 20) as "a law of war governing the interactions between combatants' forces and between those forces and noncombatants during times of military conflict." The Geneva Accords adopted in 1864, and the 1949 Geneva Conventions, organized by the ICRC and supplemented by protocols in the 1970s, define appropriate and proscribed behavior by combatants in both international and internal wars. Like UN conventions and the Helsinki Accords, these standards of conduct acquire the force of law only when a country signs them.

Organizations active in human rights are distinct from other NGOs in their style and their activities. Generally, their goal is to seek out, research, and address specific and general situations where repression occurs. Once abuses are found and documented, human rights NGOs tend first to encourage the voluntary correction of the abuse, then to pressure governments to change, and ultimately to publicly stigmatize the violator. Given this strategy, it is not surprising that these NGOs may antagonize those governments judged to be abusing human rights. International human rights NGOs also take the international community or their home governments to task for supporting abusive regimes, a process known as naming and shaming.

Some NGOs take on other roles. Peace Brigades International, a volunteer group dedicated to nonviolence, accompanies local human rights activists as they go about their work. The presence of Peace Brigades volunteers, requested by the local groups and explained to local authorities, offers a form of protection by providing international witnesses to activities of all the local actors. This witnessing function also comes into play in trial monitoring, in which human rights groups, both local and international, serve to remind the court system that outsiders are concerned about preserving fairness in the legal proceedings.

Research into possible abuses may involve NGO staff, volunteers, and members visiting selected areas as observers or monitors; gathering information from local NGOs, churches, community groups, activists, professionals, and other sources; and seeking pertinent official documentation. The task of gathering information on human rights issues can be difficult and dangerous, and local employees and groups are often at the greatest risk from persons who are hostile to the monitoring effort.

Once equipped with the necessary research data, human rights NGOs mount systematic campaigns to alert the public and officials to the plight of victims, be they individuals or entire populations. These campaigns consist of testifying before government committees, international organizations, church councils, and other influential policymaking and lawmaking bodies and reporting abuses to the world media. Testifying serves the dual purpose of educating officials and the public and exerting pressure on institutions to condemn offending parties.

The work of human rights organizations has been enhanced by the development of new information technologies, as information about human rights conditions can reach a broad international audience very quickly. For this reason, too, human rights NGOs value media attention, and they are active in alerting news resources and media in principal capitals to human rights violations. They also widely publish and distribute detailed reports, editorials, and articles. They dramatize specific cases and rally public support in the form of letter-writing campaigns, demonstrations, and fundraising campaigns.

The work of human rights NGOs is not always a stabilizing factor in a conflict, and it can run counter, at least in the short term, to peacekeeping efforts. In their direct condemnation of human rights abusers, NGOs may further antagonize parties within a conflict, criticize participants in a peacekeeping effort, and jeopardize the work of development agencies.

NGOs may also comment publicly—and often critically—on the conduct of international and national bodies, such as the United Nations and individual governments, in upholding human rights. Respect for human rights during peace and stability operations is a growing concern among a number of NGOs. One of the largest, Amnesty International, has developed a fifteen-point program for promoting human rights in international peace and stability operations targeted at the intervening entities, including the United Nations. In clear reference to the international reluctance to engage with war criminals, the second of the fifteen points calls for "no international 'silent witnesses.' All international field personnel, including those engaged in military, civilian, and humanitarian operations, should report through explicit and proper channels any human rights violations they may witness or serious allegations they receive."

Some of the better-known international human rights NGOs are profiled here.

AMNESTY INTERNATIONAL
5 Penn Plaza, 14th Floor
New York, NY 10001

Phone: 212-807-8400
Fax: 212-463-9193
E-mail: admin-us@aiusa.org
Internet: www.amnestyusa.org

Amnesty International was launched in 1961 and has an active worldwide membership with more than a million individual members, subscribers, and supporters in 162 countries and territories. Amnesty International plays a specific role in the international protection of human rights and focuses on prisoners. It seeks the release of prisoners of conscience. These are people detained anywhere for their beliefs, color, ethnic origin, language, or religion who have not used or advocated violence. Amnesty International works for fair and prompt trials for all political prisoners and on behalf of such people detained without charge or trial. It opposes the death penalty and torture or other cruel, inhumane, or degrading treatment or punishment of all prisoners without reservation.

Amnesty International's work is based on principles set forth in the United Nations Universal Declaration of Human Rights. These universal rights include the right to freedom from arbitrary arrest and detention; the right to freedom of expression, conscience, and religion; the right to a fair trial; the right to life, liberty, and security of person; and the right not to be tortured. Amnesty International works to protect these rights by its efforts to secure the release of prisoners of conscience, to encourage fair and prompt trials in political cases, and to bring an end to torture and executions. The work is impartial, and Amnesty International is a democratic, self-governing movement. Amnesty International is concerned solely with the protection of human rights involved in each case, regardless of either the ideology of the government or the beliefs of the victims.

ARTICLE 19

6-8 Amwell Street
EC1R 1UQ, London
England

Phone: 44-(0)20-7278-9292
Fax: 44-(0)20-7278-7660
E-mail: info@article19.org
Internet: www.article19.org

Article 19, founded in 1986 to campaign for the promotion and protection of freedom of expression, is named after Article 19 of the Universal Declaration of Human Rights. It seeks to achieve justice for individuals, create a dialogue with governments, influence intergovernmental bodies, build capacity and networks, and provide resources. It monitors, publishes, lobbies, campaigns, and litigates on behalf of freedom of expression.

COMMITTEE TO PROTECT JOURNALISTS (CPJ)

330 Seventh Avenue, 11th Floor
New York, NY 10001

Phone: 212-465-1004
Fax: 212-465-9568
E-mail: info@cpj.org
Internet: www.cpj.org

CPJ was founded in 1981 to monitor abuses against the press and promote press freedom around the world. It publicly reveals abuses against the press and acts on behalf of imprisoned and threatened journalists. CPJ maintains updated reports and analysis of conditions for journalists, and is a resource for journalists when covering attacks against the press, when in emergency situations, and when preparing for assignments abroad.

HUMAN RIGHTS WATCH

350 Fifth Avenue, 34th Floor
New York, NY 10118-3299

Phone: 212 290-4700
Fax: 212-736-1300
E-mail: hrwnyc@hrw.org
Internet: www.hrw.org

Human Rights Watch began in 1978 with the founding of its Helsinki division. Today, it includes five divisions covering Africa, the Americas, Asia, the Middle East, as well as the signatories of the Helsinki accords. It also includes three collaborative projects on arms, children's rights, and women's rights. Special initiative areas include academic freedom, corporations and human rights, drugs and human rights, free expression, prison conditions, and human rights in the United States.

Human Rights Watch conducts regular, systematic investigations of human rights abuses in more than seventy countries around the world. It addresses the human rights practices of governments of all political stripes, all geopolitical alignments, and all ethnic and religious persuasions. In internal wars, it documents violations by both governments and rebel groups. Human Rights Watch defends freedom of thought and expression, due process, and equal protection under the law; it documents and denounces murders, disappearances, torture, arbitrary imprisonment, exile, censorship, and other abuses of internationally recognized human rights.

INTERNATIONAL COMMISSION OF JURISTS (ICJ)

PO Box 216
81A Avenue de Chatelaine
CH-1219 Chatelaine/Geneva
Switzerland

Phone: 41-22-979-3800
Fax: 41-22-979-3801
E-mail: info@icj.org
Internet: www.icj.org

Founded in 1952, the ICJ is devoted to the promotion of the understanding and observance of the rule of law and the promotion and legal protection of human rights throughout the world. Commission membership is limited to sixty eminent jurists representing the different legal systems of the world. The ICJ emphasizes not only individual civil and political rights, but also the economic, social, and cultural rights of communities. The ICJ also advocates for development policies and social reform.

INTERNATIONAL FEDERATION OF HUMAN RIGHTS (FIDH)

(Fédération Internationale des Ligues des Droits
de l'Homme)
17 Passage de la Main d'Or
75011 Paris
France

Phone: 331-43-55-2518
Fax: 331-43-55 1880
E-mail: www.fidh.org/_contact.php3
Internet: www.fidh.org

The International Federation of Human Rights—usually known by its French acronym, FIDH—was founded in

1972 at the initiative of human rights organizations in several European countries. Today, it has 141 national league members in more than eighty countries, with a joint membership of more than 500,000. In coordination with its affiliates, FIDH carries out missions of investigation, missions to observe trials and judicial processes, and missions of training. FIDH has also sent missions of mediation and election monitors. Its goal is to promote the implementation of the Universal Declaration of Human Rights and other international instruments of human rights protection.

FIDH seeks to mobilize the community of states to prevent violations of human rights and to support civil society. It provides support and technical assistance to its affiliates and helps them bring their message to the attention of the international community. It is a network of support and solidarity, linking human rights advocates on every continent.

NGOS

INTERNATIONAL LEAGUE FOR HUMAN RIGHTS
228 East 45th Street, 5th Floor
New York, NY 10017

Phone: 212-661-0480
Fax: 212-661-0416
E-mail: info@ilhr.org
Internet: www.ilhr.org

The International League for Human Rights was formed in 1942 to defend individual human rights of advocates who risk their lives to promote the ideals of a just and civil society in their own countries. It also focuses attention on the plight of women and children in armed conflict and has special consultative status to the United Nations, the Council of Europe, and the International Labor Organization.

HUMAN RIGHTS FIRST
(Formerly the Lawyers Committee for Human Rights)
333 Seventh Avenue, 13th Floor
New York, NY 10001-5004

Phone: 212-845-5200
Fax: 212-845-5499
E-mail: feedback@humanrightsfirst.org
Internet: www.humanrightsfirst.org

Human Rights First works in the United States and abroad
to create a secure and humane world by advancing justice,
human dignity, and respect for the rule of law. It supports
human rights activists who fight for basic freedoms and
peaceful change at the local level; protects refugees in flight
from persecution and repression; helps build a strong international system of justice and accountability; and makes
sure human rights laws and principles are enforced in the
United States and abroad. Its work is impartial, holding all
governments accountable to the standards affirmed in the
United Nations International Bill of Human Rights. Its
programs focus on building the legal institutions and
structures that guarantee human rights in the long term.

Strengthening independent human rights advocacy at
the local level is a key feature of its work. Human Rights
First also plays a key role in influencing the actions of the
U.S. government in promoting the rule of law in both its
foreign and domestic policies, and it presses for greater accountability by bodies such as the United Nations and the
World Bank. Through representation of asylum seekers
and by challenging U.S. refugee policy, Human Rights First
has combined its work on international human rights and
the rights of refugees.

MINORITY RIGHTS GROUP INTERNATIONAL (MRG)

54 Commercial Street
London E1 6LT
United Kingdom

Phone: 44-(0)20-7422-4200
Fax: 44-(0)20-7422-4201
E-mail: minority.rights@mrgmail.org
Internet: www.minorityrights.org

MRG is an international NGO working to secure justice for minorities suffering discrimination and prejudice and for the peaceful coexistence of majority and minority communities. Founded in the 1960s, MRG has four main activities: researching and publishing reports and other information about minorities around the world; advocating (or lobbying for) the rights of minorities at the United Nations, in Europe, with governments, and elsewhere; educating children and teachers on minority issues in order to counter racism and prejudice; and working with organizations and activists who share its aims to build alliances, develop skills, and further minority rights worldwide.

PEACE BRIGADES INTERNATIONAL (PBI)

The Grayston Center
28 Charles Square
London N1 6HT
United Kingdom

Phone: 44-(0)20-7324-4628
E-mail: info@peacebrigades.org
Internet: www.peacebrigades.org

Founded in 1981 as a grassroots NGO inspired by Gandhi, PBI explores and promotes nonviolent approaches to peace-keeping and support for human rights. When invited, it sends teams of volunteers into areas of political repression and conflict, accompanying human rights defenders, their organizations, and others who have been threatened by political violence. Volunteers also conduct peace education workshops and spread information about the conflict situation, human rights, and nonviolent struggle for peace and social justice.

PHYSICIANS FOR HUMAN RIGHTS (PHR)

Two Arrow Street, Suite 301
Cambridge, MA 02138

Phone: 617-301-4200
Fax: 617-301-4250
E-mail: phrusa@phrusa.org
Internet: www.phrusa.org

PHR, an organization of health professionals, scientists, and concerned citizens, uses the knowledge and skills of the medical and forensic sciences to investigate and prevent violations of international human rights and humanitarian law. Since 1986, members have worked to stop torture, disappearances, and political killings by governments and opposition groups; to improve health and sanitary conditions in prisons; to investigate physical and psychological violations of humanitarian law; to defend medical neutrality; to protect health professionals who are victims; and to prevent medical complicity in torture and abuse. Its actions are bound by the Universal Declaration of Human Rights.

REFUGEES INTERNATIONAL
1705 N Street NW
Washington, DC 20036

Phone: 800-733-8433 or 202-828-0110
Fax: 202-828-0819
E-mail: ri@refintl.org
Internet: www.refintl.org

Founded in 1979 in response to the forced repatriation of thousands of Cambodian, Laotian, and Vietnamese refugees, Refugees International provides early warning in crises of mass exodus. It seeks to serve as the advocate of the unrepresented—the refugee. In recent years, Refugees International has moved from its initial focus on Indochinese refugees to global coverage, conducting more than twenty emergency missions in 2004. The organization mixes quiet diplomacy and the power of the press to advocate for refugee issues with governments and agencies of the United Nations. Its on-the-ground emergency assessment paves the way for relief agencies and human rights organizations to step in with lifesaving measures.

U.S. COMMITTEE FOR REFUGEES AND IMMIGRANTS (USCRI)
1717 Massachusetts Avenue NW, 2nd Floor
Washington, DC 20036-2003

Phone: 202-347-3507
Fax: 202-347-3418
E-mail: aseiler@uscridc.org
Internet: www.refugees.org

USCRI was founded in 1958 to coordinate U.S. participation in the United Nations' International Refugee Year (1959). Since then, USCRI has worked to protect and assist refugees in all regions of the world. It defends the rights of all uprooted people regardless of their nationality, race, religion, ideology, or social group. USCRI's work is based on the belief that once the consciences of men and women are aroused, great deeds can be accomplished. USCRI goes to the scene of refugee emergencies to talk to refugees, record human rights abuses, devise a strategy to provide temporary safety and essential relief, alert the public to the unmet needs of refugee emergencies, and take steps to restore refugees to secure, productive lives.

Civil-Society- and Democracy-Building NGOs

Currently, many countries are in need of international assistance to help heal wounds inflicted by ethnic conflict, civil war, and, in the worst cases, genocide. A number of NGOs focus particularly on supporting the development of civil institutions and democratic practices such as elections, education, free speech, and free press in these states in transition. This is of course an activity also promoted by other kinds of NGOs—humanitarian, human rights, and conflict resolution—as a natural component of their work. It is no longer unusual, however, to find NGOs not initially designed for this function playing a role in this area in the increasingly complex social situations developing in countries such as Afghanistan and Iraq.

NGOs committed to building civil society seek to empower people as citizens. The issues they address include the rights, freedoms, and responsibilities of citizens within a democracy; the infrastructure necessary for a democratic society; free and open elections; freedom of speech; and the functioning of a market-driven economy.

Education may take the form of workshops, seminars, and training programs. NGOs may serve as technical advisers to governments or run programs that explain the institutions of constitutional government, the nature of participatory government, the conduct of elections, mechanisms to protect the rights of minority groups, and the role of civil society in a democratic system.

Citizens of many countries moving toward democracy have had little experience in organizations that were not state sponsored. Civil-society building NGOs assist in the formation of a variety of nonpolitical community organizations, such as parent-teacher, voting registration, and community resource associations; professional, recreational, and volunteer membership groups; and activist organizations for advancing programs for children, women, minorities, and community health. NGOs advance the understanding that such groups are necessary to strengthen the framework of the community but depend on the initiative of local, often private, individuals.

Some NGOs send observers to monitor local elections. A number, especially those with limited resources, specifically target their services to countries that are known for their commitment to democracy. Another activity involves demobilization and job training for former combatants. In emerging democracies, rehabilitation and reintegration of former fighters is essential to prevent the restart of armed conflict.

In many places, large relief and development NGOs incorporate civil-society building in their programs by encouraging the establishment and work of citizen groups. As a grassroots presence in countries in transition—often in crisis—these NGOs support peacebuilding and help establish a foundation on which to build democratic institutions by strengthening community organizations and creating cooperatives. They dispatch teams to organize and train regional groups to define election issues and platforms, to participate in election campaigns, and to be equal partners in development.

NGOs

The following profiles focus on some of the NGOs that concentrate on building civil society and democratic institutions.

ACADEMY FOR EDUCATIONAL DEVELOPMENT (AED)

1825 Connecticut Avenue NW
Washington, DC 20009-5721

Phone: 202-884-8000
Fax: 202-884-8400
E-mail: web@aed.org
Internet: www.aed.org

AED, founded in 1961, is an independent, nonprofit service organization committed to addressing human development needs in the United States and throughout the world. Under contracts and grants, AED operates programs in collaboration with policy leaders; non-governmental and community-based organizations; businesses; government agencies; international multilateral and bilateral funders; and schools, colleges, and universities. In partnership with its clients, AED seeks to meet today's social, economic, and environmental challenges through education and human resource development; to apply state-of-the-art education, training, research, technology, management, behavioral analysis, and social marketing techniques to solve problems; and to improve knowledge and skills throughout the world as the most effective means for stimulating growth, reducing poverty, and promoting democratic and humanitarian ideals.

EUROPEAN AND EURASIA DIVISION OF THE RULE OF LAW INITIATIVE (CEELI)

American Bar Association
740 15th Street NW
Washington, DC 20005

Phone: 202-662-1950
Fax: 202-662-1597
E-mail: ceeli@abanet.org
Internet: www.abaceeli.org

CEELI, a public service project of the American Bar Association, advances the rule of law in the world by supporting the legal reform process in Central and Eastern Europe and states of the former Soviet Union. With the assistance of lawyers, judges, and law professors, it helps to build the legal infrastructure that is indispensable to strong, self-supporting, democratic, free-market systems.

CEELI has offices in twenty-two countries across Central Europe and Eurasia. Through the efforts of liaisons, who typically live in a country for a year, and other volunteers, it encourages the formation of independent bar associations, judges' associations, press associations, and other non-governmental organizations that strengthen the fabric of a free society. Volunteers have also assisted in drafting new constitutions, civil and criminal codes, and security laws and in erecting a legal framework to support modern democracies through independent judiciaries.

NGOS

CIVITAS International
77 Great Peter Street
Westminster SW1P 2EZ, London
United Kingdom

Phone: 44-(0)20-7799-6677
Fax: 44-(0)20-7799-6688
E-mail: info@civitas.org.uk
Internet: www.civitas.org.uk

CITIVAS, an international consortium for civic education, aims to strengthen effective education for informed and responsible citizenship in new and established democracies around the world. The CIVITAS consortium is composed of individuals, non-governmental associations, and governmental institutions from many countries, as well as international organizations.

CIVITAS works to maintain a worldwide network, using all available resources, including computer networking, international exchanges, and various other means, to bring the knowledge, skill, and experience of education for democracy to bear on the tasks that confront today's democracies.

The Freedom Forum
1101 Wilson Boulevard
Arlington, VA 22209

Phone: 703-528-0800
Fax: 703-284-3770
E-mail: news@freedomforum.org
Internet: www.freedomforum.org

The Freedom Forum was established in 1991 as a nonpartisan, international foundation dedicated to free press, free speech, and free spirit for all people. The foundation pursues its priorities through conferences, educational activities, publishing, broadcasting, online services, fellow-ships, partnerships, training, research, and other programs. International programs of the Freedom Forum focus on operating news and journalism libraries for journalists and journalism students in Eastern and Central Europe and Asia; supporting international institutions such as schools of journalism and journalistic associations; organizing conferences on global media issues; and providing training and guidance to international journalists through workshops, seminars, fellowships, and exchange programs. The Freedom Forum also funds the operations of the Newseum, an interactive museum of news in Washington, D.C., and the First Amendment Center and Diversity Institute in Nashville, Tennessee.

SOROS FOUNDATIONS NETWORK

c/o Open Society Institute
400 West 59th Street
New York, NY 10019

Phone: 212-548-0600
Fax: 212-548-4600
Internet: www.soros.org

The numerous nonprofit foundations and organizations created and funded by philanthropist George Soros are linked together in an informal network, the Soros Foundations Network. At the heart of this network are thirty-three autonomous organizations, known as national foundations, located throughout Central Europe, Eurasia, and Africa and in Haiti and Guatemala. These foundations share the common mission of supporting the development of open society.

The Soros Foundations Network operates and supports an array of programs and initiatives in education; civil society; independent media; Internet and e-mail communications; publishing; human rights; arts and culture; and social, legal, and economic reform. The Open Society Institute–New York and the Open Society Institute–Budapest assist these foundations and organizations by creating programs on issues common to two or more foundations and by providing administrative, financial, and technical support. Other entities created by George Soros include the Central European University, the international Science Foundation, and the Open Media Research Institute.

■   ■   ■

Although funded by the U.S. Congress, the three institutions that follow act much like NGOs and are found in post-conflict situations.

NATIONAL ENDOWMENT FOR DEMOCRACY (NED)

1101 15th Street NW, Suite 700
Washington, DC 20005

Phone: 202-293-9072
Fax: 202-223-6042
Internet: www.ned.org

NED is a private, nonprofit organization created in 1983 to strengthen democratic institutions around the world through non-governmental efforts. An independent and non-partisan board of directors governs the endowment. With its annual congressional appropriation, it makes hundreds of grants each year to support prodemocracy groups in Africa, Asia, Central and Eastern Europe, Latin America, the Middle East, and the former Soviet Union.

The endowment is guided by the belief that freedom is a universal human aspiration that can be realized through the development of democratic institutions, procedures, and values. NED believes that democracy cannot be achieved through a single election and need not be based on the model of the United States or any other particular country. Rather, it evolves according to the needs and traditions of diverse political cultures. By supporting this process, the endowment helps strengthen the bond between indigenous democratic movements abroad and the people of the United States—a bond based on a common commitment to representative government and freedom as a way of life.

INTERNATIONAL REPUBLICAN INSTITUTE (IRI)
1225 I Street NW, Suite 700
Washington, DC 20005

Phone: 202-408-9450
Fax: 202-408-9462
E-mail: iri@iri.org
Internet: www.iri.org

A nonprofit organization dedicated to advancing democracy worldwide, IRI was established as one of four institutes of the National Endowment for Democracy, which was authorized by Congress in 1984. IRI initiates and supports a wide range of programs to promote democratic ideals and institutions abroad. IRI programs are nonpartisan and adhere to fundamental American principles, such as individual freedom, equality of opportunity, and the entrepreneurial spirit that fosters economic development.

IRI programs range from basic instruction in the mechanics of building political parties and conducting campaigns for public office and civic education to training on the legislative process for newly elected parliamentarians. IRI has trained poll watchers, prepared political parties for free elections, and organized conferences in an effort to instruct prodemocracy reformers in free election campaign techniques in more than sixty countries. IRI programs place great emphasis on facilitating free, fair, and multiparty elections. Its programs may focus on analyses of electoral laws, preelection political assessments, and training seminars for local and national election commission members and poll watchers.

NATIONAL DEMOCRATIC INSTITUTE FOR INTERNATIONAL AFFAIRS (NDI)

2030 M Street NW, 5th Floor
Washington, DC 20036-3306

Phone: 202-728-5500
Fax: 202-728-5520
E-mail: contact@ndi.org
Internet: www.ndi.org

NDI is a nonprofit, non-governmental organization that was established in 1984 to strengthen democratic institutions and pluralistic values in new and emerging democracies. NDI's programs are concentrated in new democracies, societies in conflict, and nondemocratic countries with strong democratic movements. Programs address political parties, election processes, governance, civil-military relations, women in politics, and civic organizations. A major objective of NDI is the consolidation of existing democratic institutions and the nurturing of peaceful transitions to democracy.

Benefactors of NDI's work include national legislatures and local governments that function with openness and competence; broad-based political parties that are vehicles for public policy debates; election commissions that administer transparent and fair balloting; and non-partisan civic organizations that monitor elections and promote democratic values and citizen participation. Its main functional areas include improving civil-military relations and strengthening local governments, legislatures, election processes, and civic organizations.

Conflict Resolution NGOs

A significant number of NGOs focus their resources primarily on conflict resolution and prevention. In an active conflict, such NGOs may be recruited to act as impartial intermediaries, working with opposing parties, facilitating negotiations, and helping to uphold accepted solutions. In some cases, they may actually initiate and catalyze dialogue between parties; in others, they may simply monitor and expedite it. In conflict prevention, NGOs try to avert conflict or crisis. Many organizations are working in Africa, the Middle East, South Asia, and independent states of the former Soviet Union to promote innovative solutions to ethnic conflict. In both mediation and conflict prevention, the success of the project depends on the strict neutrality of the NGO.

The field of conflict resolution has many sources, including the academic disciplines of political science, international relations, psychology, sociology, anthropology, biology, economics, mathematics, and law. Other sources include the long history of domestic labor-management disputes and negotiation; the civil rights movement; and other work on racial, community, and domestic ethnic conflict. The emergence of social activism in the 1960s and 1970s, including the antiwar, feminist, and environmental movements, has played a very important part. Another influence has been the development of alternative dispute settlement mechanisms—such as arbitration and mediation

—that take place outside the domestic court system. Also influential has been the work of NGOs, including religion-based organizations dedicated to nonviolence, such as the Quakers and the Mennonites and the contribution of foreign policymakers and official practitioners whose practice of negotiation, mediation, and conflict resolution on a national and multilateral basis has long provided insights for the field.

Most NGOs in this field represent a specific approach to conflict management and resolution, many of which involve developing programs that make the participants aware of their own role in a conflict and give them tools for resolving or at least ameliorating the situation. Beneath this broad canopy lie many different approaches to conflict management and to the specific work each NGO performs, ranging from programs to improve negotiation skills to strategies to identify and resolve the underlying causes of conflict.

Some NGOs specialize in facilitating dialogue among parties to the conflict or among influential community leaders. In addition, government officials have asked NGOs to help improve conflict resolution skills, design dispute resolution systems, monitor ethnic tensions, and design new legislation that can help resolve conflicts. Collaboration is critical, and NGOs may work with local individuals, community groups, university staff, clergy, and government agencies, as well as with other international NGOs, to organize training sessions, workshops, and conferences.

Some of the large humanitarian NGOs have added a conflict resolution component to their work, recognizing that development itself can create new tensions. With their long-term, community-level presence in strife-ridden areas, these NGOs are well suited to engage in building civil society. For instance, after constructing a dam to generate electricity and a stable supply of drinking water, an aid organization found that the dominant ethnic group was preventing members of the other ethnicities from using it.

NGOs

Negotiation and conciliation were needed to ensure that all parties had access to the new resource. Subsequently, this NGO has incorporated conflict resolution components into its relief work.

The following profiles focus on some of the better-known NGOs that specialize in conflict resolution work.

ALLIANCE FOR INTERNATIONAL CONFLICT PREVENTION AND RESOLUTION

11 Dupont Circle NW, Suite 200
Washington, DC 20036

Phone: 202-822-6135
Fax: 202-822-6068
E-mail: aicpr-dc@aicpr.org
Internet: www.aicpr.org

The Alliance is a not-for-profit network of private and public organizations dedicated to increasing the effectiveness of the conflict management field and maximizing its impact on international peacebuilding. Focusing on areas affected by international and civil armed conflict, members seek to resolve conflicts without violence, facilitate post-conflict reconciliation, and promote social, economic, and political development. At present, members are working in Africa, Asia, Europe, Latin America, and the Middle East.

AMERICAN FRIENDS SERVICE COMMITTEE (AFSC)

1501 Cherry Street
Philadelphia, PA 19102

Phone: 215-241-7000
Fax: 215-241-7275
E-mail: afscinfo@afsc.org
Internet: www.afsc.org

NGOs

The AFSC is a Quaker organization committed to social justice, peace, and humanitarian service. Its work is based on the Quaker belief in the worth of every person and faith in the power of love to overcome violence and injustice. Founded in 1917 to provide conscientious objectors with an opportunity to aid civilian victims during World War I, the AFSC today has programs on issues related to economic justice, peacebuilding and demilitarization, social justice, and youth in Africa, Asia, Latin America, the Middle East, and the United States.

The Conflict Resolution Program was begun in 1992 at the New York Metropolitan Region of the AFSC. It works directly with expatriates and others with ethnic or religious connections to regional conflicts to seek peaceful and constructive means to achieve resolution and reconciliation. Through dialogues involving expatriates and others living in the New York metropolitan area, the program engages participants in a three-stage process: (1) speaking and listening to build understanding and trust; (2) problem solving focused on core issues to build common ground; and (3) joint action to express a common agenda.

CARTER CENTER: INTERNATIONAL NEGOTIATION NETWORK

One Copenhill
453 Freedom Parkway
Atlanta, GA 30307

Phone: 404-420-5100
Fax: 404-331-0283
E-mail: carterweb@emory.edu
Internet: www.cartercenter.org

Created in 1984 in partnership with Emory University, the Carter Center is guided by a fundamental commitment to human rights and the alleviation of human suffering. It seeks to prevent and resolve conflicts, enhance freedom and democracy, and improve health.

The Conflict Resolution Program (CRP) marshals the experience of peacemakers to prevent and resolve armed conflicts around the globe. It is the base for the International Negotiation Network, an informal network of eminent persons who can offer advice and assistance to resolve disputes. The CRP regularly monitors many of the world's armed conflicts in an attempt to better understand their histories, the primary actors involved, disputed issues, and efforts being made to resolve them.

CHILDREN AND ARMED CONFLICT UNIT (CACU)

The Children's Legal Centre
University of Essex
Wivenhoe Park
Colchester
Essex CO4 3SQ
United Kingdom

Phone: 44-(0)1206 873 483
Fax: 44-(0)1206 874 026
E-mail: armedcon@essex.ac.uk
Internet: www.essex.ac.uk/armedcon/unit/default.htm

The Children and Armed Conflict Unit is a project of the Children's Legal Centre, a UK registered charity, and the Human Rights Centre of the University of Essex. CACU now sits in the international section of the Children's Legal Centre, which is the lead body in this project.

Set up in 1997 following the groundbreaking report on the impact of armed conflict on children by Graça Machel, CACU's patron, CACU works around the world to improve the situation for children caught up in armed conflict and civil unrest.

CACU believes that the restoration of civil society following armed conflict provides an opportunity to ensure systems and structures are in place that fully implement children's rights.

COMMUNITÀ DI SANT'EGIDIO

Piazza S. Egidio 3/a
00153 Rome
Italy

Phone: 39-06-899-2234
Fax: 39-06-580-0197
E-mail: info@santegidio.org
Internet: www.santegidio.org

Sant'Egidio, founded in 1968, is a Catholic International Association recognized by the Holy See in 1986. Present on all five continents, it has more than 30,000 members. It tries to reconcile social commitment with a strong evangelical life, at both personal and community levels. Sant'Egidio emphasizes prayer, living the gospel, helping the poor, and ecumenical and interreligious dialogue. On the international scene, Sant'Egidio has been active in southern and eastern Africa, Asia and the Middle East, Central America, and Europe, particularly in the Balkans, contributing with projects to overcome starvation and war. In Mozambique and Guatemala, Sant'Egidio played an important role in peace negotiations that brought an end to the conflicts in those countries.

GLOBAL PARTNERSHIP FOR THE PREVENTION OF ARMED CONFLICT

European Centre for Conflict Prevention
Laan van Meerdervoort 70
2517 AN The Hague
The Netherlands

Phone: 31-(0)70 311 0970
Fax: 31-(0)70 360 0194
E-mail: info@conflict-prevention.net
Internet: www.gppac.org

The Global Partnership for the Prevention of Armed Conflict is an international network of civil-society organizations working for conflict prevention and peacebuilding worldwide. Divided into fifteen regions, the Global Partnership has worked during the past three years to develop Regional Action Agendas on conflict prevention and a Global Action Agenda, which was presented at the United Nations at the Global Conference July 19–21, 2005. At the Global Conference, the network launched a new international movement of People Building Peace to promote conflict prevention and peacebuilding globally.

INITIATIVE FOR INCLUSIVE SECURITY (FORMERLY WOMEN WAGING PEACE)

Cambridge Office
625 Mount Auburn Street
Cambridge, MA 02138

Phone: 617-995-1900
Fax: 617-995-1982

Washington, D.C., Office
2040 S Street NW
Washington, DC 20009

Phone: 202-403-2000
Fax: 202-299-9520
E–mail: information@womenwagingpeace.net
Internet: www.womenwagingpeace.net

The Initiative for Inclusive Security advocates for the full participation of all stakeholders, especially women, in peace processes. Creating sustainable peace is achieved best by a diverse, citizen-driven approach. Of the many sectors of society currently excluded from peace processes, none is larger—or more critical to success—than women. Since 1999, Inclusive Security has connected more than 400 women experts with more than 3,000 policy shapers to collaborate on fresh, workable solutions to long-standing conflicts around the globe.

Members of the Initiative for Inclusive Security network are elected and appointed government officials; directors of NGOs; lawyers, scholars, and educators; business, military, and religious leaders; representatives of multilateral organizations; and journalists. With varied backgrounds, perspectives, and skills, these women bring a vast array of expertise to the peacemaking process.

INSTITUTE FOR MULTI-TRACK DIPLOMACY

1901 North Fort Meyer Drive, Suite 405
Arlington, VA 22209

Phone: 703-528-3863
Fax: 703-528-5776
E-mail: imtd@imtd.org
Internet: www.imtd.org

Created in 1992, the Institute for Multi-Track Diplomacy seeks to promote a systems approach to peacebuilding and to facilitate the transformation of deep-rooted social conflicts. Twelve principles form the basis for multi-track diplomacy: relationship, long-term commitment, cultural synergy, partnership, multiple technologies, facilitation, empowerment, active research, invitation, trust, engagement, and transformation. The institute also has worked in partnership with organizations such as CARE and the World Bank.

INSTITUTE OF WORLD AFFAIRS (IWA)

Institute of World Affairs
1321 Pennsylvania Avenue SE
Washington, DC 20003

Phone: 202-544-4141
E-mail: info@iwa.org
Internet: www.iwa.org

IWA was founded in 1924 as a nonprofit, non-partisan, tax-exempt organization devoted to international understanding and the peaceful resolution of conflict. In support of its mission, IWA conducts a range of programs designed to prevent violent conflict and to advance post-conflict peacebuilding. These programs include training seminars, both in the United States and abroad, designed to enhance professional skills in conflict resolution and infrastructure development. IWA also operates several long-term development and post-conflict reconciliation projects in the Middle East, West Africa, and the Eastern Mediterranean.

INTERNATIONAL ALERT

346 Clapham Road
London SW9 9AP
United Kingdom

Phone: 44-(0)20-7627-6800
Fax: 44-(0)20-7627-6900
E-mail: general@international-alert.org
Internet: www.international-alert.org

Created in 1985 by human rights advocates, International Alert aims to contribute to the prevention and resolution of violent internal conflict. International Alert helps the victims of war; believes that lasting peace and security for all people can be built only on justice and the recognition of the human dignity of all people; seeks the consent and trust of all parties to a conflict; and urges adherence to international humanitarian law and respect for human rights as indispensable obligations of those parties. International Alert believes that the antagonists in a conflict—and the citizens affected by that conflict—will be the primary actors in its resolution and that sustained dialogue is a principal means to this end.

INTERNATIONAL CRISIS GROUP (ICG)

1629 K Street NW, Suite 450
Washington, DC 20006

Phone: 202-785-1601
Fax: 202-785-1630
Internet: www.crisisgroup.org

Brussels Headquarters
149 Avenue Louise, Level 24
B-1050 Brussels
Belgium

Phone: 32-2-502-9038
Fax: 32-2-502-5038
Internet: www.crisisgroup.org

Founded in 1995, ICG is a private, multinational organization committed to strengthening the capacity of the international community to understand and respond to impending crises. Teams of political analysts based on the ground in countries at risk of crisis gather information from a wide range of sources, assess local conditions, and produce regular analytical reports containing practical policy recommendations targeted at key international decision takers. ICG's reports are distributed widely to officials in foreign ministries and international organizations, journalists, and others. ICG's board is closely involved in helping to bring ICG reports and recommendations to the attention of senior policymakers around the world. ICG's advocacy efforts are reinforced by a media strategy designed to increase press coverage of key issues identified in ICG's analyses.

INTERNATIONAL WOMEN'S TRIBUNE CENTRE (ITWC)

777 United Nations Plaza
New York, NY 10017

Phone: 212-687-8633
Fax: 212-661-2704
E-mail: iwtc@iwtc.org
Internet: www.iwtc.org

IWTC is an international NGO established in 1976 following the United Nations International Women's Year World Conference in Mexico City. With a commitment to empowering people and building communities, IWTC provides communication, information, education, and organizing support services to women's organizations and community groups working to improve the lives of women, particularly low-income women, in Africa, Asia and the Pacific, Latin America and the Caribbean, Eastern Europe, and Western Asia. IWTC's work is grounded on the premise that access to information and the ability to communicate are basic to the process of women's empowerment, to women's ability to redefine development paradigms, to women's participation in the public policy arena, and to the building of democratic societies.

MENNONITE CENTRAL COMMITTEE (MCC)

21 South 12th Street
PO Box 500
Akron, PA 17501-0500

Phone: 888-563-4676 or 717-859-1151
Fax: 717-859-2171
E-mail: inq@mcc.org
Internet: www.mcc.org

MCC is the relief, service, community development, and
peacekeeping arm of the North American Mennonite and
Brethren in Christ churches. Founded in 1920, MCC has
more than fourteen hundred workers in fifty-eight countries around the world involved in food relief, agriculture,
health, education, and social services. The peacemaking
program works on arms exports, gun control, conscientious objection, and mediation and conflict resolution.

NONVIOLENCE INTERNATIONAL (NI)

4545 42nd Street NW, Suite 209
Washington, DC 20016

Phone: 202-244-0951
Fax: 202-244-6396
E-mail: info@nonviolenceinternational.net
Internet: www.nonviolenceinternational.net

Founded in 1989, NI assists individuals, organizations, and
governments striving to use nonviolent methods to bring
about changes reflecting the values of justice and human
development on personal, social, economic, and political
levels. NI is committed to educating the public about nonviolent action and to reducing the use of violence worldwide. NI believes that every cultural and religious tradition
can discover and employ culturally appropriate nonviolent
methods for positive social change and international peace.

To put its philosophy into action, NI trains individuals, organizations, and governments in nonviolent action and democratization campaigns; educates the public on nonviolent methods for change; coordinates teams of international nonviolence trainers; supports nonviolence activists and their campaigns; organizes conferences on nonviolent struggles and peacekeeping; works with gangs and local leaders to reduce street and community violence; publishes articles, newsletters, and other materials that promote nonviolence; and collaborates with international peace and conflict resolution groups in pursuit of common goals.

SEARCH FOR COMMON GROUND

1601 Connecticut Avenue NW, Suite 200
Washington, DC 20009

Phone: 202-265-4300
Fax: 202-232-6718
E-mail: search@sfcg.org
Internet: www.sfcg.org

Search for Common Ground was founded in 1982 in Washington, D.C.; the European Centre for Common Ground was established in Brussels in 1995. Both organizations share a vision of transforming the way the world deals with conflict—away from adversarial approaches and toward cooperative solutions. To implement this vision, Search for Common Ground carries out programs that aim at resolving conflict and preventing violence.

Search for Common Ground employs a wide array of means—including community forums, professional roundtables, joint action projects, policy coordination forums, television, radio, songs, publications, and training programs for schoolchildren, journalists, police, and military personnel— to counter stereotypes, promote cooperation, and foster conflict resolution, institution building, and understanding.

NGOs

WOMEN'S INTERNATIONAL LEAGUE FOR PEACE AND FREEDOM (WILPF)

1, rue de Varembe
Case Postale 28
1211 Geneva 20
Switzerland

Phone: 41-22 919-7080
Fax: 41-22 919-7081
E–mail: inforequest@wilpf.ch
Internet: www.wilpf.org

WILPF is the oldest women's peace organization in the world. It was founded in April 1915, in the Hague, the Netherlands, by some thirteen hundred women from Europe and North America, from countries at war against each other and neutral countries, who came together in a Congress of Women to protest the killing and destruction of the war then raging in Europe. WILPF is an international NGO with National Sections in thirty-seven countries, covering all continents. Its International Secretariat is based in Geneva, with a New York UN office.

Its aims and principles are to bring together women of different political beliefs and philosophies who are united in their determination to study, make known, and help abolish the causes and the legitimization of war; work toward world peace; strive for total and universal disarmament; advocate the abolition of violence and coercion in the settlement of conflict and its replacement in every case by negotiation and conciliation; support the civil society to democratize the UN system; support the continuous development and implementation of international and humanitarian law; promote political and social equality and economic equity; contribute toward cooperation among all people; and enhance environmentally sustainable development.

WILPF's mission is to further, by nonviolent means, the social and economic transformation of the international community. The aim is to establish economic and social systems in which political equality and social justice for all can be attained, without discrimination on the basis of sex, race, or religion.

Civilian Agencies of the U.S. Government

Introduction

THE ARRAY OF U.S. government agencies on the ground has expanded as U.S. participation in peace and stability operations has increased. Whether by invitation of the host country or through application of military force, and whether under a UN mandate or with the United States as the lead, the presence of civilian agency personnel in zones of conflict is a fact of life. Among the large number of U.S. government departments active in reconstruction and stabilization efforts, some, such as USAID and the State Department, have long been involved in these efforts. Recent years have seen a marked increase in the size and composition of the official U.S. presence, even before the conflict is settled. In places like Kosovo, Afghanistan, Liberia, and Iraq, it has become normal to find people from the departments of Treasury, Justice, Transportation, or Health and Human Services, as well as those from the traditional foreign affairs departments—State, Defense, Commerce, and Agriculture.

This trend is likely to continue for several reasons. The end of the Cold War has increased the likelihood of weak states disintegrating and of the international community intervening to help resolve local conflict. The resulting efforts to transform these societies require sectoral expertise beyond traditional diplomacy, peacekeeping, development assistance, or trade agreements. When a country becomes an "international project," reform of its governance structures and other key institutions, in conjunction with local leaders, takes center stage. In addition, U.S. interests dictate greater U.S. involvement in conflict transformation abroad.

As the September 11 attacks drove home to the United States, security threats today come not from large militaries in adversary countries but from small bands of extremists. Conditions of civil strife or rampant lawlessness in their home countries may be prime motivators for terrorists and criminals, but they often blame the United States and its allies when airing their grievances.

Another factor, in an ever-more-interdependent world, is that most cabinet-level departments of the U.S. government cannot avoid engaging around the globe. Managing currency reserves, prosecuting crime, protecting air travel, and safeguarding health are all areas in which U.S. personnel must operate abroad to fulfill their agencies' domestic responsibilities.

Finally, understanding of development aid has evolved with the experience of recent decades. Donors today seek to create capable institutions, incorporating market economies and representative political structures, because fostering these self-correcting mechanisms allows economic and social development to become self-sustaining.

As a result of all these factors, the profile of the U.S. government's role in peace and stability operations around the world looks very different at the opening of the twenty-first century than it did in the 1970s and 1980s. At that time, U.S. military interventions were often focused on limited security aims without attempting to reform the local society (for example, in Grenada, Lebanon, and Panama). Development aid was concerned primarily with long-term economic and social progress as planned and coordinated by host government officials. Civilian "emergency response" was essentially for humanitarian needs like refugee crises and natural disasters. In its peacekeeping practice, the United Nations avoided using U.S., or Soviet troops, or troops from other major powers and limited its involvement in the internal affairs of parties to a conflict. Peacekeeping operations tended to separate armies, monitor cease-fire agreements, and perhaps address the needs of a civilian population in a conflict zone, but not to change structures within the belligerent societies (for example, between Syria and Israel, Pakistan and Afghanistan, or Egypt and Israel in the Sinai).

The nature of international intervention began to change as the Cold War ended. UN peacekeepers, with U.S. support, took up nonmilitary tasks like organizing elections, performing transitional administration, and reforming legal systems as part of implementing complex peace agreements (for example, in Cambodia, El Salvador, and Namibia). International assistance programs retooled to promote postcommunist reform in Eastern Europe and applied this experience to the transition from dictatorships in other parts of the world.

Consequently, the 1990s saw a series of complex interventions, with a greater U.S. role (for example, in Bosnia, Croatia, East Timor, Haiti, northern Iraq, Kosovo, Macedonia, Sierra Leone, and Somalia). In these cases, U.S. embassies and missions organized a more operational type of diplomacy in support of peace agreements and international coalitions. The extent of U.S. military participation varied both with circumstances in individual countries and with a fluctuating debate about nation building. Recent experience in Afghanistan and Iraq has transformed that debate, however. Expectations now have risen both for the frequency of a military role in future situations (noncombat or otherwise) and for the degree of coordination between the military and civilian agencies.

In the aftermath of the U.S.-led interventions in Afghanistan and Iraq, the U.S. government took two important steps to improve the capacity and coordination of civilian agencies in providing stabilization and reconstruction assistance to countries emerging from violent conflict.

USG

On December 7, 2005, President Bush signed National Security Presidential Directive 44, which assigned the secretary of state responsibility for planning, coordinating, and implementing activities aimed at preventing conflict in weak and failing states and for intervening in war-torn countries. Under the directive, the State Department is to coordinate the activities of other civilian government agencies during conflict interventions. It is also to serve as the focal point for creating a Civilian Reserve Corps of experts in diplomacy, security, rule of law, public administration, and essential public services that could be deployed rapidly to assist the U.S. military in future peace and stability operations. The directive instructs the Department of State to engage with other nations and international organizations to forestall state failure when possible. In situations where violent conflict has occurred, the State Department is instructed to coordinate an effective response that promotes peace, democracy, and economic recovery.

To accomplish this mission, in 2004 the State Department created the Office of Coordinator for Reconstruction and Stability (S/CRS), which reports directly to the secretary of state. Creation of a permanent office to manage both conflict prevention and conflict intervention acknowledged the reality that the United States could not continue to rely upon ad hoc responses to each new crisis. It also acknowledged the need for a cadre of professional conflict managers who could quickly deploy at the onset of an emergency to oversee the critical start-up phase of operations. The office has the following mission: to lead, coordinate, and institutionalize U.S. government civilian capacity to prevent or prepare for state failure and post-conflict situations, and to help stabilize and reconstruct societies in transition from conflict or civil strife, so they can reach a sustainable path toward peace, democracy, and a market economy. Among its many activities, the coordinator's office has sought to create a monitoring system to identify states at risk, develop a whole-of-government planning capacity for conflict transformation, build an operational capacity for rapid deployment of civilian experts, engage with other governments and international organizations, and compile lessons learned.

Despite its impressive mandate and progress creating new tools, systems, and rapid-response mechanisms, the coordinator's office struggled in its first two years with problems related to funding, staffing, and bureaucratic authority. Congress was unwilling to provide the State Department with contingency funds for unspecified future operations, and entrenched bureaucratic forces resisted taking policy guidance from a new and untested office, particularly in crisis situations. At the same time, the creation of a new Director for Foreign Assistance (with the rank of deputy secretary of state) to both oversee USAID and create a consolidated U.S. foreign assistance strategy produced uncertainty about processes within the State Department for future operations. Similarly, the Defense Department's issuance of Directive 3000.05 on *Military Support for Stability, Security, Transition and Reconstruction Operations* made the conduct of such operations a core military mission and indicated that the Defense Department would play a larger role in shaping the U.S. response to future contingencies.

This chapter is intended as an overview of *who* and *what*: Who are the main civilian actors sent abroad by the U.S. government, and what are their main activities and mandates? It first examines the process by which policy and programs are established. Next, it addresses the question of coordination among agencies involved in implementation. Finally, it considers some of the positions and cultural characteristics active in reconstruction and stabilization efforts. While the people and agencies are hardly monolithic, some generalization is possible and useful. It is hoped this discussion will increase understanding of the U.S. government civilians typically found in stabilization and reconstruction operations as well as provide context for the descriptions of individual agencies that follow.

U.S. Government Decision-Making Process

Decisions about policy and programs for peace, stability, and relief operations usually result from an interagency process in Washington. At the top of the hierarchy is the president, whose explicit approval is required for the escalation of U.S. presence in a conflict zone, the deployment of troops, and the expenditure of resources. Typically, U.S. plans would involve consultation with Congress accompanied by a press campaign to explain the decision to the American people.

The National Security Council (NSC) considers these matters. By statute it includes the president, vice president, and secretaries of state and defense. The chairman of the joint chiefs of staff and the director of national intelligence are statutory advisers, while the national security adviser and other officials routinely participate. In practice, the NSC's Principals Committee (PC) and Deputies Committee (DC) oversee and approve most strategies. The PC consists of officials at the level of cabinet secretary or head of agency and the DC of their second in charge. Meetings are chaired by the national security adviser (NSA) or deputy NSA, with meeting documents and records produced by the NSC staff, although agencies often will circulate papers on specific issues for PC or DC consideration.

Standing members of the PC and DC, in addition to the NSC staff, include State Department, Office of the Secretary of Defense (OSD), Treasury Department, USAID, Joint Chiefs of Staff (JCS), Central Intelligence Agency (CIA), U.S. Mission to the United Nations (USUN), and the Office of Management and Budget (OMB), as well as the Office of the Chief of Staff to the President and the Office of the Vice President (OVP). Other agency representatives are invited to participate when appropriate.

While the executive branch has the lead, Congress plays a major role in exercising oversight and providing authorization and appropriations for U.S. government activities. Agency officials consult members of Congress and their staffs regularly as situations develop and responses are planned, in addition to giving formal testimony, submitting official reports, and preparing detailed budget requests regarding USG operations. Strong congressional interest in a country or program can shape the USG response, and site visits by members and staff assume top priority for USG civilian agency personnel abroad, usually preempting all other plans and activities.

Coordination in Washington and in the Field

By law, the secretary of state is the president's primary adviser on foreign policy and is responsible for the overall coordination and supervision of all U.S. government activities and operations abroad. In normal situations, U.S. relations are conducted and coordinated via embassies and diplomatic missions. The ambassadors and other chiefs of mission (COMs) abroad report to the president through the secretary of state, while foreign missions in the United States are accredited to the secretary of state.

USG

U.S. Diplomatic Mission Structure

Ambassadors and other U.S. chiefs of mission are the president's representatives and have authority over every executive branch employee in the host country or in the U.S. mission to an international organization. The only exceptions are for personnel under the authority of a U.S. area military commander or detailed to the staff of an international organization. Official instructions to COMs and reports from their posts are transmitted via State Department communications channels; this process is overseen by the assistant secretary of state responsible for a geographic region and staffed by a country desk in the geographic bureau.

In the field, the practice by which ambassadors and COMs coordinate USG activities varies from country to country and from issue to issue. A few typical institutions are likely to be found, however. The country team consists of the heads of all USG agencies in country and some other officials. Chaired by the ambassador or COM, the country team meets periodically to review developments and coordinate activities. Working groups on specific subjects—for example, democracy, rule of law, and economic development—are typical, with a subset of the country team and others added. They might be chaired by the ambassador or COM, the deputy chief of mission (DCM), or a head of a section or agency at post. While some country teams will be more formal than others in terms of agenda, goals, work plan, and minutes, most will likely be key forums for getting action, plugging gaps, and addressing overlaps.

In Washington, coordination among agencies takes place at several levels. It is useful to consider first mechanisms for coordination of policies and programs. Policy coordination committees (PCCs) on various issues meet at the assistant secretary (A/S) level and report to the DC and PC. Their composition, leadership, and mode of operation

Figure 3.1. Organization of a U.S. Diplomatic Mission

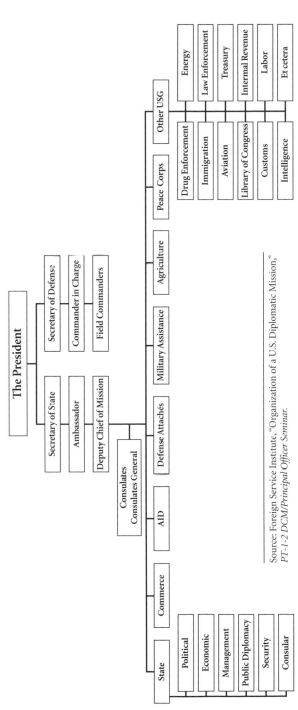

Source: Foreign Service Institute, "Organization of a U.S. Diplomatic Mission," *PT-1-2 DCM/Principal Officer Seminar.*

Figure 3.2. Inside a U.S. Embassy

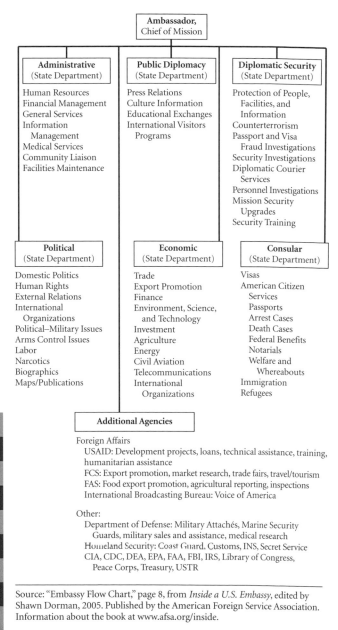

Source: "Embassy Flow Chart," page 8, from *Inside a U.S. Embassy*, edited by Shawn Dorman, 2005. Published by the American Foreign Service Association. Information about the book at www.afsa.org/inside.

vary according to the subject; their organization (and sometimes their names) tend to change from administration to administration. Regional PCCs, focused roughly by continent, are a continuing feature of the interagency landscape. Chaired by the State Department's assistant secretary for the region, PCCs exist for Africa, East Asia, South Asia, the Near East, Latin America, and Europe. In 2005, the Bush administration established a PCC for Stabilization and Reconstruction, cochaired by the new A/S-level coordinator for reconstruction and stabilization, based in the State Department, and the NSC director for stability operations. PCCs often establish subcommittees (sometimes called sub-PCCs) for specific topics.

USG peace and stability operations in Afghanistan, Bosnia, Haiti, Iraq, Kosovo, and Sudan developed certain key institutions in Washington. These institutions included an interagency decision-making group consulting frequently to sort out issues of policy and programs. Typically, the main participants are at the A/S or deputy A/S (DAS) level, and they meet face-to-face at least weekly. In addition, there is usually an expanded country desk, programs group, task force, or other office that provides staff support for the increased workload. Often, personnel from another agency are detailed to work in the State Department to support the effort. Even when members of these special staffs are not colocated, they are in constant contact and frequently meet for extended work sessions, forming a virtual secretariat. Participants often meet via secure video teleconference systems (SVTS) to exchange information or communicate with representatives in the field. SVTS meetings are usually held on a regular schedule. While they may be organized more for information sharing than decision making or assigning tasks, they can drive the schedule for reporting on developments or for defining issues that require action.

For a U.S. government engagement in a specific country that requires a comprehensive response across agencies and management of interagency civilians in the field, a new type of PCC has been proposed. Labeled a Country Reconstruction and Stabilization Group (CRSG), it is to focus USG efforts and develop coordinated conflict transformation, plans, and strategies for review by the PC and DC, acting in place of both the regional and reconstruction PCCs and designed to achieve greater unity of effort within the USG. It is designed to have a secretariat with staff drawn from involved agencies and is mostly colocated within the State Department. This staff is to support the CRSG/PCC, organize interagency groups to do strategic and tactical planning for conflict transformation, serve as a clearinghouse for information on USG efforts in country, provide mobilization and operations support for field teams, identify and mobilize resources, raise issues requiring decision makers' attention, and track progress in implementing USG strategies. The CRSG is the Washington management element of a proposed interagency response system that includes Planning Integration Teams sent to Geographic Combatant Commands to integrate civilian and military planning processes, as well as Advanced Civilian Teams (ACTs), which provide the COM with a structure for interagency coordination in the field. The first CRSG was tasked to plan for and monitor Sudan peace implementation in August 2005.

Frequently, an experienced diplomat or political figure is named as a special U.S. envoy for the crisis. Titles, organization, and mandates vary, but the person usually has a small office and staff in the State Department. The special envoy has a mediating role involving frequent travel to meet with the parties in the region and with key international partners. A senior USG official can be seconded to support a UN special representative or other international negotiator.

The PCC or CRSG, the expanded staff(s), the SVTS, and the special envoy team all play key roles in managing U.S. policy and programs. In theory, these components would dovetail and help to coordinate efforts within the USG. In practice, coordination can fall short. Bureaucratic infighting, personalities, the pace of events, and the need for confidentiality all may contribute to the breakdown of communication and cooperation among offices and agencies, particularly under pressure to respond to a crisis. Problems with coordination are likely to be reflected in the failure of the peace and stability operation to accomplish its mission. They are also likely to result in finger-pointing that only exacerbates the problem.

Another set of field coordination bodies may be found with international partners. Sometimes a lead country is named, and the embassy of that country hosts coordination meetings with participation of interested embassies and international agencies. For example, in the run-up to elections, a group—consisting of representatives from several of the most interested embassies and assistance missions, elections NGOs and other implementing partners, political foundations, and international organizations— may meet weekly to track progress in ballot preparation and voter registration and to develop a united front for the international community to use with the host government and local political parties.

Frequently the chairmanship and organizational lead may be assumed by an international organization, for example, the OSCE on elections, the United Nations on police reform, or the World Bank on economic privatization. The coordination group may meet on an ad hoc basis or be hosted on a rotating basis among the member institutions. The point here is the importance of identifying the key coordination mechanisms and plugging into them. When they do not already exist, they are almost always invented. While they are not designed to coordinate USG activities,

USG

they create a dynamic set of meetings for which the USG representative needs to be up to speed on USG programs and to represent a consistent USG position; so their effect is to foster coordination within the USG (and within other participating governments).

Characteristics of Civilian Officials in Reconstruction and Stabilization Efforts

USG civilian personnel do not lend themselves easily to stereotypes. A few general observations may prove useful, however. By and large, they are self-selected volunteers for reconstruction and stabilization assignments rather than persons ordered to a difficult place over their objections. They tend therefore to have a high degree of motivation for their work and belief in the importance of USG engagement in the country. Although they may receive additional compensation for being in a hardship or dangerous environment, few are in it for the money.

They generally have some latitude in what they are able to do and how they do it. That is, although they come from hierarchical organizations with bureaucratic rules, they are in the field to exercise judgment within the parameters of the hierarchy and bureaucracy. They will probably need to check "up their chain" on major decisions, but they will exercise some authority for the programs and funds they are managing. The degree of field initiative versus Washington oversight varies from agency to agency. For example, USAID's Office of Transition Initiatives (OTI) and Office of Foreign Disaster Assistance (OFDA) are set up and operated to foster quick response on the ground without detailed supervision from their headquarters.

Most of these personnel are overseas on a limited assignment within a longer career with an agency. Even individuals hired by an agency on a contract basis (usually called a personal services contract [PSC]) often go from contract to contract within the same agency. Consequently, they tend to exhibit a high degree of loyalty to their agency. Some may see themselves primarily as representatives of their agency rather than part of the overall U.S. government team. Again, attitudes vary greatly, but it is worth noting that a sense of teamwork cannot be taken for granted, and usually has to be built up over time.

State Department officials are likely to be skilled in political analysis, reporting, and diplomacy but inexperienced in management and administration, especially of large enterprises or government bodies. Under the Coalition Provisional Authority in Iraq, State Department foreign service officers (FSOs) were required to learn on the job how to run government ministries or municipalities. FSOs are likely to have language skills and an understanding of the foreign history and culture that will assist the entire mission. They do not, however, have the type of program and logistical resources of the U.S. military, on which they depend for transport and administrative support. In addition, the State Department and other civilian agencies lack the capacity to surge significant numbers of personnel into the field in response to a crisis. Civilian agencies' representatives are likely to be few in number and stretched thin. As an example, in 2005, the State Department was able to fill only thirteen of nineteen billets related to Provincial Reconstruction Teams in Afghanistan, where they served as political advisers to the commanders. S/CRS has established an Active Response Corps (ARC) and Standby Response Corps (SRC) of foreign and civil service State Department personnel who can deploy quickly in crisis situations to perform a wide range of diplomatic and start-up stabilization and reconstruction tasks, but the numbers are small. USAID has also piloted several surge proposals. National Security Presidential Directive 44 charges civilian agencies with developing their surge capacity for these missions. S/CRS is currently leading an interagency process to build up this civilian surge capacity in implementation of the directive, but the numbers are likely to remain limited in the near future.

Profiles of Federal Agencies Involved in Peace and Relief Operations

U.S. DEPARTMENT OF STATE

2201 C Street NW
Washington, DC 20520

Phone: 202-647-4000
Internet: www.state.gov
   (extensive online phone/fax directory)

OFFICE OF THE COORDINATOR FOR RECONSTRUCTION AND STABILIZATION (S/CRS)

Suite 7100, Dept. of State SA-3
2121 Virginia Avenue NW
Washington, DC 20521

Phone: 202-663-0323
Internet: www.crs.state.gov

Coordinating U.S. government operations in countries emerging from conflict is one of today's greatest foreign policy challenges. Reflecting a widespread consensus among independent experts and government policymakers that the United States needed to upgrade from ad hoc responses, the Office of the Coordinator for Reconstruction and Stabilization (S/CRS) was established in 2004 to begin building an institutional capacity to address these challenges more quickly, effectively, and systematically. While it will take years to build the needed institutional base, significant efforts are under way. Proposals for contingency planning, a quick-response corps, a contingency fund, and systematic identification of lessons learned were contained in the president's budget request to Congress for fiscal year 2007.

Located within the State Department to ensure consistency with foreign policy priorities and with expert understanding of foreign societies, S/CRS seeks to coordinate and strengthen the work of the agencies and bureaus engaged in conflict prevention, stabilization, and reconstruction.

S/CRS core functions include the following: to identify and plan responses for peace and stability operations and coordinate USG participation in multilateral operations; to engage interagency partners to identify states at risk of instability and focus attention on polices and strategies to prevent or mitigate conflict; to coordinate interagency efforts to integrate civilian and military planning; to provide interagency leadership on monitoring of potential states in crisis, assessing lessons learned and applying these lessons into operations and planning; to support budget requests for capacity building; to recommend resource allocations for an effective response; to develop proposals for, and eventually to manage, civilian standby capabilities for deployment; and to coordinate with international partners.

Bureau of Population, Refugees, and Migration (PRM)

Internet: www.state.gov/g/prm/

PRM is central to U.S. government efforts to provide protection and relief for millions of refugees and victims of conflict around the globe. The United States also admits tens of thousands of refugees annually for permanent resettlement.

PRM has primary responsibility for formulating policies on population, refugees, and migration and for administering U.S. refugee assistance and admissions programs.

PRM coordinates U.S. international population policy and promotes its goals through bilateral and multilateral cooperation. It works closely with USAID, which administers U.S. international population programs. PRM also coordinates U.S. international migration policy within the U.S. government and through bilateral and multilateral diplomacy.

PRM administers and monitors U.S. contributions to international and non-governmental organizations to assist and protect refugees abroad. In overseeing admissions of refugees to the United States for permanent resettlement, PRM works closely with the Department of Homeland Security, the Department of Health and Human Services, and various state and private voluntary agencies.

BUREAU OF DEMOCRACY, HUMAN RIGHTS, AND LABOR (DRL)

Internet: www.state.gov/g/drl/

DRL is committed to supporting and promoting democracy programs throughout the world. As the nation's primary democracy advocate abroad, DRL is responsible for overseeing the Human Rights and Democracy Fund (HRDF), which was established in 1998 to address human rights and democratization emergencies. DRL uses resources from HRDF, as well as those allocated to Regional Democracy Funds, to support democratization programs such as election monitoring and parliamentary development. HRDF maintains innovative programming designed to uphold democratic principles, supports democratic institutions, promotes human rights, and builds civil society in unstable countries and regions of the world.

USG

Through its Offices of Promotion of Human Rights and Democracy, Multilateral Affairs, and Country Reports and Asylum Affairs, DRL works on human rights issues. Activities include holding governments accountable to universal human rights norms; promoting respect for human, women's, media, children's, and minority rights; promoting rule of law; and coordinating human rights activities with allies. DRL's annual human rights report to Congress evaluates over 190 countries on human rights standards. It actively works to support accountability for past abuser nations, employs external U.S. pressures and promotes internal reforms to combat present human rights abusers, and maintains early warning plans to prevent future human rights abuses. DRL also forges and maintains partnerships with organizations, governments, and multilateral institutions committed to human rights.

DRL's Office of International Labor Affairs promotes the rights of workers throughout the world through universal recognition and implementation of internationally recognized core labor standards. These include freedom of association and the effective recognition of the right to organize and bargain collectively, the elimination of all forms of forced or compulsory labor, the effective abolition of child labor, and the elimination of discrimination with respect to employment and occupation.

Bureau of International Narcotics and Law Enforcement Affairs (INL)

Internet: www.state.gov/gp/inl/

INL programs support two of the State Department's strategic goals: to reduce the entry of illegal drugs into the United States and to minimize the impact of international crime on the United States and its citizens. Counternarcotics and anticrime programs also complement the war on terrorism, both directly and indirectly, by promoting modernization of and supporting operations by foreign criminal justice systems and law enforcement agencies charged with the counterterrorism mission. While attacking the core targets, INL emphasizes the need to strengthen host nation capabilities through institution building so that key countries can bolster their effectiveness in fighting international drug trafficking and crime.

In addition to its antinarcotics and anticrime programs, INL recruits U.S. police officers from all over the country to participate in international civilian police missions and trains local police officers around the world through its International Civilian Police Program (CIVPOL). Today, more than 350 U.S. police officers are contributing to public safety in UN Police forces, while another 700 are participating in bilateral programs in Iraq and Afghanistan. Additionally, INL has worked toward establishing a network of International Law Enforcement Academies (ILEAs) throughout the world to combat international drug trafficking, criminality, and terrorism through strengthened international cooperation. The United States and participating nations have established ILEAs to serve Europe, Asia, Africa and a graduate facility in Roswell, New Mexico.

BUREAU OF POLITICAL-MILITARY AFFAIRS (PM)

Internet: www.state.gov/t/pm/

PM is the principal link between the departments of State and Defense. PM provides policy direction in the areas of international security, security assistance, military operations, reconstruction and stabilization, and defense trade. PM is instrumental in the State Department's efforts to accomplish three major goals under the United States Strategic Plan for International Affairs:

USG

- Playing a key role in the global war on terrorism, which includes securing base access and overflight permission to support the deployment of U.S. military forces, coordinating the participation of coalition combat and stabilization forces, and promoting critical infrastructure protection

- Promoting stability around the world by fostering effective defense relationships with allies; regulating arms transfers; promoting responsible U.S. defense trade; controlling access to military technologies; combating illegal trafficking of small arms and light weapons; negotiating status of forces and base access agreements; and facilitating the education and training of international peacekeepers and other foreign military personnel

- Managing humanitarian demining programs around the world and working with the Defense Department to provide assistance in the event of natural disasters and other crises abroad. PM also coordinates U.S. government response to chemical, biological, radiological, and natural events overseas

HUMANITARIAN INFORMATION/ INTELLIGENCE UNIT/OFFICE (HIU)

HIU collects and stores geospatial information intelligence data. HIU exists to improve data flow during humanitarian response. It has no deployment capabilities or project funding.

USG

U.S. AGENCY FOR INTERNATIONAL DEVELOPMENT (USAID)

Ronald Reagan Building
1300 Pennsylvania Avenue NW
Washington, DC 20523-0016

Phone: 202-712-4320
Fax: 202-216-3524
E-mail: pinquiries@usaid.gov
Internet: www.usaid.gov

USAID is an independent federal government agency that receives overall foreign policy guidance from the secretary of state. It is the principal U.S. agency to extend assistance to countries recovering from disaster, trying to escape poverty, or engaging in democratic reforms. U.S. foreign assistance has the twofold purpose of furthering U.S. foreign policy interests in expanding democracy and free markets while improving the lives of citizens of the developing world. USAID works in agriculture, democracy and governance, economic growth, the environment, education, health, global partnerships, and humanitarian assistance in more than 100 countries to provide a better future for all.

With headquarters in Washington, D.C., USAID's strength is its field offices around the world. It works in close partnership with NGOs, indigenous organizations, universities, U.S. businesses, international agencies, other governments, and other U.S. government agencies. Much of USAID's work in relief and stability operations is focused on the work of several departments, identified below.

USG

OFFICE OF U.S. FOREIGN DISASTER ASSISTANCE (OFDA)

Internet: www.usaid.gov/our_work/humanitarian
_assistance/disaster_assistance/

OFDA is responsible for providing humanitarian assistance in response to international crises and disasters. The USAID administrator is designated as the president's special coordinator for international disaster assistance, and OFDA helps in the coordination of this assistance.

OFDA provides humanitarian assistance in response to a declaration of a foreign disaster made by the U.S. ambassador or the U.S. Department of State. Once an event or situation is determined to require USG assistance, OFDA can immediately provide up to $50,000 to the U.S. embassy or USAID mission to purchase relief supplies locally or to contribute to a relief organization in the affected country. USAID/OFDA can also send relief commodities, such as plastic sheeting, tents, blankets, and water purification units, from its stockpiles in Maryland, Guam, Honduras, Italy, and the United Arab Emirates. Increasingly, OFDA deploys short- or long-term field personnel to countries where disasters are occurring or threaten to occur, and in some cases, dispatches a USAID Disaster Assistance Response Team.

A large percentage of OFDA's assistance goes to disaster relief and rehabilitation projects managed by NGOs (66 percent), UN organizations (15 percent), and IOs (2 percent). Relief projects include airlifting supplies to affected populations in remote locations, managing primary health care and supplementary feeding centers, and providing shelter materials to disaster evacuees and displaced persons. A rehabilitation project might immunize dislocated populations against disease, provide seeds and tools to farmers who have been affected by disasters, drill water wells, or rehabilitate water systems in drought-stricken countries. OFDA carefully monitors the organizations implementing these projects to ensure that resources are used wisely and to determine if the project needs to be adapted to changing conditions. The goal of each project is to meet the humanitarian needs of the affected population, with the aim of returning to self-sufficiency.

OFFICE OF FOOD FOR PEACE (FFP)

Internet: www.usaid.gov/our_work/humanitarian
_assistance/ffp/

FFP, during the past fifty years, has sent 106 million metric tons to the hungry of the world, feeding billions of people and saving countless lives. The program depends on the productivity of U.S. farmers and the U.S. agricultural system. The commodities FFP relies on are grown in the fields of virtually every U.S. state. But much more than farming is involved. Merchants sell the seed and fertilizer, mechanics keep the combines running, bankers extend credit to the farmers who plant and harvest the crops, millers process the grain, forklift drivers and stevedores load the ships—all are part of this unbroken chain of production and distribution feeding the world's hungry.

Upon reaching its destination, the food is used in a variety of ways, and always for the people most vulnerable to the effects of hunger: children under age five, pregnant women, the elderly, and the poorest families in a community. In an emergency where people face the threat of imminent starvation, food—usually wheat and corn—is distributed to save their lives. If the symptoms of extreme malnutrition have already appeared, a nutritionally fortified ration with blended, fortified, and processed food is provided. In less dire circumstances, food can be used to compensate people for work, such as building roads or repairing water and irrigation systems. In turn, these projects help protect communities from future hunger by providing them access to local markets for their produce, keeping them healthy, and improving their harvests. Other methods of using food aid include the following:

- Showing farmers better ways to sow and tend their fields or providing improved seed, thus improving their harvest by linking them with American know-how
- Teaching women about nutrition, resulting in healthier babies and children
- Encouraging the production of higher-value commodities that could earn money in local markets
- Providing micronutrients, such as vitamin A, iodine, zinc, and iron, that hungry children often lack
- Feeding children at school to encourage attendance and improve academic performance

OFFICE OF TRANSITION INITIATIVES (OTI)

Internet: www.usaid.gov/our_work/cross-cutting
_programs/transition_initiatives/

OTI lays the foundations for long-term development by promoting reconciliation, jump-starting economies, and helping stable democracy take hold.

OTI specifically encourages a culture of swift response among its staff and partners. This culture is reflected in a strategic approach that continually incorporates best practices and lessons learned. OTI is funded by a separate Transition Initiatives budget account with special authorities that allow immediate spending where it is most needed. Finally, OTI created an innovative contracting mechanism that preserves the principle of competition while allowing quick start-up in new countries and direct grants to small, indigenous organizations. Some of the specific project areas of OTI include the following:

- Supporting community development programs that encourage political participation of previously marginalized groups and link constituents with their elected representatives
- Funding reintegration of ex-combatants into their communities as citizens
- Backing alternative media and public information campaigns to encourage reconciliation and informed participation in elections
- Assisting local efforts to fight corruption and promote transparent governance
- Helping governments develop action plans for key reforms
- Encouraging measures to bring the military under civilian democratic control
- Building the capacity of civil-society organizations to effectively engage government officials in dialogue and debate
- Promoting human rights through education, advocacy, monitoring, reporting, and services to survivors of rape and torture
- Helping national governments manage their strategic natural resources responsibly to avoid illegal exploitation and trafficking
- Supporting local efforts to mitigate and manage ethnic and religious conflict through training, improved communication, and confidence-building measures
- Providing opportunities for children and adolescents to engage in constructive and educational activities, reducing their vulnerability to illegal recruitment in armed forces and other forms of exploitation and abuse

USG

OFFICE OF CONFLICT MANAGEMENT AND MITIGATION (CMM)

Internet: www.usaid.gov/our_work/cross-cutting
_programs/conflict/

CMM works to assist USAID to prevent, mitigate, and manage the causes and consequences of violent conflict and fragility. CMM leads USAID's efforts to identify and analyze sources of conflict and fragility; supports early responses to address the causes and consequences of instability and violent conflict; and seeks to integrate conflict mitigation and management into USAID's analysis, strategies and programs.

CMM provides analytical and operational tools to USAID overseas missions, development officers, and program partners to enable USAID to better address the causes and consequences of conflict through its development assistance programming. Its mission is to mainstream conflict programming within USAID's traditional assistance portfolios and allow it to utilize its resources in a more strategic, cost-effective manner. CMM's primary activities include the following:

- Creating detailed conflict assessments that map out destabilizing patterns and trends in specific developing countries
- Providing USAID missions with access to concrete, practical program options; lessons learned; and options for partners, mechanisms, and monitoring and evaluation tools for implementing more-effective conflict programs
- Providing direct support for innovative conflict management programs in a number of countries
- Supporting the development of an early warning system that can help focus USAID and U.S. government attention and resources on countries that are at greatest risk for violence

OFFICE OF MILITARY AFFAIRS (OMA)
Internet: www.usaid.gov

In 2005, USAID created the Office of Military Affairs in the Bureau for Democracy, Conflict, and Humanitarian Assistance (DCHA). The office serves USAID as a whole and reflects the increased importance of effective interface with the military in reconstruction, stabilization, and humanitarian assistance operations. In addition to Washington positions, the office will have advisers in several of the key combatant commands to help link regional and field planners and managers. The office will also help build understanding and effective relations between the U.S. military and the NGO community.

BUREAU FOR GLOBAL HEALTH (GH)
Internet: www.usaid.gov/our_work/global_health/

GH supports field health programs; advances research and innovation in selected areas relevant to overall USAID health objectives; and transfers new technologies to the field through its own staff work, coordination with donors, and a portfolio of grants and contracts with an annual budget in excess of $1.6 billion. USAID's objective is to improve global health, including child, maternal, and reproductive health, and to reduce abortion and disease, especially HIV/AIDS, malaria, and tuberculosis. GH personnel also deploy into the field during humanitarian crises.

There are several means by which the GH engages in relief and stability operations. The Global Health program has strengthened USAID's ability to respond to the increasing threat of new and reemerging infectious diseases through the Infectious Disease Initiative. The initiative focuses on preventing diseases such as malaria and tuberculosis, while simultaneously strengthening the treatment and control programs that exist in the health care system and focusing on crosscutting issues of building surveillance capacity and addressing antimicrobial resistance. Additionally, the Bureau for Global Health provides technical leadership to improve emergency and transition programming in nutrition and food security. The resources for responding to complex emergencies tend to shift from immediate shelter, water, and food needs to reestablishment of livelihoods and eventual development efforts. USAID relies on food aid and emergency funding for short-term activities, including technical assistance. Another GH involvement in relief operations is the reconstruction of water supply, sanitation, and hygiene activities in areas of crises, through the Environmental Health branch of GH.

OFFICE OF DEMOCRACY AND GOVERNANCE (DG)

Internet: www.usaid.gov/our_work/democracy _and_governance/

DG is the reach-back technical office for all USAID field missions with democracy assistance programs. It consists of approximately sixty experts with experience in the areas of rule of law, elections, political processes, civil society, media, labor, anticorruption, decentralized local governance, and legislative development. DG's officers are engaged with USAID field programs in all phases, including planning, design, development, implementation, and evaluation.

DG supports the overall USAID effort to consolidate democratic change and build robust democratic institutions in three basic ways: by providing technical assistance both on-site and through electronic means to the field offices; by developing technical guidance in the emerging practice areas of democracy building; and by conducting an extensive training program for the entire agency on democracy development.

U.S. DEPARTMENT OF THE TREASURY (OTA)

Office of International Affairs
1500 Pennsylvania Avenue NW
Washington, DC 20220

Phone: 202-622-0659
Internet: www.ustreas.gov/offices/
   international-affairs/

The Department of the Treasury, through its Office of Technical Assistance (OTA), provides comprehensive technical assistance to select countries that are of strategic foreign policy importance to the U.S. government. Most of these countries are in the process of development or transformation. Others have suffered severe deterioration of their financial institutions as a result of war, civil strife, or prolonged neglect and require serious reform.

OTA services cover a range of public financial management technical assistance, focusing on five core disciplines: budget policy and management, financial enforcement, financial institutions policy and regulation, government debt issuance and management, and tax policy and administration. Financial enforcement is addressed through initiatives that combat money laundering, corruption, and the financing of terrorism. Projects may include assisting with the development or revision of laws and regulations; the development of broad strategies; the designing and implementation of financial systems to promote macroeconomic and fiscal stability; and the building of processes for efficient resource allocation, transparency, and sustainable private-sector growth.

The relationship among OTA's five disciplines requires cooperation and mutual support. The cross-disciplinary capability of OTA provides the program with greater flexibility and an increased capacity to respond to broad requests and challenges. Treasury's technical assistance program is

USG

able to respond quickly with the placement of experts to deal with crisis situations where extensive financial and institutional rehabilitation must be initiated immediately. For example, during fiscal year 2004, OTA fielded advisers in Iraq, Afghanistan, Liberia, and Haiti and also conducted an assessment mission to the West Bank/Gaza.

OFFICE OF DEVELOPMENT POLICY (IDP)

Internet: www.treas.gov/offices/international-affairs/
  iddp/dev_policy.shtml

IDP is charged with setting and helping to advance Treasury and U.S. government policy priorities aimed at promoting economic growth and poverty reduction in developing countries. One particular focus is working with governments and development institutions to define measurable results methodology and indicators that enable the public to track the use of donor and other resources to make sure they are being used most effectively. IDP provides policy advice and technical support to other offices in International Affairs, particularly those working on the multilateral development banks. IDP provides staff support to the secretary of the treasury in his or her capacity as a member of the board of directors of the Millennium Challenge Corporation. IDP also provides support for advancing international policy priorities through international and regional fora, such as the G7/G8, the Asian Pacific Economic Cooperation, and the Summit of the Americas. Current focal areas include aid effectiveness, public expenditure management, financing mechanisms and instruments, infrastructure, and social sectors, including health and education.

U.S. DEPARTMENT OF COMMERCE

U.S. Foreign Commercial Service
1401 Constitution Avenue NW
Washington, DC 20230

Phone: 800-872-87233 (Trade Information Center)
E-mail: tic@ita.doc.gov
Internet: www.export.gov

The U.S. Foreign Commercial Service was founded in 1980 to help U.S. companies, particularly small and medium-sized businesses, make sales in international markets. The agency's network includes 107 U.S. Export Assistance Centers throughout the country and more than 150 offices overseas. In 2004, the U.S. Foreign Commercial Service facilitated more than $23 billion in U.S. exports and conducted nearly 150,000 counseling sessions with American companies.

The Global Diversity Initiative (GDI) sponsors trade-related outreach and educational activities for small, women-owned, and minority-owned business and provides advocacy for these businesses in international organizations and negotiations. GDI seeks to increase awareness of trade opportunities and export assistance services among such businesses through partnering with trade and business associations, holding seminars and workshops, and providing information on U.S. government programs and trade policy issues to business owners.

U.S. DEPARTMENT OF AGRICULTURE (USDA)

Foreign Agriculture Service (FAS)
1400 Independence Avenue SW
Washington, DC 20250

Internet: www.fas.usda.gov

FAS oversees U.S. international business interests, representing U.S. agriculture abroad, collecting and analyzing production and trade data, and financing some commercial export.

FAS is also involved in development and relief efforts abroad. The U.S. Department of Agriculture (USDA) shares administration of U.S. food aid programs with USAID. USDA channels food aid through four programs to help needy people around the world: the Food for Progress Program provides donations of agricultural commodities to needy countries to encourage economic and agricultural reforms that foster free enterprise; Section 416(b) programs provide donations of Commodity Credit Corporation-owned commodities in surplus of domestic program requirements for assistance to developing and friendly countries; the McGovern-Dole International Food for Education and Child Nutrition Program provides for donations of U.S. agricultural products and financial and technical assistance for school feeding and maternal and child nutrition projects in low-income, food-scarce countries committed to universal education; and Title II of Public Law 480 (Food for Peace) provides for long-term concessional sales of U.S. agricultural commodities to support economic growth in countries that need food assistance.

FAS also carries out a broad array of international training, technical assistance, and other collaborative activities with developing and transitional countries to facilitate trade and promote food security. To increase the benefits to developing nations participating in global agricultural markets, FAS offers numerous trade-capacity-building programs.

USG

U.S. DEPARTMENT OF JUSTICE (DOJ)

Office of International Affairs (OIA)
Criminal Division
950 Pennsylvania Avenue NW
Washington, DC 20530-0001

Phone: 202-514-0000
E-mail: Criminal.Division@usdoj.gov
Internet: www.usdoj.gov/criminal/oia.html

OIA's primary mission is to secure the return of fugitives from abroad for prosecution in the United States and to obtain from foreign countries evidence, witnesses, and other assistance needed for the successful prevention, investigation, and prosecution of crimes in the United States. In this regard, OIA's mission encompasses state, local, and federal investigations and prosecutions. Necessary adjuncts to OIA's primary mission are three complementary missions: ensuring that the United States meets its reciprocal obligations to foreign countries with respect to the extradition of foreign fugitives and obtaining evidence in the United States needed for the prevention, investigation, and prosecution of foreign crimes; ensuring that there are effective treaties and other legal authorities to secure fugitives and evidence from abroad and to meet the country's reciprocal obligations; and promoting relationships with foreign counterparts, from the working level to that of the attorney general, that will foster effective international cooperation in the prevention, investigation, and prosecution of transborder crime. OIA handles thousands of international criminal cases a year; has a staff of fifty attorneys; and has field offices in Rome, Brussels, Paris, London, Mexico City, San Salvador, and Manila.

USG

International Criminal Investigative Training Assistance Program (ICITAP)

1331 F Street NW, Suite 500
Washington, DC 20530

Phone: 202-305-8190
Fax: 202-305-3335
Internet: www.usdoj.gov/criminal/icitap/

ICITAP's mission is to support U.S. criminal justice and foreign policy goals by assisting foreign governments in developing the capacity to provide professional law enforcement services based on democratic principles and respect for human rights. It was created in response to a request from the Department of State for assistance in training police forces in Latin America. Since then, ICITAP's activities have expanded to encompass two principal types of assistance projects: the development of police forces in the context of international peace and stability operations, and the enhancement of capabilities of existing police forces in emerging democracies. Assistance is based on internationally recognized principles of human rights, rule of law, and modern police practices.

ICITAP's training and assistance programs are intended to develop professional, civilian-based law enforcement institutions. This assistance is designed to enhance professional capabilities to carry out investigative and forensic functions; assist in the development of academic instruction and curricula for law enforcement personnel; improve the administrative and management capabilities of law enforcement agencies, especially capabilities relating to career development, personnel evaluation, and internal discipline procedures; improve the relationship between the police and the community they serve; and create or strengthen the capability to respond to new crime and criminal justice issues.

USG

OFFICE OF OVERSEAS PROSECUTORIAL DEVELOPMENT, ASSISTANCE, AND TRAINING (OPDAT)

Criminal Division
950 Pennsylvania Avenue NW
Washington, DC 20530-0001

Phone: 202-514-1323
E-mail: Criminal.Division@usdoj.gov
Internet: www.usdoj.gov/criminal/opdat.html

OPDAT seeks to further goals relating to criminal justice development. OPDAT has been tasked with the training of judges and prosecutors in South and Central America, the Caribbean, Russia, other newly independent states, and Central and Eastern Europe. OPDAT also serves as DOJ's liaison between various private and public agencies that sponsor visits to the United States for foreign officials who are interested in the U.S. legal system. OPDAT makes or arranges for presentations explaining the U.S. criminal justice process to hundreds of international visitors each year.

FEDERAL BUREAU OF INVESTIGATION (FBI)

Legal Attaché Offices
935 Pennsylvania Avenue NW, Room 7350
Washington, DC 20535

Phone: 202-324-3000
Internet: www.fbi.gov/contact/legat/legat.htm

The FBI maintains international offices in addition to its field offices across the United States. The FBI has more than fifty offices known as Legal Attachés, or "Legats," located around the world in U.S. embassies and consulates. Their goals are to stop foreign crime as far from American shores as possible and to help solve international crimes that do occur as quickly as possible. To accomplish these

USG

goals, Legats work with law enforcement and security agencies in their host country to coordinate investigations of interest to both countries. Some Legats are responsible for the following:

- Coordinating international investigations
- Covering international leads for domestic U.S. investigations
- Linking U.S. and international resources in critical criminal and terrorist areas that better ensure the safety of the American public here and abroad
- Coordinating FBI training classes—on everything from counterterrorism and cybercrime matters to forensic techniques to human trafficking and human rights violations—for police in their geographic areas

The purpose of Legats is coordination; they do not conduct foreign intelligence gathering or counterintelligence investigations. The rules for joint activities and information sharing are generally spelled out in formal agreements between the United States and the Legat's host country. The entire worldwide Legat program is overseen by a special agent in charge, located at FBI headquarters.

Drug Enforcement Administration (DEA)

Mailstop: AXS
2401 Jefferson Davis Highway
Alexandria, VA 22301

Phone: 202-307-1000
Internet: www.dea.gov

DEA's mission is to enforce the controlled substances laws and regulations of the United States and bring organizations and personnel involved in the growing, manufacture, or distribution of controlled substances to the criminal justice system, and to recommend and support nonenforcement programs aimed at reducing the availability of illicit controlled substances on the domestic and international markets.

In carrying out its mission, DEA's primary international commitments include the following:

- Investigation and preparation for the prosecution of major violators of controlled substances laws operating at international levels
- Management of a national drug intelligence program in cooperation with foreign officials to collect, analyze, and disseminate strategic and operational drug intelligence information
- Coordination and cooperation with foreign governments in programs designed to reduce the availability of illicit abuse-type drugs on the U.S. market through nonenforcement methods, such as crop eradication, crop substitution, and training of foreign officials
- Responsibility, under the policy guidance of the secretary of state and U.S. ambassadors, for all programs associated with drug law-enforcement counterparts in foreign countries
- Liaison with the United Nations, Interpol, and other organizations on matters relating to international drug-control programs

DEPARTMENT OF HEALTH AND HUMAN SERVICES (HHS)

Centers for Disease Control and Prevention (CDC)
1600 Clifton Road
Atlanta, GA 30333

Phone: 404-639-3311
Internet: www.cdc.gov

CDC is one of the thirteen major operating components of the Department of Health and Human Services (HHS). It is globally recognized for conducting research and investigations and for its action-oriented approach. For instance in response to the challenges for public health caused by globalization, CDC and the Agency for Toxic Substances and Disease Registry (ATSDR) have prepared a Global Health Strategy. The rationale for CDC/ATSDR's institutional commitment recognizes the increasing influence of determinants arising outside the country on U.S. health; the mutual benefits of improving the health of other countries; the advantages of sharing U.S. knowledge and public health expertise with international partners; and the need to respond to the health consequences of international emergencies. In addition, past and ongoing international work by CDC has provided a strong foundation on which to base its initiatives abroad. CDC engages in five main categories of international work:

- Public health surveillance and response
- Public health infrastructure and capacity building
- Disease and injury prevention and control
- Applied research for effective health policies
- Exchange of information and lessons learned

CDC's approaches to these categories emphasize that CDC's work will be rooted in sound science, bioethical principles, and local needs; that the primary modality for action will be through partnerships with other institutions; that CDC will engage in those areas in which it has established expertise and capability; that long-term relationships with selected countries will be pursued due to the enhanced productivity of such sustained collaborations; and that CDC will ensure that it has the workforce and administrative mechanisms required for their full implementation.

USG

The United States Military

Introduction

OPERATIONS OTHER THAN WAR" was a term that became increasingly common within the military in the 1990s. With the Cold War over and internal conflicts on the rise, the armed forces were often asked to play the roles of peacekeeper and peacebuilder in conflict-wracked societies around the globe. On other occasions, the military was called upon to secure and facilitate the distribution of emergency supplies to the victims of a daunting range of disasters, natural as well as human-made. More recently, the United States invaded Afghanistan and Iraq while fighting a global war on terrorism, and the military has continued to find itself involved in those countries after the major combat operations ceased. This involvement encompasses a wide range of activities where the military is used for purposes other than the large-scale combat operations usually associated with war. As the military has quickly discovered, relief and stability operations are among the most complex missions it is called on to undertake. Such operations often exist in an uncertain space between peace and war, a world that is neither black nor white. As in combat operations, the military forces sent in to conduct these operations must deal with numerous, often-unpredictable, threats from every side. These operations also bring their own challenges, not least the fact that the military must use neither too little nor too much force and must pursue objectives that may be ill-defined or constantly changing.

The new importance of peace and stability operations was acknowledged with the issuance of Department of

Defense Directive 3000.05, titled *Military Support for Stability, Security, Transition, and Reconstruction,* on November 28, 2005. Under the directive, stability operations were identified as a core mission of the U.S. military, commensurate with the conduct of combat operations. The directive noted that proper planning and execution of the stabilization or postcombat phase of operations was essential to achieving lasting victory and the rapid withdrawal of U.S. forces. It instructed the U.S. military to develop skills in rebuilding indigenous institutions, including security forces, correctional facilities, and judicial systems; restoring public services; organizing local governance; and initiating economic reconstruction. It also instructed the military to work closely with civilian government agencies and nongovernmental organizations to utilize their expertise in rebuilding indigenous institutions and restoring war-ravaged societies. The directive urged creation of training programs that would equip military personnel to perform essential functions until they could be transferred to civilian authorities. The directive marked a major change in doctrine and policy for the U.S. military in light of its experiences in Iraq and Afghanistan.

STABILITY OPERATIONS

Stability operations encompass many types of operations that are conducted in coordination with other instruments of national power to reestablish and maintain a safe and secure environment and provide essential government services, emergency infrastructure reconstruction, and humanitarian relief, as required. U.S. forces conduct stability operations to deter war, resolve conflict, promote peace, strengthen democratic processes, retain U.S. influence or access abroad, and support moral and legal imperatives. Through a combination of peacetime developmental, cooperative activities and coercive actions in response to a crisis, local stability operations promote and protect U.S. national interests by promoting and sustaining regional and global stability. U.S. military forces accomplish stability goals through both engagement and response. During and following hostilities, forces may conduct stability operations to provide a secure environment for civil authorities as they work to achieve reconciliation, rebuild lost infrastructure, and resume vital services. These operations usually involve a combination of air, land, sea, and special operations forces as well as the efforts of civilian government agencies functioning in a complementary fashion.

In stability operations, the missions assigned to the military are complicated by the fact that it may share the field with a local population and government and also a wide array of other U.S. government agencies, NGOs, international organizations, diplomats, and other foreign entities and individuals. A complex contingency operation is much more likely to succeed if the external actors not only understand the culture of the nation where they work but also have a fundamental appreciation for one another's methods, organization, and culture. Mutual understanding and cooperation is, in short, vital.

The purpose of this section is to give readers a very general understanding of how the military works. It addresses both macro-level issues, such as the military chain of command, relationships among the key commanders, and the role of each service, and micro-level matters, such as insignia and weaponry. To help interpret the signs, symbols, and abbreviations that are so much a part of military life, this section includes a chart showing insignia and a glossary of some of the more common military acronyms (and advice on how to pronounce them).

It should be pointed out that this section is chiefly concerned with the U.S. military. Certainly, much of the general information presented here, and even some of the detail, applies to the armed forces of other countries. Even so,

readers should not assume that what holds true for the
U.S. military is equally applicable to other militaries encountered in stability operations.

The Organization and Structure of the Military

I N THE UNITED STATES, every soldier, sailor, airman, and marine is under a chain of command that begins with the president. This chain of command is complex, to be sure, but the thread that runs from the highest elected official to the lowest-ranking soldier is never broken. The national chain of command encompasses two different branches (operational and administrative) and four different services (Army, Navy, Marine Corps, and Air Force). The services almost always conduct operations jointly within one of six geographic and four functional commands. The following description of the U.S. chain of command is stripped down to its bare essentials and is focused on the operational commands, because civilians are likely to encounter only operational personnel on the scene of a stability operation.

The National Command Structure

The U.S. Constitution stipulates that the **president** is the commander-in-chief of the military. The president is assisted in the management of the military by the **secretary of defense (SECDEF)**, a civilian member of the cabinet appointed by the president and confirmed by the U.S. Senate to manage the Department of Defense (www.defenselink.mil).

The chiefs of the four uniformed services—Army, Navy, Air Force, and Marine Corps—are members of the **Joint Chiefs of Staff (JCS)**. The president, with the advice and consent of the Senate, separately appoints the chairman (CJCS) and the vice chairman of the JCS. The CJCS is the principal military adviser to the president, the secretary of defense, and the National Security Council. The Goldwater-Nichols Act of 1986 considerably expanded the responsibilities of the JCS as a whole and of its chairman and vice chairman in particular. A growing number of joint organizations, especially the unified and combatant commands (see figure 4.1), report through the JCS. However, the CJCS does not exercise military command over any of the armed forces.

The president and the secretary of defense are assisted by the CJCS, the **National Security Council (NSC)**, and the **Joint Staff** (www.jcs.mil), and they are responsible to the American people for national defense and security. As figure 4.1 shows, authority over and command and control of the armed forces is exercised through a single chain of command that separates below the secretary of defense into two distinct branches: one operational and the other administrative.

The administrative chain runs from the president through the secretary of defense to the **secretaries of the departments of the Army, Navy and Marine Corps, and Air Force**. The president, with the advice and consent of the Senate, appoints the individual service secretaries, whose departments are tasked with the recruiting, administration, training, equipping, and financial management of the services.

The operational branch extends from the president to the secretary of defense to the commanders of **unified combatant commands**. Unified combatant commands

Figure 4.1. National Chain of Command

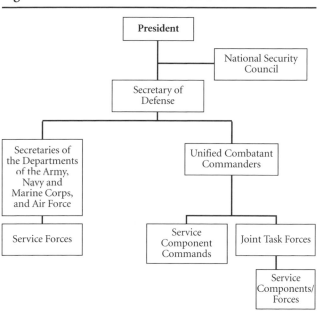

Source: U.S. Army Peacekeeping and Stability Operations Institute.

are organized on a geographic or functional basis and include forces from the various services. The document
known as the **Unified Command Plan (UCP)** establishes
these commands, identifies their specific **areas of responsibility (AORs)**, defines the authority of the commanders,
and establishes command relationships. The UCP is re-
viewed periodically by the JCS and is adjusted in response
to changes in the world situation. There are currently ten
unified combatant commands:

Geographic

- USCENTCOM: U.S. Central Command—Directs
  and coordinates the employment of U.S. forces in
  peace, crisis, or war in an area encompassing the
  Middle East and Central and Southwest Asia (www
  .centcom.mil)

- USEUCOM: U.S. European Command—Directs and coordinates the employment of U.S. forces in peace, crisis, or war in an area encompassing all of Europe (www.eucom.mil)

- USPACOM: U.S. Pacific Command—Directs and coordinates the employment of U.S. forces in peace, crisis, or war in an area encompassing the Pacific Ocean, the Indian Ocean, and East and South Asia (www.pacom.mil)

- USSOUTHCOM: U.S. Southern Command—Directs and coordinates the employment of U.S. forces in peace, crisis, or war in an area encompassing all of Central and South America, the Caribbean, including Haiti and Cuba, and adjacent waters (www.southcom.mil)

- USNORTHCOM: U.S. Northern Command—Plans, organizes, and executes homeland defense and civil support missions of the continental United States, its territories, and adjacent waters (www.northcom.mil)

- USAFRICOM: U.S. Africa Command—Directs and coordinates the employment of U.S. forces in peace, crisis, and war in Africa

Functional

- USSOCOM: U.S. Special Operations Command—Plans and employs strategic special operations forces (Army Green Berets, Navy SEALs, and Air Force Special Reconnaissance) (www.socom.mil)

- USSTRATCOM: U.S. Strategic Command—Plans and employs strategic nuclear forces; controls military space operations and information operations (www.stratcom.mil)

- USTRANSCOM: U.S. Transportation Command—Controls and coordinates all strategic lift capability, including air, sea, and ground transportation assets (www.transcom.mil)

MILITARY

- USJFCOM: U.S. Joint Forces Command—A catalyst for joint force integration in training, experimentation, doctrinal development, and testing (www.jfcom.mil)

Each of the unified combatant commands is organized under command of a **combatant commander**, who is a four-star general or admiral. The combatant commander, in turn, organizes the members of the various services assigned to him as **component commands**. The service components are commonly known by the acronyms ARFOR (Army forces), NAVFOR (Navy forces), AFFOR (Air Force forces), and MARFOR (Marine Corps forces). More specifically, individual components are referred to by acronyms that indicate the combatant command to which they are assigned. Thus, for example, Navy forces assigned to CENTCOM are known as NAVCENT. Each of the geographic combatant commands also has a special operations component known as an SOC, or special operations command; for example, the special operations command for EUCOM is referred to as SOCEUR.

The combatant commanders exercise **combatant command authority** (**COCOM**) over the forces assigned to their organization. COCOM, briefly, is the authority that allows the combatant commander to organize and employ forces, assign tasks, designate objectives, and give authoritative direction over all aspects of military operations and joint training as necessary to accomplish the missions assigned. In contrast, the military departments exercise **administrative control** (**ADCON**), the authority to form units, organizations, and agencies; to procure materials and equip units organic to that service; and to train those units in service-specific subjects. A simpler way to look at this is that the military departments use ADCON to provide forces while the combatant commands use COCOM to employ forces assigned to them by the departments.

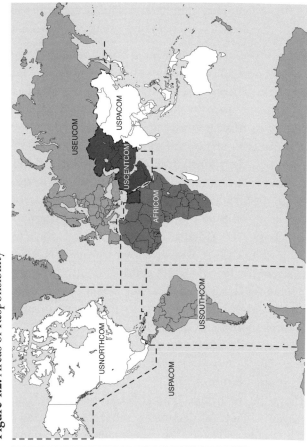

Figure 4.2. Areas of Responsibility

Source: Department of Defense, *The World with Commanders' Areas of Responsibility*, November 10, 2004, www.defenselink.mil/specials/unifiedcommands.

MILITARY

The regional nature and global focus of the commands allow the United States to quickly detect and respond to problems anywhere in the world. Joint commanders typically respond to situations within their AOR by employing a combination of forces organized into a **joint task force** (**JTF**). A JTF provides a flexible organizational structure, usually created by the responsible combatant commander, but also available at the national level in extraordinary circumstances or even to an existing JTF commander, should the need arise for a smaller, subordinate JTF. Each JTF operates for a specific purpose or to accomplish a specific mission, with forces drawn from the service components that make up the joint command. Once the mission is completed, the JTF is normally disbanded. The JTF is the primary action organization within a joint command and the one with which NGOs and IOs will have the most contact in the field during stability and support operations. A JTF is led by a **joint force commander** (**JFC**), who is normally a flag officer (a general or an admiral) and who typically reports directly to the combatant commander. In multinational operations, a JTF may combine with a variety of forces from a number of nations. In such cases, the JTF becomes a **combined joint task force** (**CJTF**).

The Services

Most countries have an army and an air force; many also possess some sort of naval capability. Some countries that have a maritime capability have an organization that projects ground military power from the sea, often engaging in amphibious operations. In the United States, as in a number of other countries, this force is known as the Marine Corps.

Although each of the U.S. armed forces has a specific and generally accepted defense function—the Army fights on land; the Navy at sea; the Marine Corps on land, usually from the sea; and the Air Force in the air—it fulfills that function through units trained and organized around various specialties. Some of these specialties exist in more than one service, but each has its own unique mission related to that service. For example, three of the services have high-performance jet aircraft, but the Marine aircraft concentrate on supporting their ground units while Navy jets concentrate on protecting the fleet.

Military personnel are very conscious of the specialties. In the Army, for instance, the specialties are grouped into branches that are identified by distinctive insignia and badges displayed on uniforms; for example, Army infantry soldiers wear a crossed rifle insignia.

UNITED STATES ARMY (USA)

Internet: www.army.mil

The United States Army's primary role is to organize, train, and equip forces to conduct sustained land combat operations. Historically, the Army has usually been the decisive element of military power, and it is typically the largest branch of militaries around the world. The United States Army has been reduced in size since the end of the Cold War, but it is still the largest of the services. Since complex contingency operations are conducted on land, the Army and, at a lower level, the Marine Corps have borne the largest share of the burden of providing units and personnel to support these operations.

The United States Army organizes its units into three general categories, which correspond to the role of the unit on the battlefield: **combat arms (CA)** (for example, infantry and armor), **combat support (CS)** (for example, communications and military police), and **combat service support** (CSS) (for example, supply and transportation). The branches for lawyers, medical personnel, and chaplains are considered special branches but perform service support functions. Additionally, the Army has many specialties that require advanced schooling and experience. These include public affairs specialists, comptrollers, and foreign area officers, who serve in U.S. embassies as military attachés. Joint operations generally require the participation of Army units from all categories, with the mix of these forces largely dependent on the nature of the given mission. In humanitarian and disaster relief operations, for example, a typical JTF is likely to include more combat support and combat service support units than combat arms units.

Individual soldiers are grouped into branches that constitute the three general categories (see table 4.1). In the Army, as in the other services, new recruits first undergo basic training (designed to enable them to function and survive on the battlefield) and then receive advanced training in a specialty appropriate to the branch to which they are assigned.

MILITARY POLICE

Military police (MP) play a critical role in stability operations, especially during periods of transitional security. The primary role of military police is to assist the military commander to accomplish his or her mission by providing security and military law enforcement. MPs provide security and protection for critical persons, facilities, and equipment. They are the initial response force to criminal and enemy attempts to demoralize, terrorize, or sabotage the military community or its operation. In detainee mission, MPs detain and safeguard prisoners of war and common criminals. During stability operations, particularly in Iraq, military police have conducted patrol operations and

Table 4.1. The Categories and Branches of Army Units

Combat Arms

- Infantry—the nucleus of the Army's fighting strength. Infantry soldiers and units fight dismounted or mounted on vehicles; includes a variety of additional specialties, such as Rangers and airborne forces.
- Armor (and cavalry)—tank or combined arms organizations that fight using fire, maneuver, and shock effect, and cavalry organizations that perform reconnaissance and provide security
- Field Artillery—employs fire support assets—that is, cannons, missiles, and rockets—in support of combat operations
- Air Defense Artillery—uses antiaircraft weapons systems in support of land operations against enemy aircraft and missile attacks to protect military forces and geopolitical assets
- Aviation—attack and support helicopters and fixed-wing support aircraft employed in combat missions, including attack and air assault operations and combat support missions; for example, intelligence/electronic warfare, personnel and materiel movement, air traffic services, and combat service support missions, such as casualty evacuation
- Corps of Engineers—mobility, countermobility, survivability, general engineering, and topographic operations, road and bridge repair, obstacle breaching, obstacle emplacement, and production and dissemination of maps. As construction engineers, they manage and control military construction programs for the Army and other Department of Defense agencies.
- Special Forces—conduct missions of unconventional warfare, direct action, foreign internal defense, special reconnaissance, and counterterrorism

Combat Support

- Signal—data and communications systems for command and control
- Military Police (MP)—maneuver and mobility support operations, including circulation and refugee movement, law-and-order operations, internment and resettlement

operations, and area security (covered in more detail in text)

- Military Intelligence (MI)—collection and analysis of information and production and dissemination of finished intelligence products
- Chemical—nuclear, biological, and chemical (NBC) defense; smoke, obscurants
- Civil Affairs—supports the commander's relationship with the civil authorities and civilian populace to promote mission legitimacy and enhance military effectiveness (covered in more detail below)

Combat Service Support
- Adjutant General Corps (AG)—personnel management and administration, postal operations, and bands; also includes soldiers from public affairs and chaplain assistants
- Finance—personnel pay; commercial vendor support; and the banking, disbursement, auditing, and accounting of funds
- Transportation—truck and boat units, movement control, maritime terminal operations, and rail operations
- Ordnance—maintenance of equipment; management, maintenance, and supply of ammunition; explosive ordnance disposal (EOD)
- Quartermaster—supplies, including most equipment, food, water, and petroleum; field services, including laundry and shower, bakery, mortuary affairs, and Army and Air Force Exchange operations; and management of dining facilities operations

Special Branches
- Judge Advocate (JAG)—legal operations, lawyers, legal advice to the commander, and military justice/criminal law; administrative law and legal assistance
- Army Medical Department—health services and hospitals, includes doctors, medics, dentists, veterinarians, nurses, medical specialists, and medical administrators
- Chaplain—religious, spiritual, moral, and ethical support to soldiers and commanders

other types of operations that have involved them in combat with insurgent forces. At the same time, U.S. military police have provided training and technical support to Iraqi police forces, conducted joint patrols, and dealt jointly with civil disturbance and other public order missions. In Iraq, U.S. military police have proven highly versatile in moving from combat support operations and training to actual law enforcement within a brief time frame, as dictated by the constantly changing requirements of their mission.

CIVIL AFFAIRS (CA) FORCES

Civil affairs units help military commanders by working with civil authorities and civilian populations in the commander's area of operations to "win hearts and minds," relieve suffering, improve local infrastructure, and increase the acceptability of U.S. military forces. Civil affairs forces support activities of both conventional and special operations forces, and are capable of assisting and supporting the civil administration in the area of operations.

Civil affairs specialists can quickly and systematically identify critical needs of local citizens in war or disaster situations. They can also locate civil resources to support military operations, help minimize civilian interference with operations, support national assistance activities, plan and execute noncombatant evacuation, and establish and maintain liaison or dialogue with civilian aid agencies and civilian commercial and private organizations.

U.S. Army civil affairs units are organized around functional specialties to provide assistance, assessment, planning, advice, and coordination at a level of expertise not normally found in military units. These units are designed to enhance the capabilities of the supported commander, who is typically a ground combat officer who may or may not have personal expertise in stability operations. While the primary purpose of CA forces is to support the commander's civil-military operations, CA soldiers normally have a more detailed knowledge of, and personal experience in, working with representatives of international and non-governmental organizations. Capabilities inherent in CA forces include expertise in a broad range of civilian sectors, including governance, rule of law, economic stability, infrastructure, police, education and information, and public health and welfare.

CA forces train on and execute a core set of functions that embrace the relationship of military forces with civil authorities. CA activities may also involve the application of CA functional specialty skills in areas normally the responsibility of the civilian government. In Afghanistan and Iraq, CA soldiers serve in Provincial Reconstruction Teams, where they concentrate on hiring local contractors to construct schools, clinics, roads, and other village improvement projects. CA soldiers operate a civil military operations center that helps coordinate the work of international and non-governmental agencies in providing relief and development assistance.

The majority of U.S. Army CA capabilities reside in the U.S. Army Reserve. Accordingly, most CA personnel hold civilian jobs, usually related to their functional specialties, and perform their military duties on a part-time basis. As part of their service obligation, reservists must participate in prescribed training on essential military skills. This training focuses on the military skill set reservists need when called to active duty. When required, reservists may volunteer or be mobilized for operations to assist active duty forces. The U.S. Special Operations Command also provides one Army active component CA battalion consisting of regionally oriented companies and structured to deploy rapidly and provide initial CA support to military operations. The unit's primary use is providing rapid, short-duration support.

CA forces are organized in to companies, battalions, and brigades and commands. Each organization is designed to augment civil military operations staffs of the geographic combatant commands' Army component, and maneuver commanders down to battalion level. They can also augment U.S. embassy country teams, other government agencies, and multinational forces. CA forces are highly flexible and can be organized based on unique mission conditions. Commanders may employ CA teams or subject matter experts to meet specific requirements.

Units

The Army is operationally organized into units of varying sizes; the larger the unit, the more numerous and diverse the specialties required to support it. For instance, the Army's largest fighting unit, a corps, usually consists of between 30,000 and 100,000 soldiers and incorporates a signal brigade, a military police brigade, and a military intelligence brigade, in addition to infantry, armor, artillery, air defense, and other combat arms, combat support, and combat service support units. The Joint Task Force normally has a similar specialty mix that can also include Air Force, Navy, and Marine elements that bring their own specialties to the task force. The size of the JTF depends on the requirements of its mission, but it is often smaller than an Army corps.

The smallest units in the Army are **squads** and **crews**. Army squads normally have six to ten soldiers, varying by the type and specialty of the unit. An Army infantry squad, for example, has nine members, whereas a military police squad has ten members. (In contrast, Marine infantry squads are composed of three four-man fire teams and a squad leader.) Crews man a specific vehicle or weapons system. Squads and crews are different in that they are led by noncommissioned officers (NCOs); all other elements in the chain typically are led by commissioned officers.

Three to five squads or crews make up a **platoon**. Three to five platoons make up a **company**. Three to five compa-

Table 4.2. Army and Marine Units

Unit	Rank of Leaders (Officer/NCO)	Number of Personnel
Squad/Crew	Staff Sergeant or Sergeant	4–13
Platoon	Lieutenant/ Platoon Sergeant/ Gunnery Sergeant	30–75
Company	Captain/First Sergeant	100–300
Battalion	Lieutenant Colonel*	250–1000
Brigade/Regiment	Colonel*	2000–5000
Division	Major General*	10000+
Corps /Marine Expeditionary Force	Lieutenant General*	50,000+

*A command sergeant major or sergeant major is the senior NCO at battalion level and above.

nies make up a **battalion**. **Brigades** and **regiments** are made up of a varying number of battalions, usually up to five or six. Two to five **divisions**, each made up of two to five brigades, make up an Army **corps**.

Brigades and larger units are very flexible in terms of the number of subordinate units assigned to them. For instance, a corps commander may move a battalion or even a brigade from one division to another to meet the needs of a given situation. To enhance their self-sufficiency, units larger than battalions are often assigned specialized units to fulfill a variety of combat, combat support, and combat service support functions. For example, in a stability operation, an army division may augment its logistical and medical capabilities with similar units.

Table 4.2 shows the type, rank of leaders, and approximate size of units found in the Army and Marines.

STAFF SECTION DESIGNATIONS

Every unit of battalion size or larger has four or more specialized staff sections, each of which is identified by an alphanumeric designation (see table 4.3). Section 1 (S1) handles personnel administration; S2 handles the processing of intelligence and tactical information for the commander; S3 handles plans, operations, and training; S4 handles all aspects of logistics—transportation, supply, ammunition, rations, and so forth. The S designation is standard for Army and Marine units up to the level of a brigade or regiment. When the unit is commanded by a general officer, the designation is G to indicate general staff. (In a JTF, each section is designated by a J instead of an S, and in a combined (or multinational) force the sections are designated by a C.) At brigade, regiment, or division level there may be an additional section, S5 (or G5), that deals with civil affairs. The officer in charge of the S5 section handles civil–military relations and is in charge of the civil–military operations center. At corps level and above, the staff sections numbered 5 or higher often deal with other specialties. Typically, staff section 5 is the planning section, staff section 6 is the communications section, and staff section 9 works on civil–military relations. The function of staff sections 7 and 8 depend on the unit's mission. The work of the various sections is coordinated and overseen by an executive officer at the battalion and brigade levels, and by a chief of staff at the division, corps, or Marine Expeditionary Force, joint and combined levels. Staff officers both plan and assist the commander in executing operations, but the leaders of staff sections are not commanders. However, when authorized and under the proper circumstances, staff officers may speak for the commander or issue orders in his name.

Table 4.3. Staff Sections

Staffs are organized by the commander of an operation to accomplish the mission. The first four sections are standard through all levels of staff.

Type/Unit	Personnel	Intelligence	Operations/ Training/ Planning	Logistics
Section (S)				
Battalion	S1	S2	S3	S4
Brigade	S1	S2	S3	S4
General (G)				
Division	G1	G2	G3	G4
Corps	G1	G2	G3	G4

Type/Unit	Personnel	Intelligence	Operations	Logistics
Joint (J)	J1	J2	J3	J4
Combined (C)	C1	C2	C3	C4

The rest of the staff organization is very much mission dependent. The portion of the table below includes some of the more traditional section designations.

Type/Unit	Civil Affairs	Communications		CMO/ CIMIC
Section (S)				
Battalion	S5			S9
Brigade	S5			S9
General (G)				
Division	G5	G6		G9
Corps	G5	G6		G9

Type/Unit	Plans/ Policy	Communications	Training	Resource Management	CMO/ CIMIC
Joint (J)	J5	J6	J7	J8	J9
Combined (C)	C5	C6	C7	C8	C9

MILITARY

ARMY TRANSFORMATION

Today, the U.S. Army is pursuing the most comprehensive transformation of its forces since World War II. The Army is transforming to a campaign-quality force with joint and expeditionary capabilities providing relevant and ready land power to combatant commanders. Campaigns are undertaken to bring about fundamental, favorable change in a crisis region and create enduring results. Many campaigns will likely entail lengthy periods of both combat and stability operations. This situation requires the Army to sustain decisive operations for as long as necessary and adapt to changes as required. At the same time, it must also sustain operational support to forces around the globe. The Army is focusing its efforts to enhance the capabilities of soldiers and units to meet the requirements of the full range of its strategic commitments.

The pace of Army transformation, particularly over the past several years, has produced important results:

- Fielding of the Stryker brigade combat team (SBCT)
- Conversion of Army units to a new structure
- Fielding of digital command capabilities to Army forces
- Fielding of enhanced joint communications capabilities

UNITED STATES NAVY (USN)

Internet: www.navy.mil

The primary role of the United States Navy is to promote and defend U.S. interests by maintaining global maritime superiority, contributing to stability and security operations, conducting operations on and from the sea, seizing or defending advanced naval bases, and conducting such land operations as may be essential to the prosecution of naval campaigns. The Navy is constantly "forward deployed" (that is, naval forces are within a relatively short distance of potential crisis areas), with ships at sea in each of the combatant commands. Because of its forward deployment, the Navy is the premier service for "power projection" (that is, the projection of national power beyond national borders), having the ability to respond quickly and with significant firepower.

The Navy is organized essentially into two major fleets: the **Atlantic Fleet** and the **Pacific Fleet**. These are further subdivided into **subordinate, numbered fleets** that are assigned to sub-areas surrounding the two largest oceans of the world. For example, the Atlantic Fleet, under control of JFCOM, consists of the Second Fleet in the Atlantic Ocean proper. The Atlantic Fleet also provides ships and other forces to the Sixth Fleet, under control of EUCOM, in the Mediterranean Sea. The Pacific Fleet comprises the Seventh Fleet, which covers the western Pacific, and the Third Fleet, which covers the eastern Pacific. Both the Atlantic and Pacific Fleets deploy forces to the Fifth Fleet, under control of CENTCOM, in the Persian Gulf and the North Arabian Sea.

Subordinate to these fleets are subcommands that are organized functionally and are known as "type commands." As their name suggests, these commands correspond to a specific type of vessel: surface vessels, aircraft carriers, or submarines.

The Navy's main fighting organization is the **carrier strike group**. Built around a large-deck aircraft carrier (most of which are nuclear powered), each carrier strike group consists of about ten vessels: the aircraft carrier, four to six surface combatants (destroyers, cruisers, or frigates armed with air defense and antisubmarine weapons, cruise missiles, and guns), one or two submarines, and an ammunition and supply vessel. With the addition of another aircraft carrier and a Marine air–ground task force, the carrier strike group becomes a **battle force** capable of a wide variety of combat missions, including amphibious operations and around-the-clock air operations. A U.S. battle force is the world's most powerful naval formation.

Naval forces can also be organized into **naval expeditionary forces**, each of which is tailored to meet specific threats and perform specific missions. Once they have accomplished their mission, they are disbanded. A JTF created to accomplish a mission requiring naval operations may use either a carrier strike group, an **expeditionary strike group (ESG)** [previously called an **amphibious ready group (ARG)**], or another naval expeditionary force, depending on the scope and nature of that mission.

The ESG is the type of naval force most relevant to stability operations, because it includes an embarked force of Marines. The ESG and its embarked force are often called upon to execute **noncombatant evacuation operations (NEOs)**, which are frequently a prelude to more protracted stability operations. The embarked Marine force is sometimes also committed to peace operations in their initial phase.

The Navy also has some deployable land-based forces, generally involved in port operations and construction. The most famous of these are the naval construction battalions, or Seabees.

UNITED STATES COAST GUARD (USCG)

Internet: www.uscg.mil

The United States Coast Guard is a military service, and during times of national emergency it does become part of the Department of the Navy. Under normal circumstances, however, the Coast Guard is subordinate to the Department of Homeland Security and is responsible for a variety of missions, most notably drug-trafficking interdiction, sea search and rescue, and harbor management.

Not surprisingly, Coast Guard personnel have many of the same specialties as the other services and maritime specialties identical to the Navy's.

UNITED STATES MARINE CORPS (USMC)

Internet: www.usmc.mil

The Marine Corps is under the administrative control of the secretary of the navy, but it is in every respect an equal partner with the other services. The Marines provide the capability to respond rapidly and forcefully to crisis worldwide. To facilitate support to the combatant commanders, Marine forces are formed into two major organizations, **Marine Forces, Atlantic**, and **Marine Forces, Pacific**.

Marine units are normally slightly larger than Army units and have similar capabilities, particularly up to battalion level. Most Army units are optimized for participation in sustained land operations, to include heavy armored forccs. In contrast, Marine units normally do not have as many heavy armored vehicles and are especially suited for amphibious or helicopter-borne operations from the sea. With the Navy, the Marines are often the first units deployed in complex contingencies, primarily because they are at sea in the vicinity of a crisis area. The Marines must have the capability to support themselves until Army units arrive. If deployed as part of a long-term operation, Marines must often utilize Army service support capabilities.

The Marine element of a JTF consists of a **Marine Air ground task force** (**MAGTF**), which may vary in size from a reinforced battalion to a reinforced division. In ascending order of size, these forces are designated as follows: **Marine expeditionary unit** (**MEU**) (a reinforced battalion); **Marine expeditionary brigade** (**MEB**) (a reinforced regiment); and **Marine expeditionary force** (**MEF**) (a reinforced division). Each MAGTF normally consists of infantry, amphibious vehicles, armor, an aviation element, and combat and service support. A MEU, for example, is structured around a Marine infantry battalion, reinforced by a tank company, artillery, engineers, service support, and aviation units. As well as tanks, a MEU has amphibious and light armored vehicles, helicopters, and vertical takeoff and landing (VTOL) ground-attack aircraft. A MEU is often the first ground force deployed in response to any complex contingency. A MEF is made up of a Marine division, a Marine air wing, and a service support group. The division is composed of three infantry regiments, one artillery regiment, a tank battalion, and supporting forces.

Though they share some of the same functions, United States Marine Corps civil affairs forces are smaller in number than their United States Army counterparts and are tactically oriented. The U.S. Marine Corps dedicated CA structure is maintained entirely within the Reserve Component (RC) and consists of two Civil Affairs Groups (CAGs). Each CAG is designed to support a MEF. While every effort is made to recruit and train Marines with a broad variety of military and civilian skills, each member of the CAG is a CA generalist.

UNITED STATES AIR FORCE (USAF)

Internet: www.af.mil

The role of the United States Air Force is to organize, train, equip, and provide forces for the conduct of sustained combat operations in the air. The Air Force is also responsible for gaining and maintaining general air supremacy, defeating enemy air forces, conducting space operations, and establishing local air superiority, as well as providing forces for air and missile defense at both the strategic and tactical levels of war. The Air Force works closely with the commander of TRANSCOM to provide strategic airlift in support of other combatant commands and services, as required. Under appropriate circumstances and when authorized by the president, Air Force transport aircraft may be used for transportation of civilian personnel, equipment, and supplies. Such support, when authorized, is often a part of a humanitarian effort. The Air Force also works closely with the commander of STRATCOM to maintain the U.S. strategic nuclear arsenal. In this way, the Air Force has a critical role to play in the overall strategic defense of the United States and its interests.

The Air Force is organized into ten **major commands**, which are categorized as either operational or support. Each major command is directly subordinate to Headquarters U.S. Air Force (HQ, USAF). The major commands are subdivided into **numbered air forces**, which in turn are subdivided into **specialized wings**: fighter, bomber, tanker, or training, depending on whether they are assigned to operational or support commands. The wings are then further subdivided into **groups**, **squadrons**, and **flights** for effective command and control.

The basic unit for generating and employing combat capability is the wing, which has always been the Air Force's primary fighting instrument. As their name suggests, **composite wings** operate more than one kind of aircraft and may be configured as self-contained units designed for quick air intervention anywhere in the world. The wing is the primary unit within the AFFOR of a combatant command and a JTF. Other wings operate a single aircraft type and are assigned as needed to air campaigns throughout the world. The fundamental components of a wing are its operations, logistics, and support groups.

OFFICERS AND ENLISTED PERSONNEL

The chain of command from the president to the combatant commanders and the military services, already outlined, continues within each service down to the individual soldier, sailor, airman, and marine.

The military hierarchy is separated into two basic groups: officers and enlisted personnel. The enlisted personnel are further subdivided into junior enlisted and noncommissioned officers. **Junior enlisted soldiers/personnel** hold ranks of private, specialist, lance corporal, seaman, or airman. (The rank title is common to both genders; thus, for instance, both men and women are referred to as "airmen" or "seamen.") **Noncommissioned officers** are corporals, sergeants, or petty officers. Exact titles vary from service to service, although several are the same within the Army, Marines, and Air Force. Figure 4.3 shows the ranks, grades, and insignia of the services. Officers are subdivided into two distinct groups: commissioned and warrant officers. The ranks are grouped to correspond with the grade of the individual holding that rank. Officers are grouped into grades beginning with *O;* enlisted personnel are grouped into grades beginning with *E.* The letters are followed by a number; the higher the number, the more senior and experienced the individual.

Officers plan operations, manage resources, and provide leadership and motivation to enlisted personnel under their supervision or command. **Commissioned officers** serve at the pleasure of the president of the United States (through the respective service of assignment) or for extended terms of service depending on rank. They exercise **command authority** (derived from the U.S. Constitution) and are held to the highest standard of responsibility for their conduct and performance. From a civilian perspective, enlisted personnel are "hired" as employees for a specific term of service and are the military's workforce. Initially terms of service are from two to six years. Thereafter, enlisted personnel reenlist for additional periods of service, typically also of between two and six years. After ten years of service, the enlistments are for an indefinite period.

Warrant officers are between commissioned officers and noncommissioned officers. These officers are appointed by the service secretary based on their demonstrated level of competence in a very specific area of expertise. Most warrant officers do not exercise command authority but rather operate, administer, and manage the equipment, support activities, and technical systems of four of the five services. There are four grades of warrant officers in the Navy, and five grades in the Marines and in the Army. The Air Force has no warrant officers. Warrant officers are often selected from the NCO ranks for advanced training in specific areas of expertise, which mirror the specialties they held as enlisted personnel. Like commissioned officers, warrant officers serve for an indefinite period and at the pleasure of the president or for as long as they choose within parameters determined by the individual service component.

Noncommissioned officers are known as the "backbone of the military," even though they cannot legally exercise command except under the most extraordinary circumstances, such as in combat when the officer in charge is incapacitated or killed. They are the first-line supervisors and trainers in the U.S. military and conduct its day-to-day activities. Senior NCOs often possess university degrees and manage complex operations and large amounts of resources. They could well be considered the midlevel management of the military.

Officers and enlisted personnel are addressed differently within the ranks of the military as well as outside the military. Enlisted personnel address officers either by their appropriate title (lieutenant, captain, major, and so on) or by using "sir" or "ma'am." Junior ranking officers address senior officers in the same way.

Figure 4.3 shows the ranks, grades, and insignia of officers.

Aside from the Marines, who routinely use rank titles in all situations, military personnel, when speaking in the

Figure 4.3. Ranks, Pay Grades, and Insignia by Service

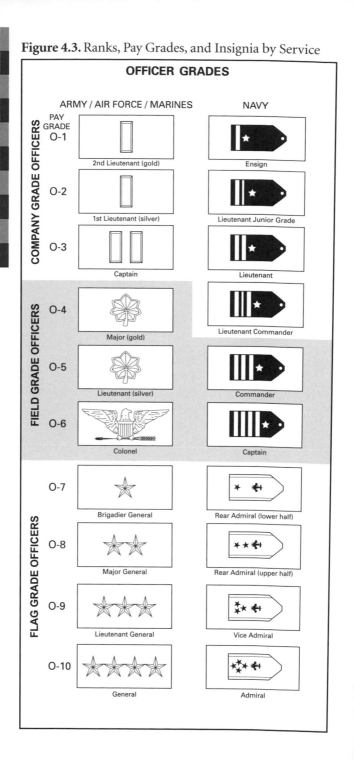

MILITARY

OFFICER GRADES

ARMY / AIR FORCE / MARINES   NAVY

COMPANY GRADE OFFICERS

PAY GRADE
O-1 — 2nd Lieutenant (gold) — Ensign
O-2 — 1st Lieutenant (silver) — Lieutenant Junior Grade
O-3 — Captain — Lieutenant

FIELD GRADE OFFICERS

O-4 — Major (gold) — Lieutenant Commander
O-5 — Lieutenant (silver) — Commander
O-6 — Colonel — Captain

FLAG GRADE OFFICERS

O-7 — Brigadier General — Rear Admiral (lower half)
O-8 — Major General — Rear Admiral (upper half)
O-9 — Lieutenant General — Vice Admiral
O-10 — General — Admiral

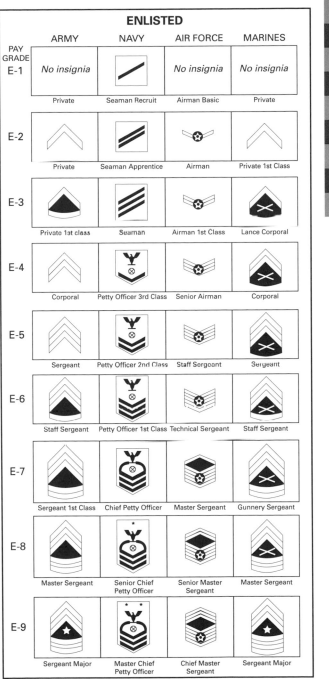

ENLISTED

PAY GRADE	ARMY	NAVY	AIR FORCE	MARINES
E-1	*No insignia* Private	Seaman Recruit	*No insignia* Airman Basic	*No insignia* Private
E-2	Private	Seaman Apprentice	Airman	Private 1st Class
E-3	Private 1st class	Seaman	Airman 1st Class	Lance Corporal
E-4	Corporal	Petty Officer 3rd Class	Senior Airman	Corporal
E-5	Sergeant	Petty Officer 2nd Class	Staff Sergeant	Sergeant
E-6	Staff Sergeant	Petty Officer 1st Class	Technical Sergeant	Staff Sergeant
E-7	Sergeant 1st Class	Chief Petty Officer	Master Sergeant	Gunnery Sergeant
E-8	Master Sergeant	Senior Chief Petty Officer	Senior Master Sergeant	Master Sergeant
E-9	Sergeant Major	Master Chief Petty Officer	Chief Master Sergeant	Sergeant Major

third person, often refer to a rank using the pay grade designation, such as "sergeant E-5," particularly at the NCO level. However, one should not address an individual by pay grade. This is primarily done to distinguish the various grades of sergeant in the Army and the Air Force and of petty officers in the Navy. Because most Army and Air Force sergeants below the grade of E-9, regardless of their rank, are addressed as "sergeant," this practice provides a way to instantly determine the seniority of the individual, an ability that is especially handy when dealing with the most junior-ranking sergeant. For instance, if one knows that a sergeant is an E-5, one instantly knows his or her status and seniority. Likewise, lieutenant colonels and colonels are identified as O-5 and O-6, respectively, because it is acceptable for both officers to respond to and describe themselves as "colonel" in everyday, informal conversation.

The Navy has a singular rank structure for commissioned officers. Some naval rank titles—such as admiral, for instance—are found only in the Navy, and some other Navy titles identify officers who are actually senior to officers in the other services who have the same title. For example, a lieutenant in the Navy is an officer in pay grade O-3, whereas in the Army, pay grade O-3 identifies a captain. However, in the Navy, a captain is an officer in pay grade O-6. The Navy no longer maintains a rank of commodore, but the term has survived as a title. Modern-day commodores are senior captains in command of groups of ships. One other nuance to the use of U.S. Navy rank is the term "captain," which is not only a rank, but is used to address the commanding officer of any ship regardless of rank.

As mentioned earlier, warrant officers in the Army and the Marines hold one of five pay grades. The most junior warrant officers are known simply as "warrant officer" (WO) and hold the pay grade of 1 (and thus are referred to as WO1); all succeeding grades of warrant officers carry the title of "chief warrant officer" and have a pay grade of between 2 and 5 (CWO2, 3, 4, or 5). Warrant officers are referred to as "Mr." or "Ms.," although once promoted to CWO2, they are typically referred to informally as "chief." In the Marines and the Navy, warrant officers are formally addressed as "sir" or "ma'am" by subordinate enlisted personnel.

All officers, commissioned and warrant, outrank all enlisted personnel. Almost invariably, officers are college graduates either from a civilian college or from one of the service academies. Many civilian colleges offer the **Reserve Officer Training Corps (ROTC)** program for students who are interested in entering the military as officers. The Army, Navy, and Air Force have academies to which qualified high school seniors may apply and compete for congressional or presidential appointments. Each of the service academies also has a preparatory school that helps selected enlisted personnel compete for an appointment. Like many nations, the United States has competitive programs through which enlisted personnel may be trained as officers. The Army has its **Officer Candidate School (OCS)**, to which appropriately qualified enlisted soldiers may be recommended by their commander. In addition, enlisted soldiers at the expiration of their enlistment may enroll in the ROTC program at a civilian college, and on completion of their degree program may be commissioned as officers.

THE ROLE OF THE RESERVE AND NATIONAL GUARD

The reserve component of the U.S. armed forces is made up of seven elements listed below.

Each of the services has a federal reserve force: **U.S. Army Reserve (USAR), U.S. Marine Forces Reserve (USMARFORRES), U.S. Navy Reserve Force (USNRF),**

MILITARY

U.S. Air Force Reserve (USAFR), and **U.S. Coast Guard Reserve (USCGR)**. These forces consist of trained units and individuals that can be called upon to provide the nation with the resources needed to deploy overseas, sustain combat forces, and conduct operations during wartime, contingencies, and peace.

The National Guard is the organized militia reserved to the states by the Constitution of the United States. The National Guard consists of the **U.S. Army National Guard (ARNG)** and the **Air National Guard (ANG)**. In peacetime, the National Guard is commanded by the governor of each state or territory and provides the first military response within states during emergencies. Most Reserve and National Guard forces train one weekend a month and two weeks in the summer. Once the force is mobilized, a period of training is required to ready it for deployment. In general, the larger the unit, the more time is required.

The president can federalize National Guard units to deal with domestic disturbances, natural disasters such as Hurricane Katrina, or for service abroad. When federalized, National Guard units are subordinate to the combatant commander of the theater in which they operate. National Guard units have fought in all the nation's wars and have served with distinction in peace operations in the Balkans. They are also serving in Iraq and Afghanistan.

As the operations tempo of National Guard and Reserve units has increased since September 11, 2001, the distinction between the active and reserve components of the U.S. military is becoming blurred. A significant number of combat support forces, such as transportation, medical, logistics, civil affairs, and military police, are in the Reserves rather than the active force. The National Guard and the Reserves have expertise in civil affairs, engineering, policing, and medicine, which makes them especially valuable in stability operations. The Defense Department is working to ensure that National Guard and Reserve personnel are fairly treated in terms of the amount of time between calls for national service.

MILITARY

Military Culture

THE MILITARY is a microcosm of the wider society. But, in certain respects, the military stands somewhat apart from the rest of society. Certainly there is a distance, if not a divide, between military personnel and civilians in terms of how they view the world in general and how they view their jobs. In part, this distinctive outlook is a reflection of the special nature of the military as an institution—of the specific tasks it is expected to accomplish and the manner in which it organizes itself to accomplish them. In part, it reflects a deep-seated set of convictions about how the world works and a set of core values about how people ought to behave.

Here, the aim is to sketch the outlines of what might be called "military thinking" and "military culture." Civilians who work with or alongside the military need to be able to recognize the instincts, characteristics, ideas, and values that drive the military.

Self-Awareness of the Military's Unique Role

Members of the military see themselves as different from civilians. As a generalization, military personnel have an almost reverent appreciation for order and precision. To the military, many civilians lack appreciation for those things the military, out of necessity, holds inviolate. This assumption leads some members of the military to look skeptically at the civilian community, particularly in stressful, unpredictable situations such as a rise in stability operations. To some people in the military, civilians seem to lack an understanding of, and an appreciation for, such key values as predictability, planning, and precision—values that are critical to the accomplishment of a military mission. However, as military experience in stability operations has grown, and as the armed forces have made greater efforts to train their personnel for stability operations, military cooperation with NGOs and other civilian-led agencies has improved.

There are excellent reasons why military personnel have such a strong self-identity. As a purely practical matter, military personnel are considered always to be on duty. They tend not to punch time cards or watch clocks; they are subject to recall from their homes at any time of the day or night should the need arise. Indeed, in times of emergency, all retired officers and enlisted personnel are subject to recall to active duty—an option that, although rarely exercised, is particularly likely to affect retired military personnel with highly specialized training. Military personnel forfeit certain rights that civilians take for granted; for example, U.S. military personnel must submit to regular, random drug testing and testing for HIV and be immunized against anthrax. This background is not unique to the U.S. military; militaries around the world recognize that to maintain the kind of discipline required to fight and win wars, certain freedoms must be sacrificed in the name of readiness. This is part of the military lifestyle and is part of what makes the military a profession.

A more profound reason for the military's sense of self-awareness is the unique role accorded the military. The primary function of the military is to fight and win its nation's wars, protecting national interests so that the citizens of that nation can enjoy peace and prosperity. This means that members of the armed forces can be placed in harm's way—in situations where the potential for killing and being killed is very real. Stability operations can be perilous undertakings, and, like the staffs of IOs, NGOs, and government agencies, military personnel may run significant risks as they perform their jobs. They accept that should their nation require it, they may be asked to make the ultimate sacrifice. To make such a commitment, military personnel must believe in what they are doing and in the country that is asking them to do it; thus, they must have a deeply ingrained sense of patriotism.

Worst-Case Thinking and the Use of Force

Largely because of the potential for catastrophic damage and widespread death caused by the lethality of modern warfare, military leaders hope for the best but plan for the worst. Militaries around the world go to great lengths to study warfare and assess potential enemies, trying to anticipate every eventuality so that, should the worst-case scenario arise, the objectives established by their nation can still be met at minimal cost. Within the U.S. military, this inclination to prepare for the worst is coupled with the belief that the application of overwhelming strength is the best way to accomplish the mission. Most military leaders around the world share this attitude. In warfare, more is usually better. However, there is a new appreciation among many officers that overwhelming force can also work against the military's interests in countering insurgencies or conducting stability operations.

Worst-case thinking is no less applicable to stability operations than it is to combat operations. The spectrum of stability operations is very broad, extending from humanitarian relief to peacekeeping to peace enforcement to combat operations, with a wide variety of missions in between. Worst-case thinking allows the unique characteristics and pitfalls of each situation to be factored into planning, thus enhancing not only the prospects for success of the mission but also the level of protection provided to the participating troops. This approach is especially valuable in light of the fact that the complexion of a stability operation can change quickly, often with little or no warning. As anyone who has participated in a stability operation knows only too well, in situations where religious, socioeconomic, or political divisions are long-standing, animosities often run very deep, and violence can erupt at a moment's notice. Belligerent parties may not only attack each other but also target outsiders, be they civilians or soldiers. A show of strength can help defuse tense situations and contribute to a more peaceful and stable environment—though it can also tempt extremists to test the resolve of the intervening force or to create conditions that discredit the force's presence.

Planning, Teamwork, and Predictability

When military forces are not fighting, they are planning and training for fighting. Just as athletes spend more time training than competing, armed forces spend more time training for warfare than conducting it. Planning and training for stability operations are as unique as the operations themselves but require the same thoroughness that the military applies to planning for war. The complexity of planning, particularly for deployment overseas, requires meticulous attention to detail. Extensive use is made of checklists to ensure that all elements deemed necessary for the success of the mission are available. The checklists themselves do not provide all the answers. Rather, they help the military

MILITARY

avoid obvious mistakes and save time in planning and preparation.

Planning of this kind achieves several things, some of which are intangible. First, troops designated to be involved in such an uncertain endeavor as a stability operation need to be assured that their needs are going to be met. Such assurance—gained from specific mission briefings by the leaders to the lower ranks—gives the troops confidence in the plan and in their leadership. If the plan is sufficiently detailed, the troops will more easily accept it and will be more likely to execute it effectively. Second, careful planning helps to create a sense of predictability in the accomplishment of a mission. Troops are much more likely to execute the plan successfully if they know the commander's intent and what will happen over time.

Teamwork is a key aspect of military organization and planning from both an individual and an organizational perspective. Every unit regardless of its size is part of a team and depends on all the other elements of that team. If the planning and training of the entire team are demanding yet realistic, each part of the team will be better able to predict the actions of the other parts. The ability to predict individual and team behavior becomes critical in situations of great stress and fatigue; this is why military units train as realistically as possible, so that they can simulate the stress and fatigue likely to be encountered in a real situation.

The military places a very high value on time—hence the emphasis on precision and punctuality, on careful planning and predictability. Intensive training and frequent deployments make time an extremely precious commodity for military personnel, especially the nearly 50 percent who are married and have children. It is important for each soldier to be able to tell his or her family with reasonable accuracy when he or she will be home. Many U.S. military leaders go to great lengths—and insist that their immediate subordinates take equal pains—to ensure that training schedules are adhered to and that the soldiers can predict with considerable certainty when they will be home. Of course, circumstances may intervene and upset these schedules, and soldiers understand that predictability sometimes cannot be maintained to the extent that the leadership would prefer.

Flexibility and Adaptability

Given the emphasis on planning and predictability, it may seem paradoxical that the military also puts a high value on flexibility and adaptability. In fact, the latter qualities are a necessary complement to the former in an institution that is fundamentally mission-oriented.

The U.S. military is notorious for frequently moving personnel from one job to another and from one geographic location to another. An individual may be moved to a new location as often as every two years, and at each location that individual may change jobs two or three times. Conventional wisdom might suggest that this practice would cause a breakdown in continuity within units or organizations and foster an overreliance on written doctrine among personnel who are not given the time to learn their job thoroughly or the opportunity to innovate. This may be true in some cases, but in most cases frequent movement results in an extremely well-developed sense of flexibility as well as the ability to adapt quickly and thoroughly to new circumstances. Such adaptability more than makes up for any rigid adherence to doctrine caused by lack of experience or continuity.

Compared with many civilian institutions, military units tend to have a short-term perspective on goals and objectives. Changes in leadership often result in changes in philosophy and direction. To plan for any period beyond two years (the typical period during which one individual is in command of a unit) is difficult.

The military's involvement in any operation, including complex contingency operations, is typically emergency in nature. For example, in humanitarian relief operations, military elements are sent because they are able to act quickly and efficiently, and because they may have equipment and capabilities (for instance, rapid water purification, mobile medical facilities, or aerial delivery capability) ideally suited to the needs of the local population. In stability operations, the military has a more political orientation. The armed forces are sent to intervene because diplomacy and negotiation have failed; because a negotiated agreement requires monitoring; or because the belligerents, not trusting one another to abide by a cease-fire or to implement a settlement, have asked for foreign intervention. Once the crisis is over, whether there has been fighting or not, the military is keen to exit and let the diplomats and the politicians resume their work. Among the many reasons the military wants to see a swift conclusion to the mission is a desire to sharpen combat skills that may have been blunted by participation in the stability operation. In all types of stability operations, the military sees its role as stabilizing the situation until appropriate civilian agencies can complete the relief effort or until the peacekeeping effort can be handed over to local authorities. Ultimately, the president decides in concert with coalition or alliance partners when the U.S. military enters and exits a stability operation.

Cohesion and Leadership

Unit cohesion at all levels, from squad to corps, is extremely important to the success of any military operation and is absolutely critical in the potentially volatile and dangerous circumstances characteristic of some stability operations. Military leaders and commanders work hard to develop cohesion in their units by focusing most of their energies on tough, realistic training—and instilling the doctrine (contained in numerous field manuals, training circulars, and regulations) that guides that training. Shared hardship tends to bring people closer together. But there is more to building cohesion than training. Cohesion is also built on the individual soldier's identification with the unit as a social and professional entity. Setting goals for the unit, offering opportunities for its members to bond through athletic competition within the unit or in conjunction with other units, and establishing family support groups that take care of the families of unit members when the need arises (for instance, when the unit is deployed) are measures that contribute to building cohesion in a unit. Leaders who realize the unit consists not only of soldiers, sailors, marines, or airmen, but also of their families, normally have cohesive units.

The military devotes a great deal of time and effort to training leaders. Many civilians misconceive the nature of leadership within the military. They assume that military leaders exercise absolute power over their subordinates, who will do exactly what they are told unquestioningly. To be sure, all members of the military are subject to regimentation. Military regulations and military culture do demand a high degree of uniformity and courtesy, especially in interactions between different ranks. But today's all-volunteer force is better educated and comes from a society that is much more informed than ever before. Soldiers, sailors, airmen, and marines all are prone to question the directions they receive. They understand that they have sworn in their enlistment to obey the officers appointed over them, but they still reserve the right to ask why something has to be done. This is not insubordination. Soldiers who understand the *why* of the mission are is in the best possible position to adjust the *how* to support that *why*. Good military leaders understand this fact and use it to their advantage, briefing their troops on the mission they are about to undertake and on the situation they are about to enter. Keeping information flowing between the leader and the led means that many of the reasonable questions that the lower ranks may have are answered before they are asked. In this way, soldiers are more likely to take ownership of the job at hand and accomplish it more efficiently. Of course, there may be no time for explanation or debate, and in such circumstances prompt and unquestioning obedience is required.

Rank is an integral part of military leadership. The visible signs of rank give the wearer instant credibility as a leader and decision maker and confer both authority and responsibility on the officer or NCO. The clarity of the military chain of command allows military personnel to easily identify their decision makers.

Military personnel may sometimes erroneously assume that the organizational principles that pertain to their world also guide civilian organizations. In general, of course, civilian organizations have looser management structures and do not have the same requirement to speak with one voice. This clash of military and civilian cultures can lead to confusion about what has actually been agreed to and how it will be implemented. Parties to a conflict may try to exploit such confusion by playing off the military and civilian components of an operation against each other.

A major aspect of military leadership, central to accomplishing the mission on the ground, is communication of intent by the commander. Soldiers can execute their mission efficiently only if they understand the leader's intent, which is the statement of how the commander envisions the mission being accomplished and how the situation should look after the job is complete.

Communication of intent is particularly important in stability operations, which are often conducted by two or more nations. A force commander is designated as such either by an agreement of the nations involved or by the United Nations. The force commander has operational control, but not command, over the multinational force; in other words, the force commander can maneuver the elements of this force regardless of their nationality, but the units that compose the force remain under the direct command of their own officers and can appeal any decision by the force commander to their own national government. Most nations will not permit their forces to be commanded by a foreign nation—that is, to be taken out of the nation's chain of command. In this sense, in multinational stability operations, there can be no unity of command, which is a fundamental principle within the U.S. military. In such operations, this principle is necessarily modified to obtain the best practical alternative: unity of effort.

The force commander must ensure that all contributing nations understand the commander's intent, take ownership of the mission, and know how the force commander intends to accomplish that mission and to use each nation's contingent. If the commander fails to do so, the coalition of nations contributing peacekeeping troops will likely begin to fray, and the success of the mission will be jeopardized.

The Challenges of Stability Operations

FORMER UN secretary-general Dag Hammarskjöld once remarked that "peacekeeping is not a job for soldiers, but only soldiers can do it." The experience of the past fifty years has largely borne out the wisdom of this observation. Although military personnel are trained and organized primarily to conduct combat operations, that same training and organization give them a unique capability to undertake many of the functions involved in a peace operation—or, indeed, any other kind of stability operation. Within the fluid, unpredictable context of a country that is teetering on the brink of chaos or struggling to return to peace and stability, the military possesses invaluable resources. For instance, the military is adept at fielding well-disciplined, cohesive, and flexible units able to shift operational gears smoothly and quickly, moving from humanitarian support to peacekeeping, to peace enforcement, to war, if necessary. Likewise, the military (particularly as demonstrated by the United States and its NATO allies) possesses the planning and logistical capability to develop and execute swift, large-scale operations to support elections, distribute food and humanitarian relief items, build and repair infrastructure, assist with refugee relocation, and conduct a host of other operations that contribute to the restoration or development of a stable environment and sustainable peace.

Yet, while the military has unparalleled capabilities to accomplish some of the most difficult tasks involved in stability operations, those operations also present the military with significant challenges—and a significant diversion from its primary purpose and mission. Here we briefly review three of these challenges: a change in paradigm, rules of engagement, and interoperability and civil–military coordination.

Paradigm Shift

The U.S. military prefers to conduct missions from a position of overwhelming strength. However, within the context of a stability operation, strength is not always a deterrent. Regardless of the amount of strength shown, one or more of the belligerents may choose to test the resolve of the military either by confronting each other or by directly challenging the stability force. In fact, the stronger the intervening forces, the more likely it is that belligerents will try to provoke an incident that will further their cause, or at least heighten their profile, in the eyes of the international community. If the stability force responds too strongly to such provocation, the credibility of the intervention will be damaged or destroyed. Conversely, if the military does not respond or responds with less force than necessary, not only will its credibility suffer, but the military and other participants may find themselves facing increasingly audacious attacks in the future.

Confrontational situations present military personnel with a dilemma for which their training and experience may have not prepared them. Combat troops are trained to close with and destroy an enemy. Yet, in a stability operation, they find themselves responsible for maintaining a peaceful environment, possibly without the use of force—

an environment, morever, that one or more belligerents often seem determined to destroy. This situation can put combat troops in an untenable situation. In short, stability operations represent a paradigm shift for the military that requires different rules and specialized training.

Rules of Engagement

Because of the need for discipline, the military operates under very strict rules. For U.S. troops participating in UN-authorized operations, these rules are gleaned not only from U.S. law and U.S. military regulations but also from host country law and the relevant UN mandate. In stability operations, the most important rules are those that govern when the military uses force. These are known as **rules of engagement** (ROE).

The political sensitivities associated with stability operations make the derivation and application of the rules critical to the success of the entire endeavor. In stability operations such as peace or humanitarian relief operations, where it may be difficult to distinguish friend from foe and where political sensitivities are always acute, ROE are specifically tailored to ensure that the neutrality or impartiality of the military is maintained. Every member of a military force involved in the stability operation must understand and observe the ROE.

As a practical matter, ROE perform three functions: they provide guidance from the national level to deployed units on the use of force; they act as a control mechanism for the transition from peacetime to combat operations; and they provide a mechanism to facilitate planning. ROE are in a very real sense the fusion of the mission requirements; national policy goals; and the rule of law as defined by the host country, by the countries of the troops involved, and/or by the United Nations in terms of how force is applied in stability operations.

Politically, ROE ensure that national policy and objectives are reflected in the action of commanders in the field—something that is particularly valuable when communication with higher authority is not possible. For example, ROE limit the number and types of targets that may be engaged, as well as the weapons systems that may be used to engage authorized targets. Among other things, this limitation can help prevent both the escalation of the conflict and the creation of an impression of political bias on the part of the intervening forces toward one or another of the belligerent parties.

Legally, ROE define the boundaries of a commander's action consistent with the applicable domestic and international law. In fact, ROE often impose greater restrictions on a commander than does the law itself.

From a military perspective, ROE provide parameters within which a force commander must operate to accomplish the mission. For example, ROE ensure that actions taken by the military force do not trigger an escalation of tensions by giving one or another belligerent an excuse to violate an agreement or a cease-fire. Generally, the initial ROE for stability operations simply allow for the protection of life and/or property. As the situation on the ground becomes either more violent and chaotic or more stable and peaceful, the ROE are adjusted accordingly.

ROE are unclassified to the maximum extent possible to ensure adequate coordination with others present in a commander's area of operations. However, some ROE are classified, or there may be both classified and unclassified versions. This precaution limits the ability of the adversary to gain insight into what limitations are placed on the use of force. Such insights might assist spoilers in gaining an advantage.

Even with the most thorough ROE, the soldier on the ground will inevitably be called upon to exercise discretion in determining whether the parameters of the ROE apply to the situation at hand, and if the use of force is warranted. Unfortunately, the decision on the use of force is often made in a stressful situation under an extreme time constraint. Consequently, all soldiers must understand the intent and limitations mandated by the ROE. Conversely, commanders must understand that overly restrictive ROE based on political considerations can be disastrous. The bombing of the U.S. Marine barracks in Lebanon in 1983 was a stark example of the latter case. The ROE were so restrictive that the guard on duty was unable to protect himself or the barracks. More than 250 people were killed as a result. Above all, then, the politicians, lawyers, and commanders who develop ROE must be cognizant of the need to balance the realities of the political situation and legitimate self-defense in any given operation. The military has developed doctrinal material to help it achieve this balance. As a final thought on ROE, the U.S. military will always retain the right to use force for self-defense. This is not always true of other nations or forces under the control of the United Nations.

Interoperability and Civil–Military Coordination

Stability operations involve troops from several countries. In some instances, such as NATO operations in Afghanistan, the troop-contributing nations may share similar organizations and training. However, in UN operations, troops may come from very dissimilar countries. This fact presents significant problems of interoperability—that is, the melding or synchronization of operations among the various national forces. Not only may the troop-contributing nations differ politically and culturally, but their militaries will inevitably differ in such matters as leadership styles, management techniques, attitudes toward the media, customs and traditions, and the off-duty behavior of their personnel. All of these differences affect how these forces interact with one another and how they operate in the field.

Obviously, not all militaries have similar or even compatible weapons, communications, or supplies. Even alliances have differences in equipment, although many alliances, such as NATO, work hard at interoperability, both in weapons and communications.

Problems of interoperability can be exacerbated when the military works alongside civilian organizations. Military personnel have been trained to function as a team, to rely on one another, and to be able to predict, with relative certainty, what each member of the team will do. Soldiers find it difficult to rely on and predict the actions of civilian organizations with which they are unfamiliar.

One of the best mechanisms for overcoming this unfamiliarity and establishing a basis for effective interaction and coordination is a **civil–military operations center** (**CMOC**). In stability operations, the CMOC serves as a coordination hub for the NGOs, IOs, other government agencies, the host nation government, and the military. For instance, through the CMOC, NGOs can request assistance from military units operating in the same area. In turn, the military can learn where the NGOs are working and can provide security for their activities as well as coordinate support for the local population. NGOs may also offer information regarding the history of belligerent parties, the nature of the public mood, and other matters that may affect the conduct of operations.

In more specific terms, a CMOC helps coordinate IOs, NGOs, and U.S. government agencies within a theater of operations in which the Department of Defense has leadership. In instances where the Department of State or other organizations share responsibility, a CMOC coordinates military operations in support of the lead agency. The staff of a CMOC is composed largely of civil affairs specialists and may be augmented by liaison officers for the Department of Defense and other U.S. government agencies, such as the Department of State and USAID.

In joint operations, the CMOC is the nerve center for the joint force commander. The CMOC may be a sub-element of a **joint civil military operations task force (JCMOTF)** and can be composed of representatives from all participating services. However, individual Army units at and above the brigade level normally have the capability to establish a CMOC in their area of operations. Regardless of the level at which a CMOC is organized, its functions are the same, even though it is flexible in terms of size and composition.

A CMOC may include or be augmented by military and/or civilian representatives of any organization that the commander considers necessary for effective civil–military operations within his or her area of responsibility. A CMOC can be managed in a variety of ways: by the U.S. commander and the multinational forces commander, by the U.S. commander alone, or by the U.S. commander and the head of the civilian agency engaged in the contingency operation. Military personnel, primarily from the Army and the Marines, staff the CMOC. In the U.S. Army these personnel are CA specialists, trained in administration and civil–military operations.

The increasingly complex and transnational nature of military involvement in stability operations has resulted in a corresponding increase in multinational or coalition responses to crisis. Despite the potential for interoperability problems resulting from language and intercultural communication issues, coalition militaries bring a wide range of skills, methodologies, and capabilities to the crisis. Contributing nations may impose restrictions or "caveats" on functions that their forces are allowed to perform. Caveats limit the ability of the military to perform effectively and efficiently. Interoperability, between the military and IOs and NGOs when desirable and possible, is subject to many of the same issues as in coalition military operations. The IO/NGO community also includes an extremely broad and diverse set of cultures, capabilities, and operational mandates that determine how it will operate.

The key to good coordination is knowing the right questions to ask. The following general questions should be asked of military personnel:

- What is your purpose for being here?
- What resources does your unit have?
- What are your rules of engagement?

Likewise, civilian organizations should be prepared to answer questions that will help the military help them to accomplish their goals and objectives

More often than not, the IO/NGO community will have an existing presence within an area affected by disaster or conflict. In conflict or disaster-response scenarios, the injection of military forces into an environment where relationships and support structures are in place among the IO/NGO community, the host government, and the affected population has the potential to affect the delivery of critical services. If the military does not have a thorough understanding of the roles played by the IO/NGO community in such scenarios, it may duplicate efforts or inadvertently disrupt IO/NGO efforts to maintain vital services. To reduce the potential for duplication of effort between the military, the host nation, and the IO/NGO community, military commanders attempt to acquire visibility of all aspects of the civil environment through the civil information management (CIM) function inherent in U.S.

CMOC operations. This capability helps military leaders at various levels understand and evaluate the complex social, cultural, and civil infrastructure dimensions of their place within the assigned area.

The combination of conflict and IO/NGO traditions of impartiality—a critical element of their mandates and of their established relationships within the affected country—often may result in situations where interoperability is undesirable or not possible. In such cases, the interaction between the military and the IO/NGO community may either be nonexistent or limited to an information exchange that stands well short of actual coordination. In some cases, the IO/NGO interest in communicating with the military may be limited to obtaining information regarding military assessments of the security of the environment. This information may then be combined with their own organization's information, or information shared internally within the IO/NGO community, so that each organization can establish its operational posture.

Other Coordination Mechanisms

In the case of a natural disaster, the military and the IO/NGO community have a common priority: humanitarian assistance and disaster recovery. Military assistance is likely to focus on filling gaps in the resources and capabilities the IO/NGO community needs to provide an effective response. This requires coordination between the military and the IO/NGO communities to provide assessments, determine priorities, and deconflict resource allocations.

In a post-conflict environment, a key IO/NGO concern is likely to be the reestablishment of security so that the IO/NGO community may continue its activities. Conflict can dramatically affect the nature of the relationship between the IO/NGO community and the military. The traditions of impartiality generally prevalent in the IO/NGO community, and necessary to perform their mandates, may result in hesitation to coordinate too closely with the militaries of either belligerent or even of the stability force.

In either case, a holistic comprehension of the operational environment requires the military commander to understand both the civilian and military aspects that impact the force's assigned area. One resource available to help the commander obtain a perspective of the civilian factors is participation in a variety of civil–military coordination mechanisms. These mechanisms may go by a variety of names depending on the particular scenario and the level at which they are established, but they all perform essentially the same function, that is, to provide a physical, doctrinal touchpoint for day-to-day information exchange and coordination between the military, the IO/NGO community, and the interested civil populace.

Civil-military mechanisms include a variety of coordination/operations centers, such as **Humanitarian Assistance Coordination Center (HACC), Humanitarian Operations Center (HOC)**, and **Coalition Humanitarian Liaison Center (CHLC)**. All are designed to provide a coordination point between the military commander and the various civilian actors. The military commander may use these organizations as a platform to help him or her fully understand and apply the complex civilian dimensions of the environment in which he or she is operating. This information may include considerations of a diverse set of factors related to legal, cultural, societal, ethnic, and critical infrastructure issues.

A combatant commander may establish an HACC within the theater to assist with early interagency coordination and planning and to provide a link between the command and other government and non-governmental agencies participating in the operation at the theater strategic level.

The combatant commander may also organize and deploy a **humanitarian assistance survey team (HAST)** to acquire information required for planning, such as an assessment of conditions and requirements for humanitarian assistance force structure. The humanitarian operations center, normally established by the United Nations or a relief agency, coordinates the overall relief strategy; identifies logistic requirements for NGOs, the United Nations, and IOs; and identifies, prioritizes, and submits requests for military support to a JTF through a CMOC in cases where a CMOC has been established. In addition, CMOCs may be established at various local or regional levels within the area to provide adequate coverage for the mission.

Whenever possible and appropriate, the military will encourage civilian humanitarian/disaster relief professionals and their organizations to mutually plan, conduct, and participate in or cooperate with civil–military operations. Sharing pertinent information, particularly that related to security, will enhance communication between the military and humanitarian organizations. It should be recognized that, by and large, the humanitarian organizations will be in the operational area long before the military arrives and long after the military departs. The military can learn from these organizations and, where appropriate, either assist in their programs, or at the least be informed of their existence to avoid duplicative civil–military operations.

The hierarchical structures of the military and IOs/NGOs are different, and this is especially apparent in the area of decision making. The military values planning, preparation, and timely staffing to provide a foundation for its leadership to make decisions. IO/NGO hierarchies often involve boards of directors and operating mandates where operational-level decision making may also be delegated and implemented at field level. Unlike in the military, however, field-level decisions are frequently made by consensus. Accordingly, the military should maintain flexibility in its dealing with IOs/NGOs and appreciate that different structures and corporate cultures are at work.

Whether the coordination mechanism involves established structures, such as CMOC-type organizations, or personal relationships, the military should understand and appreciate that NGOs, IOs, and other humanitarian players might possess information that could be relevant to civil–military operations, but they may be unable to divulge that information to the military when doing so will jeopardize their organization's charter of impartiality and independence. The appearance of partiality or lack of independence can adversely affect these organizations' ability to continue working in the operational area.

Phasing

Arranging operations is an element of planning operations, and phasing is a key aspect of this element. An operation is normally divided into phases to logically organize activities; a phase is defined as a definitive stage of an operation or campaign during which a large portion of the forces and capabilities are involved in similar or mutually supporting activities for a common purpose. Phases are distinct in time, space, and/or purpose from one another but represent a natural subdivision of the campaign. The actual phases will vary with the operation. During planning, a commander establishes conditions, objectives, or events for transitioning from one phase to another and plans sequels and branches for potential contingencies. Phases are designed to be conducted sequentially, but some activities from a phase may continue into subsequent phases. The commander will determine the number of actual phases used in an operation.

Risk Management and Force Protection

Risk management is the process of identifying, assessing, and controlling risks arising from operational factors and making decisions that balance risks with mission benefits in order to conserve combat power and resources. Risk decisions are commanders' business.

Force protection encompasses actions taken to prevent or mitigate hostile actions against personnel, resources, facilities, and critical information. These actions conserve a military unit's fighting potential so it can be applied at the decisive time and place. Force protection incorporates both offensive and defensive measures to enable the effective employment of the force while degrading opportunities for the enemy.

Force protection measures relate directly to mission accomplishment. They should enhance consensus and assist in creating the conditions for other political, economic, and humanitarian peacebuilding activities to achieve the political objectives. In stability operations, force protection measures should be consistent with the risk assessment, but they should not be excessive. A level of force protection that exceeds the risk assessment may send a psychological signal to the population that they are still in a tense and uncertain environment. It may retard the return to normalcy and lead to conditions that will prevent the peace process from continuing. Additionally, it can limit the contact between the force and local population, reducing the force's ability to gather information and to mitigate tense situations through negotiations.

Commanders attempt to accomplish a mission with minimal loss of personnel, equipment, and supplies by integrating force protection considerations into all aspects of operational planning and execution. Units meet force protection challenges through the application of a variety of capabilities, including operational security measures, information security, situational understanding, tactical deception, health and morale, safety, and avoidance of fratricide.

In stability operations, operational measures for security include communications security, impartiality, defensive positions, checkpoints, personal awareness, physical security measures, coordination, and evacuation planning.

Precautions are taken to protect positions, headquarters, support facilities, and accommodations. Precautions may include obstacles and shelters. Units must also practice alert procedures and develop drills to rapidly occupy positions. Military forces may establish and maintain checkpoints. At a minimum, the area should be highly visible and defensible with an armed overwatch.

Security measures are dependent on the situation and may include a full range of active and passive measures, such as wearing body armor, patrolling, reconnaissance, and surveillance. Even during the same operation, different nations may apply different methods and levels of force protection measures. U.S. soldiers may wear full battle gear (including helmets and protective vests) and carry weapons, while soldiers from other nations' militaries may be seen without weapons and wearing soft caps. This difference reflects the commander's risk assessment, which is based on an evaluation of the danger within the area of operations, the message sent by the appearance of the troops, and the impact of casualties both nationally and internationally. The same is true of movement restrictions commanders place on soldiers during their off time. Hostage taking is an important tool of some adversaries, and the political impact varies by nation and that nation's contribution to the operation.

Contractors

Contractors have always accompanied our armed forces. Today's complex weapons and equipment systems, high operations tempo, and limited force structure require that deployed military forces be augmented by contractor support. As these trends continue, the future battlefield will require ever-increasing numbers of critically important contractor employees. Contracted support often includes traditional goods and services support, but may include interpreters, communications, infrastructure, and other non-logistic-related support. Whether it bridges gaps prior to the arrival of military support resources, when host nation support is not available, or augments existing support capabilities, contractor support is important for operations.

Contracts may be let by contracting officers serving under the direct contracting authority of U.S. military units or by contracting officers from support organizations, such as the United States Army Materiel Command (USAMC) and the U.S. Army Corps of Engineers (USACE). They may be prearranged contracts or contracts awarded during the contingency itself to support the mission and may include a mix of U.S. citizens, third country nationals, and local subcontractor employees. Contractor activities are managed through the responsible contracting organization, not the chain of command. Commanders do not have direct control over contractors or their employees. Only contractors manage, supervise, and give directions to their employees.

When contractor employees are deployed, the U.S. force commander will provide or make available force protection and support services commensurate with those provided to U.S. government civilian personnel and authorized by law. However, local contractors may not necessarily be provided the same force protection or support.

The presence of as many as 40,000 security contractors in Iraq has drawn attention to the increasing use of commercial security and military firms in peace and stability operations. Using mostly former military and law enforcement personnel, commercial security firms perform a number of security functions, including static guards, convoy escorts, VIP protection, and, in extreme situations, combat soldiers. So-called corporate warriors guard buildings and strategic infrastructure, such as oil pipelines; escort shipments of food, medicine, and relief supplies; protect the president of Afghanistan and other dignitaries; and secure cultural sites and isolated minorities in Kosovo. In extreme cases, commercial contractors have provided security for UN and NATO installations in combat environments. The United States has hired commercial security firms to train indigenous police and military forces.

Use of such firms is controversial because of the absence of operations standards, safeguards, and licensing requirements. Especially troubling are issues related to discipline and the use of armed force. With few rules in place, armed contract guards may fail to exercise restraint in the treatment of local citizens, including the indiscriminate use of deadly force. Cost is also a consideration, as commercial security and military firms often charge exorbitant rates for their services. Reputable firms have formed a trade association, the International Peace Operations Association (http://ipoaonline.org), to set industry guidelines and lobby on behalf of such companies. Clearly, commercial security is an established and growing aspect of peace, stability, and relief operations.

Funding

Several funding programs are available to support commanders' military and humanitarian requirements. Not all funding programs available for one operation are available for another, and different-level commanders have different pots of money. Each of these funding programs comes with different restrictions on how the monies will be used, and often commanders lack flexibility in how they can expend funds.

In Iraq and Afghanistan, the Commander's Emergency Response Program (CERP) was used to provide U.S. government funds directly to tactical unit commanders for the purpose of meeting emergency needs of local civilians. Battalion-level commanders could approve projects valued up to $100,000 on their own authority. Commanders at higher levels could approve projects costing more. Money was used to engage local contractors and workers to build or improve infrastructure, such as schools, clinics, roads, and public utilities. In the immediate aftermath of the Iraq intervention, the U.S. Army 101st Airborne Division spent $28 million in CERP funds on 3,600 projects in northern Iraq. The funds were used to improve local infrastructure, including refurbishing four hundred schools and employing thousands of workers.

Uniforms, Weapons, and Other Equipment

This section describes the types of uniforms, weapons, and other equipment likely to be worn or used by the U.S. military in peace or relief operations. The descriptions are neither detailed nor exhaustive, but they should help nonmilitary personnel learn to distinguish one rank or unit from another or a Bradley fighting vehicle from an armored personnel carrier.

Reading a Military Uniform

The easiest way to distinguish among members of the military is by their uniforms and insignia. Each service has a variety of distinctive uniforms for formal and informal occasions and for field and combat duties. In the field, where most of the contact among NGOs, IO government representatives, and the military occurs, military personnel typically wear either a camouflage uniform (often referred to as a battle dress uniform/army combat uniform (BDU/ACU) in areas where green vegetation is predominant or the desert camouflage uniform (DCU) worn in desert areas. The Marines wear a similar camouflage uniform known as utilities. The Marine utilities have a different camouflage pattern than the Army's BDU/DCU. The

Army is in the process of fielding a new field uniform called the Army camouflage uniform (ACU) whose pattern is more similar to the Marine utilities than the BDU/DCU. These field uniforms do not display any of the ribbons and awards that an individual has received but may reflect some of the individual's qualifications. It is often left up to the individual to decide which, if any, qualification badges are worn.

Each service requires, as a minimum, that every individual wear a name tag or a name tape and display his or her rank. In the Army, Marine Corps, and Navy, all rank insignia for enlisted personnel or officers are worn on the collar. In the Air Force, enlisted personnel wear the rank insignia on the sleeve of the field uniform. Officer rank insignia on field uniforms are typically subdued, with black representing silver and brown representing gold. All enlisted rank insignia are black. On more formal uniforms, officer rank insignia are worn on the shoulder epaulettes and enlisted rank insignia on the sleeve; these uniforms will also display ribbons and qualification badges.

A uniform can display more than just the name and rank of the wearer. Army officers through the rank of colonel wear distinctive insignia that indicate their branch or specialty. All Army personnel wear distinctive organizational patches on their sleeves; patches worn on the left sleeve designate the person's current unit of assignment, and patches worn on the right sleeve indicate with which unit, if any, the person served in past combat. Army personnel may also wear badges that indicate qualifications—such as explosive ordnance disposal and airborne—earned at specialized schools or tabs that indicate if they are qualified as Rangers or Special Forces. Naval personnel wear badges that indicate whether they are a submariner, a surface warfare expert, an aviator, or a member of the Navy special forces (known as SEALs, or Sea-Air-Land). Air Force, Army, Navy, and Marine aviators all wear wings. Air Force, Navy, and Marine pilots also wear squadron patches on their flight jackets.

The ribbons worn on a servicemember's more formal uniforms, but not on field uniforms, give a good indication of that person's level of proficiency and experience. Members of the U.S. armed forces wear ribbons to indicate combat service, valor, and outstanding achievement. Ribbons may also indicate membership in units that have been recognized for valor or meritorious achievement by the service, the president, or a foreign government. They may also indicate participation in UN and humanitarian relief operations. Most ribbons are worn on the left side of the chest, with the arrangement of awards and decorations dictated by service regulations.

Many military operations involve the participation of units from several nations. They may be operating under a UN mandate or under a mandate from a regional security organization such as NATO. Smaller units—up to the level of a battalion—operating on the ground are often from a single nation, although smaller multinational units have been featured in recent operations. Larger units and the staffs that control their activities, however, are almost always multinational.

Generally, the rank structure of foreign militaries is similar to that of the U.S. military, although the insignia used to designate rank may be very different. Usually the rank insignia consist of stripes, stars, or some other easily identifiable icon. Care must be taken in determining foreign militaries' rank according to icon; for instance, in some armies a star indicates the lowest-ranking officer, whereas in the U.S. military one star indicates the lowest-ranking flag officer, a brigadier general.

When serving in UN operations, soldiers routinely wear their national flag on the right sleeve to indicate their nationality. All soldiers participating in UN missions wear distinctive blue headgear (helmets, berets, or baseball-style caps) that displays the UN symbol of a world map flanked by olive branches. This headgear supplements the national uniform and is the only part of the uniform that is distinctive to the United Nations.

During military operations, it is standard for the vast majority of members of the armed forces to wear a uniform. However, there are circumstances based on operational considerations when members of the armed forces may not wear a uniform, in accordance with the laws of war.

Weapons

Military personnel engaged in stability operations need weapons not only to fulfill the terms of the mandate from the United Nations or regional security organization but also to protect themselves. To some extent, they can increase their security by building bunkers or using barbed wire and in placing a variety of obstacles to establish defensive perimeters around their facilities and positions. In addition, entry controls can be used to identify visitors and control the flow of traffic into military compounds. However, although all of these measures provide the perception of security, weapons provide the substance.

SMALL ARMS

The weapons most commonly carried in peace and relief operations are referred to as small arms. These are the personal weapons common to most soldiers: pistols (sometimes termed side arms because they are normally carried on the hip or on one side of the body), rifles, and light machine guns. The standard side arm of the U.S. military is the 9 mm Beretta pistol. The weapon most commonly carried by a U.S. soldier is the M16A2 rifle. Some soldiers may carry a shortened version of the rifle designated an M4 carbine.

Within a squad or platoon, these weapons are supplemented by the squad automatic weapon (SAW): the M240 machine gun, the MK19 automatic grenade launcher, and the .50 caliber machine gun, all of which are known as crew-served weapons because they require more than one person to operate them effectively. At company and battalion level, infantry and armored units will have mortars varying in size from 60 to 120 mm. Mortars can be vehicle mounted or man-portable and normally conduct indirect fire—that is, they are fired at an unseen target, with the aim adjusted by an observer.

TRACKED AND WHEELED VEHICLES

Above the level of the personal and crew-served weapons, weapons become **weapons systems**. Of high technical sophistication, these weapons systems are likely to be mobile —either self-propelled or towed. **Tanks** are large, tracked weapons systems that carry a large cannon, normally 90 to 120 mm in diameter. Tank units maneuver on their own, and tanks are designed to fight other tanks and exploit weaknesses in enemy fortifications or defenses. The most common tank in the U.S. military is the **M1A2 Abrams**, which is widely considered to be the most effective system of its kind in the world. The Abrams is equipped with extremely sophisticated systems, allowing the crew of four to acquire and consistently hit targets at extreme range in bad weather, at night, or on the move. The tank has a turbine engine that allows it to maneuver at high speeds (up to 35–40 mph while cruising, and up to 60 mph for short periods) and a stabilization system that allows accurate firing while moving over rough terrain. The Abrams carries radios and can enable crews to see through dark, rain, dust, and fog to some extent.

Self-propelled artillery pieces are somewhat similar in design to tanks—and often are mistaken for tanks—but have a very different purpose. Artillery is designed not to conduct direct attacks but to support attacks by infantry and armor (tanks) with indirect fire. Another tracked weapons system of the artillery family is the **multiple launch rocket system (MLRS)**. These rocket launchers have a very distinctive design that features a multiple-tube pod containing twelve rockets that can be launched separately or, more often, in groups. Towed artillery pieces are generally moved around the area of operations by trucks.

Other tracked vehicles found in U.S. units that participate in peace and relief operations are the **M2** and **M3 Bradley fighting vehicles**; the **M113 armored personnel carrier (APC)**, which has a number of variants that serve diverse functions; and the **M88A2 tracked recovery vehicle**.

The **Bradley** serves two purposes: the M2 version carries infantrymen into combat, provides considerable fire support, and has an antitank capability; the M3 model is used by scouts and by armored cavalry operating ahead of larger or armored formations. The difference between the two versions is nearly imperceptible to the untrained eye. Like the self-propelled artillery pieces, the Bradley resembles a tank in that it is armored, is tracked, and has a turret, but it has a small 25 mm main gun. It also has a small pod that serves as a launcher for antitank missiles.

The M113 APC and its variants are the most commonly employed tracked vehicles in stability operations throughout the world. The M113 has been exported by the U.S. military to many friendly armies, and the United Nations has also used the M113. Small and boxlike, the M113 APC can carry up to eleven fully armed combat soldiers. It has a mount for a .50 caliber machine gun (approximately 12.7 mm), but unlike the Bradley, it has no turret. Variants of the M113 APC include one that has antitank missile pods; one with an open deck to accommodate an 81 mm or 120 mm heavy mortar; and a command-and-control version—designated **M577**—with enhanced communications capability as well as a higher upper deck to accommodate map boards and associated command and control features. Members of the M113 family of vehicles also serve as armored ambulances, reconnaissance vehicles, and transport vehicles in combat situations as well as in stability operations.

The **M88A2** is a large and mechanically powerful tracked vehicle designed to recover and tow immobile tanks, Bradleys, or APCs. The M88A2 is somewhat larger than a tank but has no turret or obvious armament other than a mount for a .50 caliber machine gun.

The **amphibious assault vehicle (AAV)** is the current amphibious troop transport of the Marine Corps. The AAV is a fully tracked armored assault amphibious landing vehicle. The vehicle carries troops in water operations from ship to shore. It also carries troops to inland objectives after ashore. It can carry twenty-one troops and is armed with .50 caliber machine gun and a 40 mm automatic grenade launcher. It is boxlike in appearance and has a small turret.

In addition to these tracked vehicles, the military employs a wide variety of wheeled vehicles, ranging from light utility vehicles to large equipment transporters and combat vehicles.

The **Stryker** is the newest combat vehicle in the U.S. Army. It is an eight-wheel-drive vehicle, transportable in a C-17, C-5, or C-130 aircraft. The Stryker can maneuver in close and urban terrain, provide protection in open terrain, and transport infantry quickly to battlefield positions. Stryker variants include the **infantry carrier** and the **mobile gun system**. The basic infantry carrier provides armored protection for the crew of two and a nine-man infantry squad. It mounts either a .50 caliber machine gun, a 40 mm automatic grenade launcher, or a 7.62 mm machine gun. The **Stryker mobile gun system** consists of the basic vehicle with a turret armed with a 105 mm cannon and a .50 caliber machine gun. Initial production of the mobile gun system began in 2005.

The **light armored vehicle-25 (LAV-25)** is used by the Marine Corps. It is also an eight-wheeled vehicle with several variants. The LAV-25 has a crew of three, and the carrier version can hold six troops. This version is armed with a 25 mm automatic cannon and a 7.62 mm machine gun. Other variants include an antitank version with an antitank guided missile system and a mortar carrier. The LAV-25 is smaller but similar in appearance to a Stryker, and it first came into use by the Marines in the mid-1980s.

The most-used vehicle in the U.S. military is the **high-mobility, multipurpose wheeled vehicle (HMMWV)**. The **Humvee**, or **Hummer**, as it is commercially known, is probably the vehicle seen most often in stability operations. It is truly a multipurpose vehicle, serving as a transport, a tactical fighting or weapons platform, and an ambulance—and can operate in any type of weather on any type of terrain. It has several configurations and the capability to handle complicated communications arrays. The vehicle can mount several types of machine guns and antitank missile launchers. Versions used in Afghanistan and Iraq have armored protection and are referred to as up-armored Humvees.

Heavier vehicles include the **2^1/$_2$-ton** and **5-ton utility trucks**, which serve as troop transports and as medium-to-heavy lift platforms for transporting food, packaged fuel, and other humanitarian relief items. The trucks can tow artillery and several kinds of logistical support trailers (such as the 400-gallon water trailer). **Heavy equipment transporters (HETs)**, using lowboy trailers, are employed primarily to transport tanks over improved roads to save wear and tear on the tanks' tracks while protecting the road surface. HETs can also be used to haul supplies or other heavy equipment, such as bulldozers. **Heavy expanded**

mobility tactical trucks (HEMTTs) are found in almost all U.S. ground units, especially in mechanized formations. Able to be configured in a number of ways, they serve a variety of functions: as wreckers for heavy-wheeled vehicles, as fuel transporters, and as medium-lift vehicles.

MILITARY

AIRCRAFT

Most U.S. military aircraft (both fixed- and rotary-winged) have an alphanumeric designation that indicates their function. Although these designations are not painted on the aircraft, military personnel typically refer to aircraft according to these combinations of letters and numbers. The letter *A* designates attack aircraft; *B*, bomber; *C*, cargo; *E*, electronics; *F*, fighter; *H*, helicopter; *K*, tanker; *M*, special operations; and so forth. These combinations make up the nomenclature of the aircraft. These letters are sometimes used in combination to specify the aircraft capability or to indicate that it is a variant of the original design. For instance, EH-60 is the designation of a Blackhawk helicopter configured to conduct electronic surveillance and jamming, whereas UH-60 designates the utility-configured Blackhawk.

Several types of aircraft are either integral to U.S. ground units or fly consistently in support of them. Most of the aircraft in the former category are helicopters. All the U.S. armed forces tend to use the same two types of utility helicopters and their variants: the UH-1 and the UH-60. Their alphanumeric designations and nicknames can vary from service to service, but generally retain the specific *H* designation.

The oldest and best known of these single-rotor troop and equipment transporters is the **UH-1**, commonly known as the **Huey**. The UH-1 can lift up to eight combat-equipped troops and can serve as an aerial command, control, and communications platform. The **UH-60**, or **Blackhawk**, is a more recently fielded and more versatile utility helicopter designed to ultimately replace the Huey. It can carry up to 11 combat troops or 4-tons of cargo. Medium-to-heavy lift capability is supplied by the **CH-47 Chinook**, a double-rotor aircraft capable of carrying 33 combat-loaded troops or lifting up to 13 tons of cargo. The Marines have a smaller version of the CH-47 called the **CH-46 Sea Knight**, which can carry 14 troops or two tons of cargo. The Marines also have a heavy lift helicopter, known as the **CH-53 Sea Stallion**, which can carry 37 troops or 16 tons of cargo.

Two types of attack helicopters are designed exclusively to support ground combat troops in either an antitank or an antipersonnel role. The older of these is the **AH-1 Cobra**, which, like the Huey, dates from the Vietnam War. A modernized, twin-engine version called the **Super Cobra** is still used extensively by the Marine Corps. The Super Cobra has a distinctive narrow body design and carries machine guns and rocket pods. The more recent of the attack helicopters, the **AH-64 Apache**, is both more versatile and more lethal in its capability. Larger than the Cobra but somewhat similar in appearance, the Apache can operate in nearly any weather and at night. It has advanced optical systems to complement equally advanced fire control and target-acquisition systems. Its design supports its primary mission, which is to detect and destroy enemy armor using the infrared Hellfire antitank missile. The Apache also has a nose-mounted 30 mm cannon for ground support in combat situations. In stability operations, the Apache flies in support of utility helicopters, particularly where the situation on the ground is uncertain.

Among fixed-winged aircraft used in stability operations, transport aircraft predominate. Some combat aircraft, such as high-performance fighter-bombers and ground combat support aircraft, may also be present, if it is necessary to demonstrate resolve or stage a show of force.

Transport aircraft have a *C* designation. The **C-130**, known as the **Hercules**, is the most recognizable of this group of transport aircraft. It is used by many nations as an aerial lift workhorse. It is a versatile aircraft, capable of medium-to-heavy lift, but it is confined by a relatively short flying range (2,356 miles fully laden). The most attractive feature of the aircraft is its capability of operating on unimproved and short runways. The C-130 is also used for airborne operations. It can accommodate 90 combat troops, 64 fully loaded paratroopers, or 74 nonambulatory patients when configured as an air ambulance.

The **C-141 Starlifter** is the primary strategic lift aircraft in the U.S. inventory. The versatile and reliable C-141 can carry up to 200 combat troops, 155 paratroops, or 103 nonambulatory patients when configured as an air ambulance, or up to 68,725 pounds of cargo. It has nearly unlimited range because of its in-flight refueling capability. With its large payload capacity, the C-141 is well suited to support humanitarian assistance operations by bringing large quantities of supplies to marshalling areas, from which they can be distributed by C-130s or helicopters to areas in need.

The **C-5 Galaxy** resembles the C-141 in design but is much larger—it is indeed one of the largest aircraft in the world and certainly the largest in the U.S. inventory. It can carry outsized cargo over intercontinental distances, taking off and landing in relatively short distances.

The newest addition to the U.S. strategic airlift fleet is the **C-17 Globemaster**. The C-17 was designed to deploy large amounts of cargo and troops to hot spots around the world very quickly. It has less cargo capacity than the C-5 but costs less to build and is easier to maintain. Like the C-141, it has in-flight refueling capability and can transport troops, medical patients, or cargo, but unlike the C-141 it can land on airstrips only 3000 feet long and 90 feet wide.

Aerial refueling is conducted by the **KC-135 Stratotanker,** a modified version of a Boeing 707 commercial aircraft. Equipped with an aerial boom through which it pumps fuel, the KC-135 can refuel aircraft in flight. It has a range of 1,500 miles when fully loaded for in-flight refueling. When used as a cargo aircraft, it has a range of up to 11,015 miles, making it a good alternative to other strategic lift aircraft in an emergency.

Other Equipment

Much of the armed forces' equipment is analogous to equipment used by civilian organizations and can be extremely useful to the NGOs and IOs involved in peace operations. The military has tremendous lift capability—that is, the ability to transport supplies, personnel, and equipment quickly from one place to another. Various military units specialize in creating communications systems; providing medical supplies and expertise; or delivering such items as clothing, tents, blankets, food, water, and petroleum.

Although military regulations usually prohibit the use of military equipment by civilians, such equipment can be made available in support of actions and programs likely to foster stability within the theater of a stability operation. These programs, sometimes referred to generically as civic action programs, involve the military using its expertise and capabilities to improve conditions on the ground for the local population. In a country devastated by conflict, civic action programs can make a substantial contribution to efforts—usually undertaken once the belligerents have demonstrated a willingness to cease hostilities—to reestablish and rebuild infrastructure. Indeed, these programs can form part of the initial nation-building efforts undertaken by the United Nations. The situation on the ground and the status of the peace operation will drive the availability of equipment for civic action programs; in all

instances, the requirements of the military forces supporting the peace operation will take precedence.

Nonmilitary agencies and organizations can make specific requests for assistance directly either to local or
higher-level unit commanders or, more formally, through
the CMOC.

Table 4.4. Common Military Abbreviations and Acronyms

ACU	army camouflage uniform
AFFOR	Air Force forces (of a combatant command)
ANG	U.S. Air National Guard
AOR	area of responsibility
APC	armored personnel carrier
ARFOR	Army forces (of a combatant command)
ARG	amphibious ready group
ARNG	U.S. Army National Guard
BDU	battle dress uniform
C-cubed, or C3	command, control, and communications
CJCS	chairman, Joint Chiefs of Staff
CJTF	combined joint task force
CMC	commandant, Marine Corps
CMO	civil–military operations
CMOC	civil–military operations center
CNO	chief of naval operations
COCOM	combatant command authority
CS	combat support
CSA	chief of staff, Army
CSAF	chief of staff, Air Force
CSS	combat service support
CWO	chief warrant officer
DCU	desert camouflage uniform
HEMTT	heavy expanded mobility tactical truck
HET	heavy-equipment transporter
HMMWV	high-mobility, multipurpose wheeled vehicle, pronounced Hum vee
HQ	headquarters
JCMOTF	joint civil–military operations task force
JCS	Joint Chiefs of Staff

JFCOM	Joint Forces Command *(combatant command)*
JTF	joint task force
MAGTF	Marine air–ground task force
MARFOR	Marine forces *(of a combatant command)*
MEB	Marine expeditionary brigade, *pronounced* meb
MEF	Marine expeditionary force, *pronounced* meff
MEU	Marine expeditionary unit, *pronounced* mew
MLRS	multiple launch rocket system
MOOTW	Military Operations Other than War, *pronounced* moo-twa *(also called* OOTW*)*
NAVFOR	Naval forces *(of a combatant command)*
NCO	noncommissioned officer
NEO	noncombatant evacuation operation
NMS	national military strategy
NSC	National Security Council
NSS	national security strategy
OCS	Officer Candidate School
OOTW	Operations Other than War, *pronounced* oo-twa *(also called* MOOTW*)*
OPCON	operational control
ROE	rules of engagement
ROTC	Reserve Officer Training Corps
SAG	surface action group
SAW	squad automatic weapon
SECDEF	secretary of defense, *pronounced* sek def
SOFA	status of forces agreement
SOMA	status of mission agreement
UCP	Unified Command Plan
USAF	United States Air Force

Table 4.4. *(cont.)*

USAFR	United States Air Force Reserve
USAFRICOM	U.S. Africa Command
USAR	United States Army Reserve
USCENTCOM	United States Central Command *(combatant command)*, *pronounced* u s sent com
USCG	U.S. Coast Guard
USCGR	U.S. Coast Guard Reserve
USEUCOM	United States European Command *(combatant command)*, *pronounced* u s you com
USJFC	U.S. Joint Forces Command
USMARFORRES	U.S. Marine Forces Reserve
USMC	United States Marine Corps
USN	United States Navy
USNORTHCOM	United States Northern Command *(combatant command)*, *pronounced* u s north com
USNRF	U.S. Navy Reserve Force
USPACOM	United States Pacific Command *(combatant command)*, *pronounced* u s pay com
USSOCOM	United States Special Operations Command *(combatant command)*, *pronounced* u s so com
USSOUTHCOM	United States Southern Command *(combatant command)*, *pronounced* u s south com
USSTRATCOM	United States Strategic Command *(combatant command)*, *pronounced* u s strat com
USTRANSCOM	United States Transportation Command *(combatant command)*, *pronounced* u s trans com
WO	warrant officer

Additional Resources

Published Resources

The following resources include books, scholarly publications, official reports, and articles on topics related to peace, stability, and relief operations. The section is divided into civil society and NGOs, economics, governance, humanitarian operations, the security environment and the military, and further reading to help the reader quickly narrow down the area of interest when searching for additional resources. Additionally, the Online Resources section suggests online databases, continually updated best-practices resources, and official Web sites of influential institutions in the fields of peace, stability, and relief operations.

CIVIL SOCIETY AND NON-GOVERNMENTAL ORGANIZATIONS

Anderson, Mary B. 1999. *Do No Harm: How Aid Can Support Peace—or War.* Boulder, Colo.: Lynne Rienner.

Anderson, Scott. 1999. T*he Man Who Tried to Save the World: The Dangerous Life and Mysterious Disappearance of Fred Cuny.* New York: Doubleday.

Arulanantham, Ahilan T. 2000. "Restructured Safe Havens: A Proposal for Reform of the Refugee Protection System." *Human Rights Quarterly,* vol. 22, no. 1, 1–56.

Bergman, Carol. 2003. A*nother Day in Paradise: International Humanitarian Workers Tell Their Stories.* Maryknoll, N.Y.: Orbis Books.

Center for Stabilization and Reconstruction Studies, Naval Postgraduate School. 2005. *Workshop Report: Humanitarian Roles in Insecure Environments,* January 13–14, Washington, D.C.

Davis, Jan, and Robert Lambert. 2002. *Engineering in Emergencies: A Practical Guide for Relief Workers.* 2nd ed. London: ITDG.

Department for International Development. 2002. *Tools for Development.* London: Author.

Dobbins, James, et al. 2005. *The UN's Role in Nation Building: From the Congo to Iraq.* Santa Monica, Calif.: RAND.

Donini, Antonio, Norah Niland, and Karin Wermester. 2004. *Nation-Building Unraveled? Aid, Peace and Justice in Afghanistan.* Bloomfield, Conn.: Kumarian Press.

ECHO. 2004. *Report on Security of Humanitarian Personnel: Standards and Practices for the Security of Humanitarian Personnel and Advocacy for Humanitarian Space.* Brussels: Author.

Fawcett, John, ed. 2003. *Stress and Trauma Handbook.* Monrovia, Calif.: World Vision.

Frohardt, Mark, Diane Paul, and Larry Minear. 1999. "Protecting Human Rights: The Challenge to Humanitarian Organizations." In *Occasional Paper* No. 35. Medford, Mass.: Tufts University, Watson Institute.

Gallagher, Anne. 2001. "Human Rights and the New UN Protocols on Trafficking and Migrant Smuggling: A Preliminary Analysis." *Human Rights Quarterly,* vol. 23, no. 4, 975–1004.

Glaser, Max P. 2003. "Humanitarian Engagement with Non-State Actors." *Network Paper: Humanitarian Practice Network* 51.

Gutman, Roy, and David Rieff, eds. 1999. *Crimes of War: What the Public Should Know.* New York: W. W. Norton.

Muggah, Robert. 2003. "Small Arms Survey, In the Line of Fire: Surveying the Impact of Small Arms on Civilians and Relief Workers." *Humanitarian Exchange* no. 25, 20–23.

Paris, Roland. 2004. *At War's End: Building Peace after Civil Conflict.* Cambridge, U.K.; New York: Cambridge University Press.

Reed, Holly, and Roundtable on the Demography of Forced Migration. 2002. *Demographic Assessment Techniques in Complex Humanitarian Emergencies: Summary of a Workshop.* Washington, D.C.: National Academy Press.

Roberts, David Lloyd. 1999. *Staying Alive: Safety and Security Guidelines for Humanitarian Volunteers in Conflict Areas.* Geneva: International Committee of the Red Cross.

Smillie, Ian, and Larry Minear. 2004. *The Charity of Nations: Humanitarian Action in a Calculating World.* Bloomfield, Conn.: Kumarian Press.

Sphere Project and Isobel McConnan. 2000. *Humanitarian Charter and Minimum Standards in Disaster Response.* Geneva: International Committee of the Red Cross. www.sphereproject.org/content/view/27/84/lang.English/

United Nations General Assembly, 2005. *In Larger Freedom: Towards Development, Security, and Human Rights for All* (A/59/2005). New York: United Nations.

United Nations General Assembly, 2005. *Letter dated 24 March 2005 from the Secretary-General to the President of the General Assembly* (A/59/710). New York: United Nations.

United Nations High Commissioner for Human Rights. 1948. *Universal Declaration of Human Rights.* New York: United Nations.

United Nations Office for the Coordination of Humanitarian Affairs. 2003. *Secretary-General's Bulletin: Special Measures for Protection from Sexual Exploitation and Sexual Abuse* (ST/SGB/2003/13). New York: United Nations.

United Nations Office of the Secretary-General. 1997. *Renewing the United Nations: A Programme for Reform* (A/51/950). New York: United Nations.

United States Institute of Peace. 2005. *American Interest and UN Reform.* Washington, D.C.: United States Institute of Peace Press.

ECONOMICS

Duffield, Mark. 2001. *Global Governance and the New Wars: The Merging of Development and Security.* London and New York: Zed Books.

Forman, Shepard, and Stewart Patrick, eds. 2000. *Good Intentions: Pledges of Aid for Postconflict Recovery.* Boulder, Colo.: Lynne Reinner.

Galama, Anneke, and Paul van Tongeren, eds. 2002. *Towards Better Peacebuilding Practice: On Lessons Learned, Evaluation Practices and Aid and Conflict.* Amsterdam: European Centre for Conflict Prevention.

Office of Foreign Disaster Assistance. 2004. *OFDA's Field Operations Guide 4.0.* Washington, D.C.: U.S. Government Printing Office.

Oliker, Olga, et al. 2004. *Aid during Conflict.* Santa Monica, Calif.: RAND.

Orr, Robert C., and Center for Strategic and International Studies. 2004. "Winning the Peace: An American Strategy for Post-Conflict Reconstruction." *Significant Issues Series,* vol. 26, no. 7. Washington, D.C.: CSIS Press.

GOVERNANCE

Benomar, Jamal. 2004. "Constitution-Making after Conflict: Lessons for Iraq." *Journal of Democracy,* vol. 15, no. 2, 81–95.

Brahimi, Lakhdar. 2004. *The Political Transition in Iraq: Report of the [United Nations] Fact-Finding Mission February 6–13.* New York: United Nations.

Chopra, Jarat. 1998. *The Politics of Peace-Maintenance.* Boulder, Colo.: Lynne Rienner.

Diamond, Larry. 1999. *Developing Democracy: Toward Consolidation.* Baltimore: Johns Hopkins University Press.

Fukuyama, Francis. 2004. *State-Building: Governance and World Order in the 21st Century.* Ithaca, N.Y.: Cornell University Press.

Holsti, K. J. 2004. *Taming the Sovereigns.* Cambridge, U.K.: Cambridge University Press.

Kumar, Krishna. 1998. "After the Elections: Consequences for Democratization." In *Postconflict Elections, Democratization, and International Assistance,* ed. K. Kumar. Boulder, Colo.: Lynne Rienner.

Liberman, Peter. 1996. *Does Conquest Pay?* Princeton, N.J.: Princeton University Press.

Lijphart, Arend. 1999. *Patterns of Democracy.* New Haven, Conn., and London: Yale University Press.

Mansfield, Edward D., and Jack L. Snyder. 2002. "Democratic Transitions, Institutional Strength, and War." *International Organization,* vol. 56, no. 2, 297–337.

Ottaway, Marina. 2003. "Promoting Democracy after Conflict: The Difficult Choices." *International Studies Perspectives,* vol. 4, no. 3, 314–322.

Peceny, Mark. 1999. *Democracy at the Point of Bayonets.* University Park: Penn State Press.

Snyder, Jack, and Edward Mansfield. 1995. "Democratization and the Danger of War." *International Security,* vol. 20, no. 1.

Stedman, Stephen John, Donald S. Rothchild, and Elizabeth M. Cousens. 2002. *Ending Civil Wars: The Implementation of Peace Agreements.* Boulder, Colo.: Lynne Rienner.

Zakaria, Fareed. 2003. *The Future of Freedom.* New York: W. W. Norton.

HUMANITARIAN OPERATIONS

Holzgrefe, J. L., and Robert O. Keohane. 2003. *Humanitarian Intervention: Ethical, Legal, and Political Dilemmas.* Cambridge, U.K.; New York: Cambridge University Press.

Ignatieff, Michael. 2003. *Empire Lite: Nation-Building in Bosnia, Kosovo, and Afghanistan.* Toronto: Penguin Canada.

International Commission on Intervention and State Sovereignty, Gareth J. Evans, Mohamed Sahnoun, and International Development Research Centre (Canada). 2001. *The Responsibility to Protect: Report of the International Commission on Intervention and State Sovereignty.* Ottawa: IDRC.

International Committee of the Red Cross (ICRC). International Humanitarian Law: Answers to Your Questions." 2002. Available from http://www.icrc.org/web/eng/siteeng0 .nsf/iwpList104/0CA6FC89781FC094C1256DE800587554.

International Development Research Centre. 2003. *Resource Pack on Conflict Sensitive Approaches to Development, Humanitarian Assistance and Peacebuilding.* Ottawa: IDRC.

Janz, Mark, Joann Slead, and World Vision International. 2000. *Complex Humanitarian Emergencies: Lessons from Practitioners.* Monrovia, Calif.: World Vision.

Kent, Randolph. 2004. "Humanitarian Futures: Practical Policy Perspectives." *Humanitarian Practice Network Paper* 46.

Independent Commission on Kosovo. 2001. *Kosovo Report.* London: Oxford University Press.

McHugh, Gerard, and Lola Gostelow. 2004. *Provincial Reconstruction Teams and Humanitarian-Military Relations in Afghanistan.* London: Save the Children.

Pirnie, Bruce R. 1998. *Soldiers and Civilians: Achieving Better Coordination.* Santa Monica, Calif.: RAND.

Regan, Patrick M. 2000. *Civil Wars and Foreign Powers: Outside Intervention in Intrastate Conflict.* Ann Arbor: University of Michigan Press.

Reychler, Luc, and Thania Paffenholz. 2001. *Peacebuilding: A Field Guide.* Boulder, Colo.: Lynne Rienner.

Terry, Fiona. 2002. *Condemned to Repeat? The Paradox of Humanitarian Action.* Ithaca, N.Y.; London: Cornell University Press.

United Nations High Commissioner for Refugees. 1999. *Handbook for Emergencies.* 2nd edition. New York: United Nations.

United Nations Office for the Coordination of Humanitarian Affairs. 2001. *Use of Military or Armed Escorts for Humanitarian Convoys.* New York: United Nations.

United Nations Office of the Humanitarian Affairs. 2003, March. *Guidelines on the Use of Military and Civil Defence Assets to Support United Nations Humanitarian Activities in Complex Emergencies* New York: United Nations. (March 2003).

United Nations Office of the Humanitarian Affairs. 2004, June 28. *Civil-Military Relationship in Complex Emergencies,* ed. IASC. Reference Paper New York: United Nations.

United Nations Office of the Deputy Special Representative of the Secretary-General the United Nations Assistance Mission for Iraq. 2004. *Guidelines for Humanitarian Organisations on Interacting with Military and Other Security Actors in Iraq.* New York: United Nations.

United Nations Office of the Secretary-General. 2004. "A More Secure World: Our Shared Responsibility." *Report on the Secretary-General's High Level Panel on Threats, Challenges, and Change* (A/59/565). New York: United Nations. www.un.org/secureworld.

Weiss, Thomas George. 2004. *Military-Civilian Interactions: Humanitarian Crises and the Responsibility to Protect.* 2nd ed. Lanham, Md.: Rowman & Littlefield.

Weissman, Fabrice, and Médecins sans frontières. 2004. *In the Shadow of 'Just Wars': Violence, Politics, and Humanitarian Action.* Ithaca, N.Y.: Cornell University Press.

SECURITY ENVIRONMENT AND THE MILITARY

Bonn, Keith E., and Anthony E. Baker. 2000. *Guide to Military Operations Other Than War: Tactics, Techniques, and Procedures for Stability and Support Operations: Domestic and International.* Mechanicsburg, Pa.: Stackpole Books.

Center for Strategic and International Studies and the Association of the United States Army. 2002. *Post-Conflict Reconstruction: Task Framework.* Washington D.C.: Author.

Cornwallis Group (Lester B. Pearson Canadian International Peacekeeping Training Centre), A. E. R. Woodcock, David F. Davis, Cornwallis Group, and Lester B. Pearson Canadian International Peacekeeping Training Centre.

2002. *The Cornwallis Group VI: Analysis for Assessment, Evaluation, and Crisis Management.* Clementsport, Nova Scotia: Canadian Peacekeeping Press.

Darcy, James. 2003. "Iraq: Protection, Legitimacy, and the Use of Armed Force." *Humanitarian Exchange* No. 23, 2–3.

Department of Defense. 2006. *Military Support for Stability, Security, Transition, and Reconstruction Operations* (3000.05). Washington, D.C.

Finnemore, Martha. 2003. *The Purpose of Intervention: Changing Beliefs about the Use of Force.* Ithaca, N.Y.: Cornell University Press.

Guttieri, Karen. 2004. "Civil-Military Relations in Peacebuilding." *Sicherheitspolitik und Friedensforschung,* vol. 2, 79–85.

Hillen, John. 2000. *Blue Helmets: The Strategy of UN Military Operations.* 2nd ed. Washington, D.C.: Brassey's.

Macrae, Joanna, and Adele Harmer, eds. 2003. "The Global War on Terror and the Implications for Humanitarian Action: A Review of Trends and Issues." In *Humanitarian Policy Group Report.* HPG Briefing 9. London: Overseas Development Institute.

Oakley, Robert B., Michael J. Dziedzic, and Eliot M. Goldberg. 1998. *Policing the New World Disorder: Peace Operations and Public Security.* Washington, D.C.: National Defense University Press.

Perito, Robert. 2003. *Where Is the Lone Ranger When We Need Him? America's Search for a Postconflict Stability Force.* Washington, D.C.: United States Institute of Peace Press.

Shawcross, William. 2001. *Deliver Us from Evil: Peacekeepers, Warlords, and a World of Endless Conflict.* New York: Touchstone Books.

United Nations High Commissioner for Refugees. 1995. *Handbook for the Military on Humanitarian Operations.* New York: United Nations.

United Nations, Peacekeeping Best-Practices Unit, Department of Peacekeeping Operations. 2003. *Handbook on United Nations Multidimensional Peacekeeping Operations.* December 2003 2003b [cited January 20, 2004]. Available from www.pbpu.unlb.org/pbpu/library/Handbook%20 on%20UN%20PKOs.pdf

United States Defense Science Board, 2004. *Transition to and from Hostilities.* Washington, D.C.: Office of the Under-Secretary of Defense for Acquisition and Logistics.

Yamashita, Hikaru. 2004. *Humanitarian Space and International Politics: The Creation of Safe Areas.* Aldershot, U.K.; Burlington, Vt.: Ashgate.

FURTHER READING

Berdal, Mats R., and Mónica Serrano. 2002. *Transnational Organized Crime and International Security: Business as Usual?* Boulder, Colo.: Lynne Rienner.

Bi-Partisan Commission on Post-Conflict Reconstruction, Center for Strategic and International Studies and the Association of the United States Army. 2003. *Play to Win.* Washington: CSIS and Association of the U.S. Army.

Dorman, Shawn, ed. 2005. *Inside a U.S. Embassy: How the Foreign Service Works for America.* Washington, D.C.: American Foreign Service Association.

George, Alexander. 1999. *Bridging the Gap: Theory and Practice in Foreign Policy.* Washington, D.C.: United States Institute of Peace Press.

Hampson, Fen Osler, and Pamela Aall, ed. 2007. *Leashing the Dogs of War: Conflict Management in a Divided World.* Washington, D.C.: United States Institute of Peace Press.

Head, Ivan L., Obiora Chinedu Okafor, and Obijiofor Aginam. 2003. *Humanizing Our Global Order: Essays in Honour of Ivan Head.* Toronto: University of Toronto Press.

Online Resources

The Web site of the United States Institute of Peace—www.usip.org—provides links to a wide variety of relevant sites, including homepages not only of organizations, but also of governments and foreign ministries.

INTERNATIONAL NETWORK TO PROMOTE THE RULE OF LAW (INPROL)

Internet: www.inprol.org

The United States Institute of Peace has created the **International Network to Promote the Rule of Law (INPROL)**, a Web-based network of rule of law practitioners and experts, to promote information sharing and address the immediate information needs of officials in the field. Given the ad hoc and urgent nature of post-conflict rule of law activities, practitioners often work in isolation, without access to outside expertise and the benefits of past experience. INPROL seeks to foster an integrated approach to the rule of law by including judges, prosecutors, defense attorneys, civilian police, stability police, corrections officials, legal advisers, and judicial administrators in one network, crossing organizations and missions. INPROL works in consultation with international organizations, such as the United Nations, the Organization for Security and Co-operation in Europe (OSCE), and the European Union to make INPROL effective by gathering documentation and assessing the needs of practitioners in the field.

Aid Workers Network: www.aidworkers.net/resources/
unhcr-handbook.html

Bonn International Center for Conversion—Bonn, Germany: www.bicc.de

Center for Stabilization and Reconstruction Studies, Naval
Postgraduate School: www.nps.edu.CSRS/

Department for International Development—United
Kingdom: www.dfid.gov.uk/

FIRST—Security and Development specific search engine:
http://first.sipri.org/index.php

Geneva Center for Security Policy: www.gcsp.ch/e/
index.htm

Geneva Forum—Geneva, Switzerland: www.geneva-forum.org

Humanitarian Practice Network: www.odihpn.org/

International Alert—London, United Kingdom: www
.international-alert.org/

International Committee for the Red Cross—Geneva,
Switzerland: www.icrc.org

International Conflict Research (INCORE): www. incore
.ulst.ac.uk/

Monterey Institute of International Studies, Program on
Security and Development: http://sand.miis.edu/

Project Ploughshares: www.ploughshares.ca/ index.html

Relief Web: www.reliefweb.int

Safer Africa—Pretoria, South Africa: www.saferafrica.org

Saferworld—London, United Kingdom: www.saferworld
.co.uk

Stockholm International Peace Research Institute: www
.sipri.org

UNDP Bureau for Crisis Prevention and Recovery—New
York: www.undp.org/bcpr/

UN Office for the Coordination of Humanitarian Affairs'
Relief Web: www.reliefweb.int/w/rwb.nsf

United Nations Peacekeeping basics: www.un.org/Depts/
dpko/dpko/intro/index.htm

UN Peacekeeping Web site: www.un.org/Depts/dpko/
dpko/home.shtml

UN Peace Operations Year in Review 2005: www.un.org/
Depts/dpko/dpko/pub/year_review05

Map of UN Peacekeeping Operations: www.un.org/
Depts/Cartographic/english/htmain.htm

Viva Rio—Rio de Janeiro, Brazil: www.vivario.org.br

World Bank, Post-Conflict and Reconstruction Unit:
http://web.worldbank.org/WBSITE/EXTERNAL/TOPICS
/ E X T S O C I A L D E V E L O P -
MENT/EXTCPR/0,,menuPK:407746~pagePK:149018~pi
PK:149093~theSitePK:407740,00.html

Index

United States Institute of Peace

The United States Institute of Peace is an independent, non-partisan institution established and funded by Congress. Its goals are to help prevent and resolve violent conflicts, promote post-conflict peace-building, and increase conflict-management tools, capacity, and intellectual capital worldwide. The Institute does this by empowering others with knowledge, skills, and resources, as well as by its direct involvement in conflict zones around the globe.

Chairman of the Board: J. Robinson West
Vice Chairman: María Otero
President: Richard H. Solomon
Executive Vice President: Patricia Powers Thomson
Vice President: Charles E. Nelson